Also by Sonja L. Connor, M.S., R.D., and William E. Connor, M.D.

The New American Diet
The New American Diet System

The

More Than 250 All New
Low-Fat/High-Flavor Recipes
from the Creators of
the Bestselling <u>New American Diet</u>

New

AMERICAN DIET

cookbook

Sonja L. Connor, M.S., R.D.,
and
William E. Connor, M.D.

Simon & Schuster

SIMON & SCHUSTER
Rockefeller Center
1230 Avenue of the Americas
New York, NY 10020

SIMON & SCHUSTER and colophon are registered trademarks
of Simon & Schuster Inc.

Designed by Elina D. Nudelman

Manufactured in the United States of America

1   3   5   7   9   10   8   6   4   2

Library of Congress Cataloging-in-Publication Data
Connor, Sonja L.
The new American diet cookbook :
more than 250 all new low-fat, high-flavor recipes from the creators of the
bestselling new American diet / Sonja L. Connor and William E. Connor.
p.   cm.
Includes index.
1. Low-fat diet—Recipes.   2. Cookery, American.   I. Connor, William E., date.
RM237.7.C644   1997
641.5′638—dc21   96-45252
CIP
ISBN 0-684-81422-6

ACKNOWLEDGMENTS

The 21st century is fast approaching! Since our last book was published in 1991, there has been a surge of interest in lighter cooking and in vegetarian fare. Many have mastered the basic cooking skills for removing fat from the diet; we refer to this as "Low-Fat Cooking 101." The next step is to focus on complex carbohydrates and seafood. Recipes in *The New American Diet Cookbook* emphasize vegetables, grains, beans, fruits, and seafood from a broad spectrum of cultures. These recipes will not be completely foreign because our "melting pot" cuisine has been naturally enriched as people from one culture after another have immigrated to the land of the free. It has been exhilarating to look ahead and develop new recipes that will take our cooking into the 21st century.

The New American Diet Cookbook would not have been possible without the help of many people. Special appreciation goes to Joyce Gustafson and Cindy Francois, who were instrumental in the development and production of this cookbook. Joyce and Cindy are great cooks who adeptly developed recipes, cooked recipes, analyzed recipes—and did it over and over and over again, especially during the last three years! Thanks also go to Joyce's husband, Dick, and Cindy's husband, Adam, for tasting recipes from the first test (not always a fantastic experience) to the last test.

Special appreciation also goes to David Korvik, our agent, who assisted us in writing and has provided the clever reader-friendly style to all of our books. Without Joyce, Cindy, and David, there would be no *New American Diet Cookbook* and we are grateful to them for their creativity and their dedication and hard work.

We are very appreciative of those who played a major role in the development and testing of the recipes—often in their own homes on their own time: Sandy Bacon, Reba Clow, Carol DeFrancesco, Donna Flavell, and Lauren Hatcher.

The recipes were prepared for our "official tasting" in the Oregon Health Sciences University Clinical Research Center Metabolic Kitchen, which is under the direction of Lauren Hatcher. Many thanks go to the good cooks who prepared recipes many times over (the names of the primary cooks during the last year of recipe testing are italicized): Dave Belknap, Lisa Feathers, Lisa Feringa, *Cheryl Laughlin*, *Allison Livingston* (who also helped with recipe analyses and typing) and Mary Miller, the head cook in the Clinical Research Center.

Many, many thanks go to the members of our Lipid-Atherosclerosis Research Group who were invaluable to the recipe development process and did the official "taste testing" over the last six years—our testing and tasting were low-key the first three years, moderate the next two years, and intense the last year—a challenge for the taste buds! These people were not casual "tasters." They took it very seriously and always gave thoughtful, frank, honest evaluations and helpful suggestions. Because of their dedication and the fact that many people participated, we were able to develop recipes that have sustained appeal across a broad range of tastes. We are eternally grateful to our taste testers (the names of people who participated during the last year are italicized): April Adams, *Jennifer Adu-Frimpong*, *Greg Anderson* (whose comments often made our day), Frank Arrington, Sabine Artaud-Wild, Nancy Becker, *Paula*

Bisaccio, Lisa Blanchard, Linda Bolewicz, Reba Clow, Sonja Connor, William Connor, Shirley Dai, Carol DeFrancesco, Bart Duell, Joni Elms, Donna Flavell, Jill Foehringer, Cindy Francois, Glenn Gerhard, Roxanne Griswold, Joyce Gustafson, Fay Hagemenas, Kathy Hagemenas, Michelle Haselbacher, Lauren Hatcher, Eileen Hollins, Roger Illingworth, Mary Kalez, Mogens Larsen, Barbara Lastelic, Cheryl Laughlin, Robert Leatherman, Don Lin, Stacey Lipps, Allison Livingston, Cullen MacPherson, Carol Marsh, Christine Minarik, Vicki Moffet, Ken Newcomb, Jean O'Malley, Shirley Papé, Anu Pappu, Jim Prihoda, Tina Rutter, Azar Sardari, Erik Berg Schmidt, Linda Seward, Amy Shultz, Pam Smith, Paul Steager, Samina Van Winkle, Robin Virgin, Jody Wagner, Dave Wheaton, Lois Wolfe, and Nancy Zhu.

We are grateful to the myriads of people who gave us ideas for recipes. These include family, friends, colleagues, patients, and people who attended our talks. Some of the stories are included with the recipes. Thanks go to David Rorvik's enthusiastic associate, Dennis Seals, for providing inspiration to develop creative and wonderfully tasty vegetarian dishes.

We discovered that tastes have changed over the last six years:

⮑ Ethnic tastes have broadened and many have acquired a taste for the flavors of the Thai and Indian cuisines, which means that cilantro is in!

⮑ We like recipes that mix cuisines—see our recipes for Butternut Squash Enchiladas with Spicy Peanut Sauce and Spicy Thai Pizza.

⮑ The saltiness level was very difficult to find—in fact, there is no single salt level that pleases most people. There is a wide range of preferences, from those who want little or no salt in their foods to those who like their foods quite salty. More of the recipes in this cookbook are closer to our upper limit for sodium than has been the case in the past.

⮑ When it comes to spicy—meaning hot—there are two groups. One group wants just a hint of "hot" and one group wants "fire." We have listed a range for the spicy ingredients in our recipes (e.g., $1/4$ to $1/2$ teaspoon red pepper flakes); the lesser amount for those who want just a hint of "hot" and the greater amount for the "fire eaters."

⮑ We find the same thing for sweetness—there are two groups. One group wants very little sugar while recipes are never too sweet for the second group. We aimed for the middle. You can make your own adjustments.

We are most grateful for the decades of research support from the General Clinical Research Centers of the Division of Research Resources of the National Institutes of Health and for the financial support of medical research by U.S. taxpayers. This support has made it possible for us to conduct metabolic research studies, a community study in 233 families—The Family Heart Study—and to translate 90 years of scientific research to the practical aspects of shopping, cooking, and eating.

ACKNOWLEDGMENTS

To our faithful taste testers, who know full well if something tastes wonderful it will never be served again—because we are forever working on the next 10 recipes none of us can live without.

◆

To our patients, who keep asking for recipes they can enjoy and which also bring good health.

CONTENTS

INTRODUCTION

Welcome to a New World of High-Flavor, Low-Fat Cuisine

At the dawn of the new century, a genuine revolution in the way we eat in the Western world is in progress on two major fronts. The high-fat, meat-dominated diet of the past century is being replaced by a low-fat, plant-dominated diet. Irrefutable scientific evidence has shown the capacity for a high-fat diet (also high in salt and sugar and low in plant foods) to inflict malaise and mayhem in the human body. This mayhem includes, but is not limited to, heart disease, stroke, various cancers, high blood pressure, diabetes, osteoporosis, and obesity.

These chronic diseases have developed because of sweeping lifestyle changes that have taken place in the United States and other countries of the Western world during this last century. Dramatic advances in technology have reduced drastically the amount of physical exertion involved in daily life—so much so that we now have to exercise intentionally. At the same time, other advances have made a diet characterized by large amounts of meat, fat, salt, and sugar readily available and affordable for the first time in human history. These developments, coupled with the inability of our genes to cope with such large changes in so short a time, are responsible for the explosion in chronic diseases.

This explosion of ill health has resulted in a "wake up call" for millions of us. The so-called traditional Western diet is giving way to what is the *genuine* tradition (one that has characterized human evolution for eons) of an eating style that emphasizes grains, beans, vegetables, and fruits.

But the revolution is proceeding on another front, too. It isn't enough to simply throw out the old; you have to offer something new—something large numbers will embrace. When we devoted ourselves to this task in the 1970s and 1980s, our goal was to create the *healthiest* diet U.S. Americans of all ages and circumstances would accept in significant numbers—a diet that would allow people to live out their lives as healthy as their genes and the marvels of modern medicine would allow. There's no trick to creating a healthy diet on paper—but it's a real challenge, we discovered, to create a healthy diet that contains foods people enjoy, not just for a faddish few months, but for years and lifetimes.

Our five-year major study of 233 U.S. families, funded by the National Institutes of Health, culminated in our book *The New American Diet*, which was first published in 1986. This book provided, we believe, the most detailed and effective alternative to the standard U.S. diet presented to that date. Others, however, were contributing on parallel fronts. Since that time, there has been an explosion in the efforts to provide palatable, healthful alternatives to the diet of the past century.

Suddenly, the Western world was no longer being asked to give up its meats, gravies, cheeses, creams, and high-fat desserts for what, previously, had been the only apparent alternative—odd-looking and strange-tasting soy concoctions, sprouts, and other "rawbits" that starved the palate and caught in the collective craw of all but those who wore the sturdiest Birkenstocks. Instead, we're now treated to a cornucopia of low-fat, high-flavor alternatives, fueled not only by the imaginations of cooks around the world but also by the food industry itself, which is beginning to respond positively and energetically to the demand for healthy change.

Healthy eating is no longer a fringe activity indulged in by the few who eat in offbeat "health food" restaurants. The revolution has gone mainstream, with the multi-billion-dollar food industry working overtime to make food products that are not only good for your health but also useful in combining with other foods to make great-tasting recipes the "lighter" way.

Vegetarianism and near-vegetarianism are rapidly outgrowing their longtime minority status. A recent national survey conducted by Yankelovich Clancy Shulman revealed that Americans are now becoming vegetarians at an unprecedented rate—20,000 new vegetarians *per week!* That brings the total of those who say they are strictly vegetarian to more than 12 million U.S. Americans. The number who are becoming semivegetarian is growing at an even faster pace. This includes many "boomers" as well as many who have passed the 50-year mark, who have discovered the current sedentary U.S. lifestyle demands that they eat lighter as they head into their fifties, sixties, and beyond.

Vegetarian diets recently received endorsement by the new *Dietary Guidelines for Americans* from the U.S. Department of Agriculture and the National Institutes of Health. Vegetarian diets meet the Recommended Dietary Allowances for nutrients, including protein, provided a wide variety of foods is consumed. Such diets must, of course, meet the fat and cholesterol guidelines, as suggested in this cookbook.

Still other recent surveys, conducted by the Grocery Manufacturers of America, Health Focus, and others, showed that 46 percent of all Americans now agree it is not necessary to eat meat every day (a notion most recoiled from even a decade ago), 36 percent of all U.S. Americans now look for lighter meatless entrées when eating out, and 40 percent of U.S. Americans say they now put nutritional value ahead of price and even taste in making their food choices.

The New American Diet Cookbook is our celebration of the new cuisine that is beginning to sweep the Western world. It is the product of extensive testing by people who love to cook and eat good food. We believe we have some of the best cooks in the world on our staff at Oregon Health Sciences University, and they come from all over the world—Europe, Africa, Asia, Australia, and the Americas. Every recipe in this book is new—and every recipe has been carefully analyzed for its nutrient content and must meet strict nutritional standards and even stricter taste tests.

What The New American Diet Cookbook Delivers

The New American Diet Cookbook emphasizes vegetables, grains, beans, fruits, and fish, but also includes some chicken dishes. Calorically, this cuisine is "light." As the baby boomers begin to enter their fifties, surveys show they want to eat lighter fare; this is partly due to our growing health consciousness and partly because of our changing metabolism. As we age, we need to eat less to avoid obesity. Thus, it becomes even more important that the foods we eat provide all the nourishment we need. Whether you're a child, a teenager, a boomer, an in-betweener, or a senior, our recipes are packed with optimal nutrition.

In the typical U.S. diet, over 60 percent of the calories come from fat, sugar, and alcohol, and have little nutrition other than calories. During much of this last century, we have had to rely on about 35 percent of our calories to provide the wide range of vitamins, minerals, and other important nutrients. In the New American Diet eating style, almost 70 percent of the calories come from foods that are packed full of nutrients that science suggests are associated with optimal health throughout life.

By selecting and trying a wide variety of dishes from this cookbook, some of the recipes will become part of your everyday eating style. This will move you toward the following nutritional goals, which decades of research have shown can reduce the risk of coronary heart disease by as much as 40 percent and help protect you and your family from heart disease (atherosclerosis), stroke, various cancers, high blood pressure, obesity, and other degenerative processes such as osteoporosis.

The nutritional goals to prevent these diseases are:

· To reduce the average U.S. cholesterol consumption from its current 400 to 500 milligrams per day to less than 100 milligrams per day.

· To reduce fat intake by about one-half, so that only 20 percent, rather than the current average of 37 percent, of all calories are derived from fat, three-fourths of which are "invisible" in the current U.S. diet.

· To decrease saturated fat intake by two-thirds so that, instead of getting 14 percent of our calories from this type of fat, we get only 5 or 6 percent from this source.

· To increase the omega-3 polyunsaturated fat intake from both seafood and plant foods.

· To increase carbohydrate intake from the present 45 percent of total calories to 65 percent, with emphasis on increased intake of complex carbohydrates and fiber from grains and beans.

· To decrease the intake of refined sugar from 20 percent of calories to 10 percent.

· To cut salt intake substantially—by half (from the equivalent of 10 pounds of salt a year to 5 pounds a year).

What these goals mean in terms of food:

· Eating no more than 3 to 4 ounces of seafood, chicken, or lean red meat a day.

· Eating 2 fish meals a week.

· Using nonfat dairy products (milk, cheeses, ice creams, etc.).

· Reducing the fat in baked goods by one-third.

· Using only small amounts of oils and margarine (4 to 7 teaspoons a day—half in cooking and baking and half for spreads and salad dressings).

- Doubling your intake of complex carbohydrates and fiber by eating all of the following:

  Two to 5 servings of grains per meal.

  Cereal and toast for breakfast.

  Soup and crackers, a vegetarian sandwich, or leftovers for lunch.

  Rice, pasta, or potatoes and bread for dinner.

  Bagels, low-fat muffins, baked chips, and low-fat crackers for snacks.

  Three to 5 cups of legumes a week.

  Two to 3 cups of vegetables a day.

  Two to 3 pieces of fruit a day.

- Using Lite Salt (contains one-half the sodium of table salt) or no salt.

- Cutting sugar in half (using small amounts to sweeten sour fruits, breads, and desserts).

Obviously, explaining all the ins and outs of these goals goes beyond the scope of a cookbook, but they are provided in detail in our previous books, *The New American Diet* (about making changes slowly and gradually) and *The New American Diet System* (contains our table of the calories, fat, and the Cholesterol–Saturated Fat Index (CSI) for 1,000 foods; we call it the *Encyclopaedia Britannica* of the kitchen), both available through our publisher, Fireside Books.

Good news! It is not necessary to commit these goals to memory, or even to post them on your refrigerator. We have done all the work for you by translating the scientific goals to food. All you have to do to meet these goals is to use our New American Diet recipes—and not slather margarine or pour olive oil on everything (our motto is "If it has fat in it, don't put fat on it"), *and* be selective about eating out. Using these recipes regularly will move you in the direction of achieving an eating style that promotes optimal health for life.

The health benefits of using recipes like these to help decrease your fat intake and increase your complex carbohydrate intake are now convincingly documented. Until recently, it was thought the complex carbohydrate foods did little more than simply replace fats in the diet. There have been numerous scientific reports recently showing that vegetables, fruits, grains, and beans are loaded with antioxidants that can protect the body from "free radicals," by-products of metabolism that inflict damage on cells and contribute to heart disease, various forms of cancer, and autoimmune disorders. Examples of antioxidants are vitamins C and E and beta carotene. These and other disease-fighting substances are plentiful in the ingredients we favor in our recipes (especially the red, green, orange, and yellow fruits and vegetables). Science has also identified other protective factors in plant foods such as soluble fiber and saponins. Other protective factors are likely to be identified in the future.

The cuisine from *The New American Diet Cookbook* favors stronger bones, as well as stronger hearts and immune systems. Osteoporosis, a thinning of bone mass that many of us suffer from as we get older, increases when more calcium is excreted from the body. Excess intake of animal protein, salt, coffee, and alcohol—all of which are diminished in our fare— contributes to calcium excretion and increased risk for osteoporosis.

The New American Diet Cookbook also emphasizes fish. There is overwhelming evidence that eating fish two or three times a week can cut the risk of premature fatal coronary heart disease in half. The omega-3 fatty acids contained in fish oils lower triglyceride concentrations in the blood, reduce the formation of blood clots, make the blood thinner, and reduce the risk of disturbances in the rhythm of the heart. Omega-3 fatty acids may also have favorable effects on some inflammatory disorders, such as reducing the symptoms of rheumatoid arthritis.

How to Use the Recipes

If your family is just beginning to make the transition from a high-fat, meat-dominated diet to an eating style that focuses more on grains, beans, vegetables, and fruits, our recipes are designed to make life a lot easier for you. Flavor is the key. There are more ways than one to skin a fat; when we take the fat *out* we put enough flavor back *in*, through an alchemy of international seasonings and blending of ingredients, to please most palates. Not *every*time for *every*member of the family, mind you—but we give you enough recipes to experiment with that we think you will have little difficulty in making our New American Diet cooking a tasty staple of your life.

Extensive taste testing indicates that many hardened fat fiends won't even know what's missing when they consume our fare. Try a few of our desserts if you—or your family members—need convincing. Our Roxy Road Cheesecake, for example, or our Lemon Gelati are good for starters. Intersperse our fish and chicken dishes—let's see who can resist our East Indian Chicken with Apricot Rice or Mrs. Plancich's Barbecued Salmon—with such vegetarian taste treats as our Spicy Thai Pizza, our Yakisoba Stir-Fry, or our Peppers Stuffed with Red Lentils and Drizzled with "Fire."

If you want to try something from our kitchens that you or other family members consider really unusual, introduce it first as a side dish, along with fare that is more familiar to your family. In general, make changes *gradually*. This is of great importance in making healthful changes stick. For example, don't start cooking with skim milk right away. Move gradually from 2 percent to 1 percent and then to skim.

And to make sure that you continue in the right direction, keep the best food choices/ingredients on hand at all times, so that you won't be tempted to backslide. Staples we like to keep on hand are provided later.

We also find it helpful if cooks avoid repeating recipes too soon. If you find that a particular recipe is a great hit with your family, let it rest on its culinary laurels awhile before repeating it. Every now and then, we get enthusiastic about the magic of beans. Early on, after we had served our family numerous bean dishes, including even a cake made with refried beans, our kids started asking if they were going to find beans in the fruit salad or nestled in their next bowl of popcorn. Red Bean and Cilantro Dip, Black Bean Picante Soup, Prawns and Beans Tuscan Style, and Black Bean Pizza are all terrific, tasty and brimming with healthful nutrients, but it would be a mistake to serve them all in a week's time to a family that hasn't had beans since last summer's camping trip.

Another tip: Serve enough so that all get their fill. Remember, when you are serving "lighter" fare, you are not only reducing the amount of fat but also the number of calories. This is great for the majority of us who aspire to lose a little weight. But for the growing child or the teen with a voracious appetite or the strenuous exerciser, less is not going to be regarded as "better" —they will be hungry in an hour if you don't serve enough. The beauty of this food is that you can eat more and it will still be good for you.

Finding Recipes That Suit Your Tastes

It's not always easy to identify "your type of recipes" in a new cookbook. Toward that end, our cooks and taste testers helped us identify three groups of recipes: one group of recipes that are very ethnic, spicy, and/or mostly vegetarian, another group of recipes that are easy to prepare, and a third group of recipes that are more involved and take more time to prepare.

Ethnic, Spicy, Mostly Vegetarian Recipes

Skordalia
Tzatziki

Chai (Indian Tea)
Finland's Sima

Round Rye Bread
Sweet Potato Muffins
Raap-Wal-O (Great Hot Cereal)

Blackeye Pea Salad
Roasted Eggplant and Bean Salad
Indonesian Pasta Salad
Curried Chicken and Rice Salad with Grapes

African Peanut Soup with Rice Balls
Curried Apple Soup
Moroccan Stew
Spicy Peanut Soup

Butternut Squash Enchiladas with Spicy Peanut Sauce
Grilled Pepper, Eggplant, and Zucchini Sandwiches
Vegetables Middle Eastern Style
Bangon Aloo (Eggplant and Potatoes)
Kate Aloo (Cut Potatoes)
Potatoes Bhaji
Angry Penne
Pad Thai
Thai Fusilli

Savory Eggplant Sauce with Pasta
Spicy Si-Cuan Noodles
Gobi Pilaf
Polenta with Late Summer Garden Vegetables
Peppers Stuffed with Red Lentils and Drizzled with "Fire"
Blackeye Peas and Plantains (Red Red)
Kung Pao Vegetarian Style

Paella

Fruit Cassis Sorbet
Grapefruit Tequila Sorbet

Easy-to-Prepare Recipes

Black Bean Dip

Strawberry Lemonade

Baked Onion Twists
Blackberry Muffins

Allison's Caesar Salad
Cindy's Potato Salad

Black Bean Picante Soup
Donna's Easy Bean Soup

Mediterranean-Style Spaghetti Squash
Garlic Mashed Potatoes
Parmesan Potatoes
Angel Hair Pasta with Tomatoes and Basil
Cranberry Rice Pilaf
Baked Corn Casserole
"Pile-Ons" (Our Favorite Tostada)

Lemon Garlic Halibut
Fish Nuggets with Tartar Sauce
Halibut Olé

Chicken with Cranberries
La Paz Chicken and Corn Stir-Fry

Chocolate Mint Cookies
Chocolate Cherry Cheesecake
Quick Fruit Sherbets
Three Berry Cobbler

More-Involved Recipes

Layered Mexican Bean Dip
Salmon Pâté

Cranberry Wassail

Homemade English Muffins
Lemon Blueberry Muffins
Oven-Baked French Toast with Cranberry Maple Syrup

Greens and Apple Salad with Garlic Dijon Dressing
Greens with Strawberries and Poppy Seed Dressing
Marinated Asparagus or Broccoli
Sourdough Bread Salad with Roasted Vegetables
Jane's Asian Pasta Salad

Em's Black Bean Soup
Special Minestrone Soup

Italian Marinara Sauce
Sweet Onion Bake
Roasted Potatoes and Mushrooms with Fennel
Party Mashed Potatoes
Santa Fe Potatoes
Apple and Dried Fruit Bread Dressing
Black Bean Pizza

Chilean Sea Bass with Ginger Sesame Sauce
Dungeness Crab Cakes with Red Pepper Sauce
Fresh Fish with Mediterranean Herbs

Chicken and Spinach with Creamy Ginger Sauce

Paula's Date Nut Bars
Soft Ginger Cookies
Lemon Gelati
Fabulous Fruit Tart

Stocking Your Pantry

> The keys to maximizing success in moving toward the lighter New American Diet cooking are:
> ·﹣Using high-quality ingredients.
> ·﹣Knowing when and how to use low-fat and nonfat foods.
> ·﹣Having the necessary ingredients on hand.

We have inventoried our pantries and come up with a starter list for you. With these foods on hand, you should be well prepared to tackle the New American Diet recipes without having to make too many trips to the store.*

Bottled products that add special flavor to many recipes:

Kikkoman Lite Soy Sauce
Dijon-style mustard (we like *Watkin's*)
Balsamic vinegar
S&W Vintage Lites Red Wine & Herb Vinegar Dressing
Consorzio Vignette Flavored Vinegars (mango, passion fruit, raspberry, tomato)
Worcestershire sauce
Fish sauce (used in Pad Thai recipe)
Sesame oil (the dark variety)
Liqueurs or syrups (crème de cassis, amaretto, Grand Marnier)

Dry sherry (not cooking sherry—it contains salt)
Extracts (vanilla, almond, coconut)
Black bean sauce with chili or chili paste with garlic
Thai chili sauce
Skippy Reduced Fat Peanut Butter Spread
Nonfat mayonnaise or *Miracle Whip* or *Best Foods Low Fat Mayonnaise* (1 gram fat/tbsp)
Apricot preserves
Currant and/or raspberry jelly

Canned and packaged goods we like to keep on hand:

Vinegars (balsamic, rice, white wine, etc.)
Nonstick cooking spray
Oils (olive, canola, sesame, etc.)
Flours (unbleached white, whole wheat, rye, etc.)
Dried beans (white, black, pinto, etc.)
S&W Lite Beans (black, garbanzo, kidney)
Refried beans (pinto and black)

Swanson Natural Goodness 100% Fat Free 1/3 Less Sodium Chicken Broth
Vegetable broth
Campbell's Healthy Request Cream of Mushroom Soup, Cream of Chicken Soup, and Tomato Soup
Couscous
Bulgur

* Certain products are listed in italics to provide examples of food items on the market that are acceptable choices for a person wishing to comply with the New American Diet nutritional goals. Often there are other products of similar composition with different trade names that are also acceptable to use.

B&M Baked Beans 99% Fat Free
Unsalted tomatoes (we like S&W Ready-Cut
    Peeled Tomatoes)
Unsalted tomato sauce
Unsalted tomato paste
Meatless spaghetti or marinara sauce (we like
    Diomonde Mediterranean Spaghetti Sauce)
Canned salmon
Canned crab
Salsa, fresh and S&W Salsa with Cilantro
Green taco sauce
Sliced water chestnuts
Roasted red peppers
Jalapeño pepper slices
Pineapple (crushed, sliced, and chunks)
Mandarin oranges
Cherry pie filling
Evaporated skim milk
Parmesan cheese
Brown rice
Basmati rice

Spaghetti and other pastas (penne, angel hair,
    fusilli, rotini, linguine)
Low-fat ramen noodle soup
Rice noodles (for Pad Thai)
Somen noodles
Chuka soba noodles
Oatmeal
Cornmeal
Grape-nuts cereal
Graham crackers (regular and chocolate)
Raisins
Currants
Dates
Dried apricots
Dried cranberries
Mini semisweet chocolate chips
Fat-free soda crackers
Carr's Table Water Crackers (plain and pepper)
Nabisco Harvest Crisps
Baked tortilla chips
Baked potato chips

A variety of spices is essential:

Buy top quality. Purchase small quantities because the flavors are volatile and quickly lose their "punch." Be very selective in choosing ground spices as some will give a bitter aftertaste; this is why we generally suggest using leaves. Some spices that we especially like to keep on hand are:

Morton's Lite Salt
Black pepper
Spicy Pepper Seasoning (Spice Islands) or other
    seasoned pepper (without salt)
Red pepper flakes
Cayenne pepper
Tabasco sauce
White pepper
Oregano leaves (we like Watkin's)
Basil leaves
Marjoram leaves
Thyme leaves
Dillweed
Nutmeg
Cloves

Fennel seeds
Cumin seeds
Sesame seeds
Garlic powder
Ground cumin
Ground ginger
Ground cardamom
Chili powder
Curry powder (we like Sharwood's Mild)
Mustard powder
Sage
Saffron
Cinnamon
Allspice

Fresh foods we like to keep on hand (we buy fish, chicken, and breads just before we use them):

Lemons

Lots of other fruits

Gingerroot

Garlic (LOTS)

Cilantro

Parsley

Onions

Potatoes (bakers, small red, Yukon Gold)

Bell peppers (red, yellow, green)

Mushrooms

Celery

Carrots

Lots of other vegetables

Skim milk

Nonfat plain yogurt

Buttermilk

Eggs (for the whites)

Egg substitute

Nonfat cream cheese

Nonfat sour cream (we like *Land O' Lakes*)

Light part-skim mozzarella cheese

Jarlsberg Lite Reduced Fat Swiss Cheese

Fat-free Cheddar cheese

Whole wheat bread

Foods we like to keep in the freezer:

Bags of frozen fruit (strawberries, mixed berries, cranberries, etc.)

Vegetables (corn, peas, carrots)

Icelandic cod

GardenSausage and *Gardenburger* (Wholesome and Hearty Foods)

Nonfat frozen yogurt (vanilla and chocolate)

Vegetable broths from recipes on pages 162 to 163

Whole wheat bread—just in case

Addresses for Special Products

Mediterranean Spaghetti Sauce is sold under the brand name Diomonde Foods. Outside the Portland, Oregon, area it may be obtained by writing Diomonde Foods, P.O. Box 69351, Portland, OR 97201-0351.

Consorzio Vignettes (flavored vinegars) can be found in specialty grocery stores or obtained through Williams-Sonoma (1-800-541-2233).

GardenSausage and Gardenburger can be found in the natural foods section of supermarkets, in health food stores, or be obtained from Wholesome and Hearty Foods, Inc. (1-800-636-0109).

Thai Chili Sauce can be found in the Asian-food section of supermarkets or in Asian grocery stores.

Menus for All Occasions

We created a selection of menus to give you some ideas about using our New American Diet recipes (indicated in italics). Many of the menus can be made simpler by substituting convenience foods for some of the recipes (e.g., bottled salad dressings and store-bought frozen yogurts and sorbets, for which there are many delicious flavors available).

Sunday Brunch with a West African Accent

Fruit Slush Cups
African Peanut Soup with Rice Balls
Marinated Asparagus
Round Rye Bread
Fabulous Fruit Tart

A Wedding Shower Brunch

Fresh-Squeezed Orange Juice or *Switchel*
Baked Chicken Sandwich
Fresh Fruit Platter with Strawberry Sauce
Tiny Pineapple Muffins with Orange Glaze

An Everyday Breakfast

Grapefruit Half
Raap-Wal-O
Whole Wheat Toast with Honey

Lunch with a Bit of Thai

Thai Sandwiches
Fresh Fruit
Paula's Date Nut Bars

Weekend Lunch

Spicy Si-Cuan Noodles or *Pad Thai*
Luscious Black Grapes

Friday-Night Suppers

Grilled Pepper, Eggplant, and Zucchini Sandwiches
Baked Potato with Yogurt and Chives
Greens with *Salad Dressing à la Mango*
Fresh Blueberries and Raspberries

Em's Black Bean Soup or *Black Bean Picante Soup*
Chile Cheese Dinner Muffins
Greens with *Spicy Tomato Vinaigrette Salad Dressing*
Fresh Apples and Pears

Fresh Corn and Zucchini Chowder
Greens with *Ginger Vinaigrette Dressing*
Sweet Potato Muffins
Chocolate Mint Cookies

Summer-Evening Suppers

Chicken Couscous Salad with Lemon Dressing
Vegetables Middle Eastern Style
Warm Pita Bread
Fresh Blackberry Quick Fruit Sherbet

Indonesian Pasta Salad
Sliced Tomatoes
Onion Nann (east Indian bread, purchased in an Indian specialty store)
Fresh Peaches and Blueberries
Chai (Indian Tea) served over crushed ice

Casual Mexican Dinner

Black Bean Enchiladas with *Fresh Tomato Salsa,* Yogurt, and Green Onions
Baked Corn Casserole
Greens and Apple Salad with Garlic Dijon Dressing
Papaya with Lime Wedges

Asian Dinner

Colorful Hot and Sour Soup
Kung Pao Vegetarian Style
Steamed Jasmine Rice
Thai Cucumber Salad
Fresh Ginger Cake

Spanish Dinner

Crisp Vegetables with *Spanish Sour Cream Dip*
Paella
Allison's Caesar Salad
Crusty French Bread
Grapefruit Tequila Sorbet

Italian Dinner

Special Minestrone Soup
Sausage and Mushroom Spaghetti Torta
Allison's Caesar Salad
Focaccia Bread
Tiramisù or Fruit Cassis Sorbet

Dinner with a Taste of India

Potatoes Bhaji
Steamed Rice
Sliced Cucumbers and Sliced Tomatoes
Garlic Nann (an east Indian bread)
Orange Wedges
Chai (Indian Tea) served steaming hot

Birthday Dinner

Tzatziki with Pita Triangles
Dungeness Crab Cakes with Red Pepper Sauce
Party Mashed Potatoes
Greens with Strawberries and Poppy Seed Dressing
Steamed Broccoli
Sourdough Rye Rolls
Devil's Food Cake with *Devil's Frosting*

Dinners for Busy Nights

"Pile-Ons" (Our Favorite Tostada)
Mexican Corn
Fresh Peaches or Pears

Angel Hair Pasta with Tomatoes and Basil
Greens with *Honey Dijon Dressing*
Warm Garlic Bread
Melon

Chicken with Cranberries over Steamed Rice
Broccoli with a Splash of Light Soy Sauce
Whole Wheat Sourdough Baguette with Walnuts

La Paz Chicken and Corn Stir-Fry
Tossed Green Salad with S&W Vintage Lites Red Wine & Herb Vinegar Dressing
Soft Breadsticks

Weekend Family Get-Together

Breaded Honey Dijon Salmon
Best Ever Black Beans
Sweet Onion Bake
Cranberry Spinach Salad
Whole Grain Baguette
Dorothy's Lemon Sponge Cake with Glazed Berry Topping

Company Dinners

Fresh Fish with Mediterranean Herbs
Roasted Potatoes and Mushrooms with Fennel
Greens and Apple Salad with Garlic Dijon Dressing
Baked Onion Twists
Cranberry Orange Crisp with Frozen Maple Yogurt

Salmon Pâté with Crackers
Baked Chicken with Caramelized Onions
Corn on the Cob
Apples and Greens with Toasted Walnuts
Rosemary Baguette
Three Berry Cobbler

Paula's Italian Eggplant, Pepper, and Potato Casserole
Rice and Currant Pilaf
Greens with Molly's Balsamic Vinegar Dressing
Rosemary Baguette
Italian Biscotti

Scallops à la Mistral
Curried Rice
Molly's Spinach Salad
Sourdough Whole Wheat Baguette
Summer Fruit on Lemonade Squares

A Special Dinner

Cherry Tomatoes Filled with Boursin
Chilean Sea Bass with Ginger Sesame Sauce
Steamed Jasmine Rice
Sourdough Bread Salad with Roasted Vegetables
Seeded Sourdough Whole Wheat Baguette
Chocolate Cherry Cheesecake

Backyard Barbecues

Grilled Garden Burgers and Garden Dogs on Whole Wheat Buns
with
Lettuce, Tomatoes, Sweet Onions, and Condiments
Barbecued Bean Salad with Chips
Japanese Slaw
Watermelon

Strawberry Lemonade
Mrs. Plancich's Barbecued Salmon
Jane's Asian Pasta Salad
Fresh Fruit Salad
Rosemary Baguette
Roxy Road Cheesecake

Nutrients and <u>The New American Diet Cookbook</u> Recipes

All recipes included in *The New American Diet Cookbook* meet the following nutrient standards:

	CSI†	Fat	Calories	Sodium
NUTRIENT STANDARDS FOR NEW AMERICAN DIET RECIPES*		(amount in one serving)		
Main dishes	9	10 gm	300 or 500‡	600 mg
Other dishes	5	5 gm	300	500 mg

* These guidelines represent upper limits.
† Cholesterol–Saturated Fat Index. The higher the number, the greater the cholesterol and saturated fat content of the recipe (see following explanation).
‡ If a recipe contains pasta, rice, or beans.

You may not be familiar with the Cholesterol–Saturated Fat Index (CSI). This index, which we consider revolutionary in its own right, enables us to rank foods using *one number* with respect to their *combined* cholesterol and saturated fat content. Both—not cholesterol alone and not just saturated fat alone—need to be taken into account in assessing the heart-healthiness of any recipe. The lower the CSI, the better. To be considered for this cookbook, a main dish recipe could have a CSI of no more than 9 for a reasonable serving size. For example, a typical piece of lasagna has a CSI of 30, whereas the same serving size of our Roasted Vegetable Lasagna has a CSI of 3. Also, to be considered for this cookbook, other dishes (appetizers, salads, soups, desserts, etc.) could have a CSI of no more than 5 for a reasonable serving size. For example, one serving ($^1/_{12}$ of the recipe) of the original version of Roxy Road Cheesecake has a CSI of 27, whereas our version has a CSI of less than 1.

Our research on the cuisines of some 40 countries worldwide demonstrated conclusively that those countries with the highest CSIs have the highest death rates from heart disease and, conversely, those with the lowest CSIs have the lowest death rates. France is the one exception. It has the same high CSI intake of other countries in the Western world but has less heart disease. Our study showed that France has a higher intake of foods that contain protective factors against heart disease, namely, more plant foods, especially vegetables that contain antioxidants, soluble fiber, etc.

NOTE: The nutrient content of each and every recipe was computed using Versions 2.6 and 2.7, Nutrient Calculation System, Nutrition Coordinating Center, University of Minnesota, Minneapolis, Minnesota. The calories, sodium, fiber, total fat, saturated fat, cholesterol, and Cholesterol–Saturated Fat Index (CSI) for one serving, or a specified amount, are listed at the bottom of each recipe. The numbers have been rounded to the nearest whole number. We have listed *trace* for amounts less than 0.5 but greater than 0. When a range of amounts was given for an ingredient (e.g., 1 to 3 tablespoons lemon juice), the midpoint of the range was used in the nutrient analysis (e.g., 2 tablespoons lemon juice). When more than one choice was given for an ingredient, we used the first ingredient listed in the nutrient analysis. For example, if dried beans are listed first and canned beans second, the sodium content of the recipe was computed using dried beans. Therefore, if you prepare the recipe using canned beans, the sodium content of the recipe will be higher than is listed in the recipe. The different choices for an ingredient generally will not alter the calories, fat, saturated fat, cholesterol, or CSI significantly. When *optional* was listed after an ingredient, we did not include that ingredient in the nutrient analysis.

The new

AMERICAN DIET

recipes

Developed under the direction of:
Sonja L. Connor, M.S., R.D., and William E. Connor, M.D.

Produced by the Lipid-Atherosclerosis Research Nutrition Staff:
Joyce R. Gustafson, B.S., R.D., Cindy Francois, M.S., R.D.

Sandra R. Bacon, R.N., Reba J. Clow, B.S., R.D.,
Carol DeFrancesco, M.A.L.S., R.D., Donna P. Flavell, B.A., R.D.,
Lauren F. Hatcher, M.S., R.D.

Appetizers

Black Bean Dip

A quick one! Canned black beans have really made our lives easier.

1 cup fresh salsa, mild or hot (bottled
can also be used)

2 tablespoons chopped fresh cilantro

1 can (15 ounces) black beans,
drained and rinsed*
or 2 cups cooked black beans,
drained

1 tablespoon chopped fresh cilantro,
for garnish

Place salsa, cilantro, and drained black beans in a food processor, reserving ½ cup beans to add later. Process until smooth. Stir in remaining ½ cup unmashed beans. Heat through in the microwave oven or on stovetop on medium heat and serve warm. Decorate with chopped cilantro. Accompany with baked tortilla chips.

* S&W has a 50% Less Salt product available.

⁓ Per ¼ Cup ⁓	
Calories:	67
Sodium:	300 mg
Fiber:	4 gm
Total fat:	1 gm
Saturated fat:	Trace gm
Cholesterol:	0 mg
Cholesterol—saturated fat index:	Trace

Boursin

This recipe came from Sonja and Bill's friend Ruth. She has given it to friends and family as a holiday gift for many years. Ruth gradually modified the recipe over the years away from the traditional cream cheese and butter. We adjusted hers to this current tasty version. Make the spread several hours or even a day before serving to allow the flavors to blend. To serve, put Boursin *in a small colorful pottery bowl and surround it with Carr's Table Water Crackers with Cracked Pepper or use as filling in hollowed-out cherry tomatoes.*

6 ounces fat-free cream cheese
1 tablespoon margarine, softened
   (we use Light I Can't Believe
   It's Not Butter)
1 clove garlic, minced

¹/₄ teaspoon dried oregano leaves
¹/₈ teaspoon dried thyme leaves
¹/₈ teaspoon dried basil leaves
¹/₈ teaspoon dried marjoram leaves
¹/₈ teaspoon dried dillweed

Mix all ingredients together and place in a small bowl. Cover and chill for several hours. Serve cold with a small knife for spreading on low-fat crackers.

⁓ Per Tablespoon ⁓	
Calories:	18
Sodium:	97 mg
Fiber:	Trace gm
Total fat:	1 gm
Saturated fat:	Trace gm
Cholesterol:	Trace mg
Cholesterol–saturated fat index:	Trace

Chinese-Style Salad Rolls

·— Makes 9 servings (2 salad rolls each).

These tasty salad rolls have a wonderful flavor—and they're not deep fried. The original recipe came from a woman who made them for her own wedding rehearsal dinner— only many times this amount! We've shortened and simplified the recipe for you. The vegetable filling would also taste great in pita bread for a light lunch.

Zesty Stir-Fry Sauce
1/4 cup lower-salt chicken broth*
3 tablespoons dry sherry
1 tablespoon lower-sodium
   soy sauce †
1 1/2 teaspoons cornstarch
2 1/2 teaspoons hoisin sauce ‡
1 teaspoon dry mustard

Vegetable Filling
2 teaspoons vegetable oil
1 teaspoon minced garlic

1 teaspoon grated fresh gingerroot
1/2 cup finely chopped onion
1/4 cup finely chopped celery
1/2 cup finely chopped zucchini
1/4 cup finely chopped carrots
1/4 cup finely chopped green
   bell peppers
1/4 cup finely chopped
   water chestnuts

18 rounds (8-inch diameter)
   rice paper

To make Zesty Stir-Fry Sauce, combine chicken broth, sherry, soy sauce, cornstarch, hoisin sauce, and dry mustard. Set aside.

To make the Vegetable Filling, heat the oil in a skillet or wok. Add garlic and ginger; sauté until garlic is lightly browned. Add the onion, celery, zucchini, carrots, bell peppers, and water chestnuts and the Zesty Stir-Fry Sauce to the skillet and stir-fry 5 to 7 minutes or until vegetables are crisp-tender.

Soak rice paper rounds in warm water, one at a time, about 1 minute each or until soft and pliable. Lay flat on paper towels and blot dry. To assemble rolls, top each with 1 tablespoon filling. Fold in sides and roll up as tightly as possible. Arrange on a serving platter and serve with Chinese mustard (dry mustard mixed with water), if desired.

·— Per Serving —·	
Calories:	64
Sodium:	91 mg
Fiber:	1 gm
Total fat:	1 gm
Saturated fat:	Trace gm
Cholesterol:	0 mg
Cholesterol–saturated fat index:	Trace

* Swanson Natural Goodness with 1/3 less sodium is available.
† Kikkoman Lite Soy Sauce is available.
‡ Available in the Asian section of most supermarkets.

Fresh Tomato Salsa

We find this makes a wonderful addition to all Mexican dishes. There are many delicious salsas available commercially, but we like to make our own, especially when the tomatoes are plentiful in our gardens. This version is much lower in sodium than store-bought salsa.

2¹/₂ cups finely chopped tomatoes
1¹/₂ cups finely chopped onion
¹/₄ cup finely chopped fresh cilantro
2 tablespoons bottled salsa,
    hot *or* mild

1 tablespoon freshly squeezed
    lime juice
2 cloves garlic, minced

Combine all ingredients, cover, and refrigerate so flavors can blend. Keeps well for several days when tightly covered and refrigerated.

— Per ¹/₄ Cup —	
Calories:	13
Sodium:	16 mg
Fiber:	1 gm
Total fat:	Trace gm
Saturated fat:	Trace gm
Cholesterol:	0 mg
Cholesterol—saturated fat index:	Trace

Grandma's Party Crab Dip

This is a dip Cindy's grandmother makes at Thanksgiving. The fresh crabmeat that Grandma cracks herself is a real treat.

8 ounces fat-free cream cheese, softened

¼ cup low-fat mayonnaise (we like Best Foods Low Fat)

or ¼ cup nonfat mayonnaise

½ pound fresh crabmeat, broken up and picked over

¾ teaspoon Worcestershire sauce

¼ cup chopped green onions

2 tablespoons chopped fresh parsley

4 teaspoons freshly squeezed lemon juice

1 teaspoon Tabasco sauce

Combine all ingredients, saving 1 tablespoon parsley for garnish. Allow to chill for at least 1 hour before serving. Garnish with remaining parsley. Serve warm or chilled with low-fat crackers.

⌐ Per ¼ Cup ⌐	
Calories:	53
Sodium:	317 mg
Fiber:	Trace gm
Total fat:	1 gm
Saturated fat:	Trace gm
Cholesterol:	26 mg
Cholesterol–saturated fat index:	1

Great Garbanzo Spread

·⤳ Makes 1½ cups.

This is our latest version of hummus with a unique blend of spices. It is great on low-fat crackers or pita bread and topped with alfalfa sprouts.

1 can (15 ounces) garbanzo beans,
   drained and rinsed*
2 tablespoons tahini†
¼ cup freshly squeezed lemon juice
3 cloves garlic, minced
1 teaspoon cumin

¼ teaspoon cayenne pepper
¼ teaspoon chili powder
¼ teaspoon paprika
2 to 3 tablespoons water
¼ cup chopped fresh cilantro

Combine garbanzo beans, tahini, lemon juice, garlic, cumin, cayenne pepper, chili powder, paprika, and water in a food processor or blender and blend until smooth. Add chopped cilantro, stir, and serve.

* S&W has a 50% Less Salt product available.
† Tahini (sesame seed butter) is available at most supermarkets.

·⤳ Per ¼ Cup ⤳·	
Calories:	152
Sodium:	14 mg
Fiber:	4 gm
Total fat:	5 gm
Saturated fat:	1 gm
Cholesterol:	0 mg
Cholesterol–saturated fat index:	1

Herbed Pita Triangles

Makes 60 chips (about 12 servings).

A great crunchy chip! They are delicious served "as is" or with a dip. When there is pita bread in their house, Sonja is likely to find Bill in the kitchen cutting it up to make pita triangles. This always seems to happen about 11:00 P.M.

1 teaspoon dried tarragon
1 teaspoon dried basil leaves
1 teaspoon dried thyme leaves

5 (8-inch diameter) whole wheat
   pita breads

Preheat oven to 325°. Combine herbs. Split each pita bread into 2 round pieces. Cut each half into 6 triangles with kitchen scissors. Put triangles on baking sheet in single layers. Spray triangles with nonstick cooking spray and sprinkle with herbs. Do a few at a time until all are prepared. Bake 8 to 10 minutes or until lightly browned and very crisp. Serve immediately or store in a container with a tight lid.

~ Per 5 Chips ~	
Calories:	108
Sodium:	215 mg
Fiber:	3 gm
Total fat:	1 gm
Saturated fat:	Trace gm
Cholesterol:	0 mg
Cholesterol–saturated fat index:	Trace

Jenny's Shrimp Dip

A friend of ours recently served this dip at an engagement party. It was such a success the bowl was quickly emptied.

8 ounces fat-free cream cheese,
   softened
1/2 cup Campbell's Healthy Request
   Tomato Soup, undiluted
1/2 cup low-fat mayonnaise (we like
   Best Foods Low Fat)
   or 1/2 cup nonfat mayonnaise
1 cup shrimpmeat (tiny shrimp
   about 1/2 inch in size)
   or chopped cooked shrimp

2 tablespoons grated onion
1 tablespoon freshly squeezed
   lemon juice
1 teaspoon dry mustard
1/4 to 1/2 teaspoon Tabasco sauce
1/8 teaspoon Salad Seasoning
   (by Spice Islands)

In a mixing bowl, combine all ingredients. Stir until well combined. Chill and serve with fresh vegetables or low-fat crackers.

~ Per 1/4 Cup ~	
Calories:	53
Sodium:	273 mg
Fiber:	Trace gm
Total fat:	1 gm
Saturated fat:	Trace gm
Cholesterol:	24 mg
Cholesterol–saturated fat index:	1

Layered Mexican Bean Dip

Now that baked corn chips are widely available, we decided it was time to make a 1990s version of the much-loved layered Mexican dip. Rosarita's refried black beans give a new twist to this favorite four-layer appetizer. Our staff members and our families said the taste was great—after they had wolfed it all down!

Bean Layer
1 can (16 ounces) refried black beans
1 clove garlic, finely minced
¹/₄ cup diced green chiles

Sour Cream Layer
¹/₂ cup nonfat sour cream

Guacamole Layer
1 ripe avocado, mashed
2 teaspoons freshly squeezed
    lemon juice
1 tablespoon salsa (optional)

Salsa Layer
1¹/₂ cups finely chopped tomatoes
¹/₂ cup finely chopped green onions
2 tablespoons finely chopped
    fresh cilantro
1 to 2 tablespoons chopped jalapeño
    peppers *or* salsa
2 teaspoons freshly squeezed lemon
    or lime juice

Baked tortilla chips

Prepare each layer in separate bowls so the dip can be quickly assembled. Mix refried beans with garlic and chiles. Stir sour cream until smooth. Mash avocado, add lemon juice and salsa, if using. Combine tomatoes, green onions, cilantro, peppers, and lemon juice.

To assemble and serve, spread bean mixture on a 10- to 12-inch platter to make a 9-inch circle. Cover refried beans with plastic wrap and heat in the microwave oven 1 to 2 minutes. Remove plastic wrap and spread sour cream over beans. Spread guacamole over sour cream. Spoon salsa over the top and serve immediately. Pass baked tortilla chips to use as "dippers."

•→ Per Serving (Not Including Chips) →•	
Calories:	93
Sodium:	244 mg
Fiber:	4 gm
Total fat:	3 gm
Saturated fat:	1 gm
Cholesterol:	Trace mg
Cholesterol–saturated fat index:	1

Pineapple Salsa

This quick "extra" is fun to serve with any bean chili, but we especially like it with Halibut Olé (page 249).

1 can (20 ounces) crushed
   juice-packed pineapple, drained,
   or 2 cups finely chopped fresh
   pineapple
1 clove garlic, minced

3 tablespoons chopped fresh mint
   or 1 tablespoon dried mint
2 tablespoons freshly squeezed
   lime juice
2 to 4 drops Tabasco sauce

Combine all ingredients; cover tightly and chill. Serve at room temperature.

·~ Per ¼ Cup ~·	
Calories:	45
Sodium:	4 mg
Fiber:	1 gm
Total fat:	Trace gm
Saturated fat:	Trace gm
Cholesterol:	0 mg
Cholesterol–saturated fat index:	Trace

Piquant Artichoke Dip

By adjusting the amount of Tabasco sauce, you can make this dip as spicy as you want.

1 can (14 ounces) water-packed
   artichoke hearts
½ cup nonfat mayonnaise
½ cup nonfat plain yogurt
½ cup grated Parmesan cheese

2 cloves garlic, minced
1 can (4 ounces) diced green chiles
1 to 3 teaspoons Tabasco sauce
½ cup sliced green onions

Preheat oven to 350°. Cut each artichoke heart into 6 pieces. Combine all ingredients in a mixing bowl, reserving 2 tablespoons of green onions to add later. Put into a 3-cup ovenproof baking dish coated with nonstick cooking spray. Bake for 20 to 30 minutes or until lightly browned. Garnish with remaining green onions. Serve with low-fat crackers or French bread.

~ Per ¼ Cup ~	
Calories:	52
Sodium:	320 mg
Fiber:	1 gm
Total fat:	2 gm
Saturated fat:	1 gm
Cholesterol:	4 mg
Cholesterol–saturated fat index:	1

Red Bean and Cilantro Dip

This delicious bean spread can be used as a sandwich filling or as an appetizer with whole grain crackers or Melba toast. Prepare ahead of time so the garlic can do its thing!

1 can (15 ounces) kidney beans,
    drained and rinsed*

1 tablespoon red wine vinegar

2 tablespoons water

¹/₄ cup finely chopped red onion

2 cloves garlic, minced

¹/₄ cup finely chopped fresh cilantro

¹/₂ teaspoon Tabasco sauce

¹/₂ teaspoon (or less) Lite Salt

Put beans, vinegar, and water in a blender or food processor and process until mixture is slightly lumpy. Place beans in a bowl; add remaining ingredients and mix well. Cover and refrigerate 8 hours or so before using.

* S&W has a 50% Less Salt product available.

·~ Per ¹/₄ Cup ~·	
Calories:	61
Sodium:	292 mg
Fiber:	4 gm
Total fat:	Trace gm
Saturated fat:	Trace gm
Cholesterol:	0 mg
Cholesterol—saturated fat index:	Trace

Salmon Pâté

This recipe was developed when we had a mound of leftover grilled salmon. Everyone fights over this pâté, including our grandchildren. On a cross-country skiing outing on Mt. Hood, the smell was so enticing, we had to share the pâté with friends. The pâté has a wonderful taste when made from salmon that has been cooked over mesquite-type coals. Carr's Table Water Crackers with Cracked Pepper or thin slices of French bread are excellent to spread it on.

1³/₄ cups cooked salmon
  or 1 can (15 ounces) red salmon,
  drained
1 tablespoon nonfat mayonnaise
¹/₂ cup nonfat plain yogurt
2 cloves garlic, minced
¹/₄ teaspoon Tabasco sauce

1 to 2 teaspoons dried dillweed
¹/₄ teaspoon (or less) Lite Salt
  (omit if using canned salmon)
¹/₄ cup chopped green onions
2 teaspoons freshly squeezed
  lemon juice
1 tablespoon chopped fresh parsley

Remove skin and bones from the salmon. Combine all ingredients and mix thoroughly with a fork (not a food processor). Cover and chill in refrigerator. Serve with low-fat crackers or thinly sliced French bread.

⌐ Per ¹/₄ Cup ⌐	
Calories:	71
Sodium:	101 mg
Fiber:	Trace gm
Total fat:	3 gm
Saturated fat:	1 gm
Cholesterol:	23 mg
Cholesterol—saturated fat index:	2

Skordalia

This dip is full of garlic, hence the name from the Greek word for garlic, skorda. We always order it when our staff has lunch at a Greek restaurant, so we decided to make it ourselves. Serve as a dip with thinly sliced baguette.

2 cups packed white bread
   (ten 1-ounce slices)
1 tablespoon minced garlic
2 teaspoons olive oil

1 to 2 tablespoons freshly squeezed
   lemon juice *or* vinegar
1 to 1¼ cups water, divided

Remove crusts from bread. Cut bread in quarters and pack very tightly to measure. In a food processor or blender, mix bread and garlic until texture is very fine (makes 2¾ cups crumbs). Place mixture in a bowl, add oil and lemon juice or vinegar, and 1 cup water. Mix well by hand. If needed, add remaining ¼ cup water, 1 tablespoon at a time, until Skordalia is thick but spreadable.

◞ Per ¼ Cup ◞	
Calories:	38
Sodium:	52 mg
Fiber:	Trace gm
Total fat:	1 gm
Saturated fat:	Trace gm
Cholesterol:	Trace mg
Cholesterol–saturated fat index:	Trace

Spanish Sour Cream Dip

‑ Makes 2 cups.

1 cup nonfat sour cream (we like
    Land O' Lakes)
1/2 cup nonfat plain yogurt
1/2 cup sliced black olives,
    well drained
1 cup finely chopped green onions

3/4 cup chopped tomatoes
1/4 cup finely chopped fresh cilantro
2 tablespoons freshly squeezed
    lemon juice
2 cloves garlic, minced
1/4 to 1/2 teaspoon Tabasco sauce

Combine all ingredients; cover and chill before serving. Serve with raw vegetables or breadsticks.

‑ Per 1/4 Cup ‑	
Calories:	68
Sodium:	122 mg
Fiber:	1 gm
Total fat:	1 gm
Saturated fat:	Trace gm
Cholesterol:	Trace mg
Cholesterol–saturated fat index:	Trace

Spoon Bread Triangles   *‑ Makes 16 servings (2 triangles each).*

Joyce was served this custardlike corn bread as an appetizer in historic Williamsburg, Virginia. We think it would also taste great topped with honey or salsa and served with bean soup or chili.

1½ cups water	1½ teaspoons sugar
2 cups skim milk	2 tablespoons margarine
1½ cups cornmeal	1¼ cups egg substitute
1 teaspoon (or less) Lite Salt	1 tablespoon baking powder

Preheat oven to 350°. In a medium saucepan, combine water and skim milk; heat until warm. Add cornmeal, Lite Salt, sugar, and margarine and cook over medium heat, stirring vigorously until mixture thickens. Remove from heat. In a separate bowl, beat egg substitute with baking powder until light and fluffy. Add to cornmeal mixture and mix well. Pour into a 9-by-13-inch baking dish that has been coated with nonstick cooking spray. Bake 45 to 50 minutes.

Cut into 8 pieces and then cut each piece into 4 triangles. Serve hot with honey or salsa, if desired.

‑ Per Serving ‑	
Calories:	81
Sodium:	213 mg
Fiber:	1 gm
Total fat:	2 gm
Saturated fat:	Trace gm
Cholesterol:	1 mg
Cholesterol–saturated fat index:	Trace

Thai Salad Rolls

This is a favorite Thai appetizer. Cindy's husband likes them so much he prepares them himself. The Thai Peanut Sauce *in this recipe is very good, but we also like to use the* Peanut Sauce *from our* Spicy Thai Pizza *(page 177).*

Thai Peanut Sauce
1 teaspoon sesame oil
4 cloves garlic, minced
1/4 teaspoon red pepper flakes
1 tablespoon tomato paste
3 tablespoons reduced-fat
   peanut butter
3 tablespoons hoisin sauce*
1/2 teaspoon sugar
3/4 cup water

Salad Rolls
1 ounce dry bean threads
   (cellophane noodles)*

1 tablespoon rice vinegar
2 large Boston lettuce leaves
8 rounds (8-inch diameter)
   rice paper
2 tablespoons chopped
   unsalted peanuts
1 green onion, sliced diagonally
   into 2-inch strips
1/4 cup grated carrot
1/4 cup thinly sliced Chinese
   or napa cabbage
1/4 cup chopped fresh mint
1/4 cup chopped fresh cilantro

To prepare Thai Peanut Sauce: In a small saucepan, heat sesame oil and sauté garlic and pepper flakes until garlic is slightly browned. Add tomato paste, peanut butter, hoisin sauce, sugar, and water and bring to a boil, whisking constantly. Reduce heat and simmer, whisking, until sauce is thickened, about 1 minute. Serve at room temperature. The sauce can be made a few days ahead of time and stored in the refrigerator until ready to use. Bring to room temperature before serving. *This recipe makes 1 cup sauce; we recommend 1/4 cup for 4 salad rolls, so freeze remaining 3/4 cup sauce for later use.*

To prepare Salad Rolls: In a bowl, soak bean threads in very hot water for 15 minutes and drain. Chop into 4-inch pieces. In a small bowl, toss bean threads with rice vinegar. Tear lettuce leaves in half, discarding ribs. Soak rice paper rounds in warm water, one at a time, about 1 minute each or until soft and pliable. Lay flat on paper towels and blot dry.

To assemble rolls, overlap 2 rounds of rice paper. Arrange a lettuce leaf half on top of the rice paper rounds. Top with 1/4 each of the bean threads, peanuts, green onion, carrot, cabbage, mint, and cilantro. Fold in sides and roll up as tightly as possible. Repeat to make 4 rolls. Serve rolls chilled with 1/4 cup Thai Peanut Sauce.

* Available in the Asian-food section of most supermarkets.

• Per Salad Roll and 1 Tablespoon Thai Peanut Sauce •	
Calories:	106
Sodium:	33 mg
Fiber:	1 gm
Total fat:	4 gm
Saturated fat:	1 gm
Cholesterol:	0 mg
Cholesterol–saturated fat index:	1

Toasted Puffs

2 tablespoons very finely chopped
  red onion
1/4 cup grated Parmesan cheese
1/4 cup nonfat mayonnaise *or* low-fat
  mayonnaise (we like Best Foods
  Low Fat)

24 low-fat crackers (Melba toast *or*
  Carr's Table Water Crackers with
  Cracked Pepper work well)

Combine onion, Parmesan cheese, and mayonnaise. Cover well and chill 2 to 3 hours. When ready to serve, preheat broiler and then spread 1 teaspoon of cheese mix on each cracker. Place under broiler until they are puffy and lightly browned (about 4 minutes). Watch closely while broiling to make sure they don't burn. Serve immediately.

Per Serving	
Calories:	75
Sodium:	265 mg
Fiber:	1 gm
Total fat:	3 gm
Saturated fat:	1 gm
Cholesterol:	3 mg
Cholesterol–saturated fat index:	1

Tzatziki

·– Makes 6 servings (¹/₄ cup each).

This is a very popular Greek appetizer. To achieve a thick, creamy yogurt like the one you would find in Greece, drain the yogurt overnight or for several hours. Add garlic according to your taste, but the original Greek dish has lots of it! When assembled, Tzatziki will keep a day or two in the refrigerator. Serve with small pieces of thickly sliced whole grain bread.

2 cups nonfat plain yogurt
1 small cucumber
    or ¹/₂ long European cucumber

1 to 3 large cloves garlic, minced
Pinch of freshly ground pepper
¹/₂ teaspoon (or less) Lite Salt

Line a strainer with cheesecloth or a linen napkin. Place over a bowl and pour in the yogurt. Refrigerate overnight, or for several hours, while it drains. The yogurt should be quite thick.

Peel cucumber, scoop out seeds, and grate. Let dry for a few minutes on a paper towel.

Beat thickened yogurt (a wire whisk works well for this) until creamy. Add minced garlic, pepper, Lite Salt, and grated cucumbers. Mix well and store in refrigerator. Serve chilled.

·– Per ¹/₄ Cup ·–	
Calories:	51
Sodium:	144 mg
Fiber:	Trace gm
Total fat:	Trace gm
Saturated fat:	Trace gm
Cholesterol:	1 mg
Cholesterol–saturated fat index:	Trace

Beverages

Chai (Indian Tea)
Citrus Mint Iced Tea
Cranberry Wassail
Finland's Sima
Strawberry Lemonade
Switchel (A Cold Drink)

Chai (Indian Tea)

We first drank this tea at The India House, a restaurant in downtown Portland. It was a cold, rainy night and the tea really hit the spot. Chai recently has become a popular drink in Portland. It is available in supermarkets at a cost many times greater than when prepared at home. There were two clear preferences among our tasters. One group preferred a stronger tea flavor, less honey, and less milk. Another group preferred less tea, more honey, and more milk (see footnote for amounts to use for this version).

¹/₄ cup black tea leaves (we like Darjeeling)*	1 teaspoon cardamom seeds
5 cups water*	10 whole cloves
2 teaspoons grated fresh gingerroot	5 peppercorns
1 star anise, broken into small pieces	1 teaspoon vanilla
1 teaspoon grated orange peel	¹/₄ to ¹/₃ cup honey*
2 three-inch pieces stick cinnamon, each broken in half	3 cups skim milk*

Place tea leaves, water, ginger, anise, orange peel, cinnamon, cardamom, cloves, and peppercorns in a pan. Bring to a boil, reduce heat to low, stir, cover, and boil 20 minutes. Strain, then add vanilla, honey, and milk. Heat thoroughly (do not boil) if serving hot. Pour over crushed ice if serving cold.

* Three tablespoons tea, 4 cups water, ¹/₃ cup honey, 4 cups skim milk, and the spices as indicated.

·~ Per Cup ~·	
Calories:	80
Sodium:	60 mg
Fiber:	Trace gm
Total fat:	Trace gm
Saturated fat:	Trace gm
Cholesterol:	2 mg
Cholesterol–saturated fat index:	Trace

Citrus Mint Iced Tea

We like herbal teas very much, but this delicious hot-weather drink can be made with any black tea. Serve over ice and garnish with a sprig of fresh mint for a wonderful treat.

8 tea bags Celestial Seasonings Iced
   Herb Tea Original Delight
   or 12 tea bags decaffeinated
   Constant Comment (or any
   decaffeinated black tea)
12 large fresh mint leaves
¹/₂ cup sugar
4 cups boiling water

1 can (6 ounces) frozen orange juice
   concentrate, thawed
1 can (6 ounces) frozen lemonade
   concentrate, thawed
12 cups cold water
Small sprigs of mint leaves as
   garnish (optional)

Place tea bags, mint leaves, and sugar in large bowl, pitcher, or glass jar. Pour boiling water over them and steep 10 to 15 minutes. Remove tea bags and mint. Add orange juice and lemonade concentrates and cold water. Stir and chill. Serve very cold over ice. Garnish with sprigs of mint leaves, if desired.

‿ Per Cup ‿	
Calories:	67
Sodium:	3 mg
Fiber:	Trace gm
Total fat:	Trace gm
Saturated fat:	Trace gm
Cholesterol:	0 mg
Cholesterol–saturated fat index:	Trace

Cranberry Wassail

The aroma of this hot beverage starts any holiday function off with a good beginning! It has been served at our staff holiday party for 25-plus years. During the holiday season of 1994, a group of us spent a morning decorating gingerbread houses and sipping this delicious drink. The two events are now tied together.

6 tea bags (we like Celestial
  Seasonings Iced Herb Tea)
¼ teaspoon allspice
¼ teaspoon cinnamon
¼ teaspoon nutmeg
2½ cups boiling water

½ cup (or less) sugar
2 cups cranberry juice cocktail
1½ cups water
½ cup orange juice
⅓ cup freshly squeezed lemon juice

Place tea bags, allspice, cinnamon, and nutmeg in a 3-quart container and cover with boiling water. Let steep 5 minutes and remove tea bags. Add sugar and stir to dissolve. Add cranberry juice cocktail, water, and orange and lemon juices; heat just to boiling. Serve hot.

~ Per ½ Cup ~	
Calories:	102
Sodium:	6 mg
Fiber:	Trace gm
Total fat:	Trace gm
Saturated fat:	Trace gm
Cholesterol:	0 mg
Cholesterol–saturated fat index:	Trace

Finland's Sima

One of our good friends brought this recipe for a fun drink from Finland. She said they make this drink on May Day for the workers' festivities. Some think it tastes a bit like beer, but sweeter. It came to us in metric measurements, so we made a few changes for you.

21 cups water, divided
2 lemons, sliced
1 pound brown sugar
³/₄ cup sugar

³/₄ cup beer (optional)
¹/₄ teaspoon yeast
Raisins

In a large kettle, bring 10 cups water to a boil. Add lemons, sugars, and beer, if using. Boil 5 minutes. Remove from heat and stir in 11 cups cold water; let mixture stand until it reaches room temperature. Stir in yeast. Cover, but leave the cover ajar, and let stand 24 hours at room temperature. Strain, discard lemons, and pour liquid into glass jars, each containing 4 or 5 raisins. Cover loosely and let stand at room temperature until the raisins rise to the top, 2 to 3 days. Remove raisins, cap tightly and refrigerate. Finland's Sima lasts for a week in the refrigerator unopened; once opened, it goes flat in a few hours.

⌐ Per Cup ⌐	
Calories:	93
Sodium:	7 mg
Fiber:	Trace gm
Total fat:	Trace gm
Saturated fat:	0 gm
Cholesterol:	0 mg
Cholesterol–saturated fat index:	Trace

Strawberry Lemonade

Oregon strawberries have a shelf life of 3 seconds. We all know that necessity is the mother of invention, or, as Joyce always says, "When our backs are to the wall, we can really produce." This was the case when we were faced with a mountain of strawberries. In desperation, we puréed some of the berries and added them to lemonade. A tablespoon of crème de cassis makes this wonderful drink even better.

I can (12 ounces) frozen lemonade
   concentrate, thawed
8 cups cold water

1 cup strawberries
1 tablespoon crème de cassis
   (optional)

Combine lemonade concentrate and water in a large pitcher. Stir until mixed. Clean strawberries and put in blender. Add a small amount of lemonade and blend berries. Add to lemonade. Add crème de cassis, if desired. Stir and chill. Serve over ice.

~ Per Cup ~	
Calories:	83
Sodium:	6 mg
Fiber:	1 gm
Total fat:	Trace gm
Saturated fat:	Trace gm
Cholesterol:	0 mg
Cholesterol–saturated fat index:	Trace

Switchel (A Cold Drink)

This is adapted from an old Shaker recipe found in New England. Hardworking men in the fields consumed quantities of this refreshing beverage, especially during haying time. Joyce was served this drink when she ate lunch at The Herbfarm, a very popular restaurant in the Seattle area. She was inspired to develop a variation on it. We think it's a tasty beverage for a warm day!

2 tablespoons sugar

6 tablespoons water

$1/4$ cup freshly squeezed lemon juice

$1/4$ cup freshly squeezed orange juice

$1/2$ cup finely chopped fresh mint

  or 3 tablespoons dried mint

2 quarts chilled ginger ale

Combine sugar and water in a small saucepan and bring to a boil. Add fruit juices to the hot sugar syrup. Remove from the heat. Add chopped mint and let steep, covered, for about 1 hour.

Strain mixture through a fine strainer and chill. When ready to serve, add 2 quarts of chilled ginger ale and serve very cold.

~ Per Cup ~	
Calories:	113
Sodium:	28 mg
Fiber:	Trace gm
Total fat:	Trace gm
Saturated fat:	0 gm
Cholesterol:	0 mg
Cholesterol–saturated fat index:	Trace

Yeast Breads

Baked Onion Twists
Focaccia Bread
Homemade English Muffins
Orange Cardamom Yeast Bread
Pumpkin Dinner Rolls
Stuffed Breadsticks

Quick Breads

Fresh Pear Bread
Raisin Wheat Bread
Round Rye Bread
Sour Cream Prune Bread
Tipsy Prunes and Pecan Bread

Muffins

Blackberry Muffins
Chile Cheese Dinner Muffins
Cinnamon Applesauce Bran Muffins
Fresh Apple and Pumpkin Spice Muffins
Lemon Blueberry Muffins
Pear Almond Muffins
Pie Cherry Muffins
Raisin Bran Muffins
Sweet Potato Muffins
Tiny Pineapple Muffins with Orange Glaze

Breakfasts and Brunches

Apricot Prune Coffee Cake
Baked Chicken Sandwich
Calico Strata
Cranapple Dutch Baby
Cranberry Apricot Scones
Fruit Slush Cups
Oatmeal Buttermilk Waffles
Oven-Baked French Toast with Cranberry Maple Syrup
Poppy Seed Pancakes
Raap-Wal-O (Great Hot Cereal)
Sweet Potato Pancakes

Baked Onion Twists

You will be surprised that these delicious twists are so easily prepared, and your guests will love them!

1 can (11 ounces) refrigerated soft breadsticks	¹/₂ teaspoon garlic powder
1 egg white, lightly beaten	1 teaspoon dried minced onion
1 tablespoon grated Parmesan cheese	¹/₂ teaspoon dried basil leaves

Preheat oven to 350°. Unroll dough and separate into 8 strips. Twist each dough strip and shape into a ring; pinch ends together. Place on a baking sheet that has been sprayed with nonstick cooking spray.

Brush top of each breadstick with egg white. In a separate bowl, combine Parmesan cheese, garlic powder, minced onion, and basil; sprinkle on breadsticks. Bake 15 minutes, or until golden brown.

·~ Per Twist ~·	
Calories:	117
Sodium:	311 mg
Fiber:	1 gm
Total fat:	3 gm
Saturated fat:	1 gm
Cholesterol:	1 mg
Cholesterol–saturated fat index:	1

Focaccia Bread

Focaccia bread tastes best fresh out of the oven. A variety of herbs can be used, but we like rosemary.

1 package yeast
1 cup warm water
2 teaspoons sugar
1¹/₂ teaspoons (or less) Lite Salt
1 tablespoon olive oil
1¹/₄ cups white flour
1¹/₄ cups whole wheat flour

Topping
1 teaspoon olive oil
1 teaspoon dried *or* chopped
   fresh rosemary
3 tablespoons grated
   Parmesan cheese

In a large bowl, sprinkle yeast over warm water and let stand 5 minutes. Stir in sugar, Lite Salt, and olive oil. Add 1 cup white flour and 1 cup whole wheat flour; stir just until blended. With a wooden spoon, beat until dough is elastic, about 5 minutes.

Turn dough onto a lightly floured surface (use remaining flours); knead until dough is smooth and springy, 10 to 15 minutes. Place in a bowl sprayed with nonstick cooking spray. Turn dough to coat top. Cover and let rise in a warm place until doubled in size, about 1 hour.

Punch dough down; knead briefly on a lightly floured board. Roll and stretch dough to fit bottom of a 10-by-15-inch shallow baking pan that has been sprayed with nonstick cooking spray. Leave uncovered and let dough rise again until doubled in size.

About 10 minutes before bread is ready to bake, preheat oven to 450°. Brush top of dough with olive oil. With your fingers or the end of a spoon, press holes in dough at 1- to 2-inch intervals. Sprinkle rosemary and Parmesan cheese on top. Bake 12 to 15 minutes or until lightly browned. Cut into wedges and serve warm.

⁃ Per Serving ⁃	
Calories:	115
Sodium:	152 mg
Fiber:	2 gm
Total fat:	2 gm
Saturated fat:	1 gm
Cholesterol:	1 mg
Cholesterol–saturated fat index:	1

Homemade English Muffins

Bill's brother, John, has been very upset that we have not included an English muffin recipe in any of our cookbooks. We have always assumed that people would rather buy them than go to all the trouble of making them. Our staff tried them and gobbled them up, so we have finally, and happily, succumbed to John's persistent requests.

1 cup lukewarm skim milk	1¹/₂ cups white flour
1 package yeast	1 cup whole wheat flour
2 tablespoons margarine, softened	About 1 tablespoon yellow
1 tablespoon sugar	*or* white cornmeal
1 teaspoon (or less) Lite Salt	

Combine lukewarm milk and yeast in a large mixing bowl. Let sit for 5 minutes. Stir and add margarine, sugar, and Lite Salt. Add flours gradually and then beat thoroughly for 5 minutes. Add additional flour to make the dough just barely firm enough to handle. You may want to knead it with your hands. When well mixed, return to mixing bowl, cover it with a cloth and let rise in a warm place in your kitchen for about 1 hour.

After dough has risen, place it on a board that has been sprinkled with the cornmeal. Pat out dough with your hands to ¹/₂ inch thickness. Using a 3-inch-diameter glass, cut into 12 circles. Chill for about 10 minutes and then cook on an electric griddle set at 400° or a heavy skillet over medium-high heat for 7 to 10 minutes on each side. Keep uncooked rounds in refrigerator while first batch cooks.

Serve immediately while they are warm (split in half with a fork or slice with a knife) or reheat under the broiler. Serve with jam.

Per Muffin	
Calories:	123
Sodium:	118 mg
Fiber:	2 gm
Total fat:	2 gm
Saturated fat:	Trace gm
Cholesterol:	Trace mg
Cholesterol–saturated fat index:	Trace

Orange Cardamom Yeast Bread

This bread has been made for years, most often when there is a glut of zucchini from Bill's garden. It is great toasted.

1 cup warm water	2 cups white flour, divided
1 tablespoon yeast (1 packet)	1 teaspoon (or less) Lite Salt
1 tablespoon melted margarine	1 teaspoon grated orange peel
3 tablespoons firmly packed	2 teaspoons cardamom
brown sugar *or* honey	1½ cups grated zucchini
1½ cups whole wheat flour	¾ cup currants *or* raisins

In a large mixing bowl, combine water and yeast; let stand 5 minutes to soften. In a small bowl, combine margarine and brown sugar; cool to lukewarm. Stir together whole wheat flour, 1 cup white flour, Lite Salt, orange peel, and cardamom. Stir brown sugar mixture and about half the flour mixture into the yeast. Add zucchini and currants or raisins; stir to blend. Gradually stir in remaining flour mixture to make a stiff dough.

Use the remaining 1 cup white flour during the kneading process. Turn dough out onto a well-floured board and knead 10 minutes, or until dough is smooth and elastic, adding flour as necessary to prevent sticking. Place dough in a bowl that has been sprayed with nonstick cooking spray and turn to coat top. Cover with a towel that has been lightly sprinkled with water. Let rise in a warm place until doubled in size, about 45 minutes.

Punch down dough and divide in half. Shape each piece into a small loaf and place in a 3⅝-by-7⅜-inch loaf pan that has been sprayed with nonstick cooking spray. Cover and let rise in a warm place, about 45 minutes, until dough doubles.

Bake at 350° for 40 to 45 minutes or until tops are a deep brown and loaves sound hollow when tapped. Remove from pans and cool on wire rack.

·⁓ Per Slice ⁓·	
Calories:	68
Sodium:	37 mg
Fiber:	1 gm
Total fat:	1 gm
Saturated fat:	Trace gm
Cholesterol:	0 mg
Cholesterol–saturated fat index:	Trace

Pumpkin Dinner Rolls

·⤳ Makes 36 rolls.

The pumpkin makes these rolls quite moist. We like this because we can make and freeze them ahead of time, and they are still moist when we thaw and serve them. We make these rolls every Thanksgiving—ahead of time, of course. One of our staff members, Reba, thinks they would be good to serve for breakfast or brunch.

1/2 cup sugar
2 tablespoons yeast (2 packets)
1 cup warm water
1 tablespoon melted margarine
1 teaspoon (or less) Lite Salt
1/2 cup nonfat milk powder

1 cup pumpkin
1 1/2 teaspoons cinnamon
3/4 teaspoon cloves
3/4 teaspoon nutmeg
3/4 teaspoon ginger
5 cups flour

In a large mixing bowl, combine sugar, yeast, and water. Let stand 5 minutes. Add melted margarine, Lite Salt, milk powder, pumpkin, cinnamon, cloves, nutmeg, and ginger, and mix well. Stir in flour 1 cup at a time. When dough becomes too thick to stir, put remaining flour and dough on a cutting board or other surface and knead for 8 to 10 minutes. Spray a large bowl with nonstick cooking spray. Put dough in bowl and turn over to coat top. Cover with a towel that has been lightly sprinkled with water. Let rise until double in size, 45 to 60 minutes. Place dough on lightly floured board, punch down and knead a few times to remove all the air bubbles. Shape into 36 walnut-sized balls and place in two 9-inch round cake pans that have been sprayed with nonstick cooking spray. Cover and let rise until double, 45 to 60 minutes.

Preheat oven to 375°. Bake rolls 30 minutes. Remove from pans and place on wire rack to cool 10 minutes. Serve warm.

NOTE: If you plan to make these rolls ahead of time, bake 20 minutes. Remove from pans and place on wire rack until completely cooled. Wrap in foil and freeze. To serve, remove from freezer, let thaw in foil and heat (still wrapped in foil) in 350° oven for 10 minutes.

·⤳ Per Roll ·⤳	
Calories:	85
Sodium:	38 mg
Fiber:	1 gm
Total fat:	1 gm
Saturated fat:	Trace gm
Cholesterol:	Trace mg
Cholesterol–saturated fat index:	Trace

Stuffed Breadsticks

Frozen dinner rolls make this recipe easy to prepare. The breadsticks can be baked ahead of time and frozen, although they taste best fresh out of the oven.

12 large (2 ounces each) frozen
white dinner rolls, cut in half,
or 24 small (1 ounce each)
frozen dinner rolls
or any yeast bread recipe

1/4 cup egg substitute
1/3 cup grated Parmesan cheese
3/4 cup chopped green onions
1 clove garlic, minced

1 tablespoon sesame seeds

Filling
8 ounces fat-free cream cheese,
softened

The day before: Remove dinner rolls from freezer and defrost in refrigerator overnight. *Rolls can be defrosted in the microwave oven immediately before preparation, although timing is critical to avoid cooking the dough.*

Prepare filling: Blend cream cheese and egg substitute together in a small mixing bowl. Add Parmesan cheese, green onions, and garlic.

Roll each dinner roll into an oblong shape, about 7 inches by 4 inches, on an unfloured or lightly floured surface. *If using homemade bread dough, divide into 24 equal parts and roll into the same-size pieces.* Spread 1 scant tablespoon of filling in the center of each roll (do not spread filling to the edges). Fold all 4 sides inward so they overlap, pinching to seal them. Place folded side down on a baking sheet that has been sprayed with nonstick cooking spray. Rub a small amount of water on each breadstick and sprinkle with sesame seeds. Let rise for about 1 hour at room temperature, or until size doubles. Bake at 350° for about 10 to 15 minutes, until golden brown. Serve warm.

– Per Breadstick –	
Calories:	94
Sodium:	192 mg
Fiber:	Trace gm
Total fat:	2 gm
Saturated fat:	Trace gm
Cholesterol:	1 mg
Cholesterol–saturated fat index:	Trace

Fresh Pear Bread

‣ Makes 1 loaf (16 slices).

A delicious and quickly prepared bread. Use fresh pears, if available, but canned ones work well, also. The lower fat and sodium contents of the Reduced Fat Bisquick allow us to use it in our recipes.

2 large fresh pears (mashed with
    a fork to make 1 cup)
    or 1 can (16 ounces) juice-packed
    pears, drained
2 cups Reduced Fat Bisquick
$1/2$ cup sugar

$1/4$ teaspoon nutmeg
$1/2$ teaspoon baking soda
4 egg whites, lightly beaten
$1/2$ cup nonfat plain yogurt
$1/3$ cup chopped walnuts

Preheat oven to 350°. Peel, core, and mash pears with a fork. Combine Bisquick, sugar, nutmeg, and baking soda. Mix beaten egg whites and yogurt. Combine all ingredients with chopped nuts and put batter into a lightly oiled 9-by-5-inch loaf pan. Bake for 50 minutes or until wooden pick inserted in the center comes out clean.

‣ Per Slice ‣	
Calories:	123
Sodium:	223 mg
Fiber:	2 gm
Total fat:	3 gm
Saturated fat:	Trace gm
Cholesterol:	Trace mg
Cholesterol–saturated fat index:	Trace

Raisin Wheat Bread

This round loaf of bread has a delightful crunchy texture. It is good to serve at a Sunday brunch and makes a nice accompaniment to a curry dish. The raisins can be omitted when serving the bread with soup or chowder.

1 tablespoon vegetable oil
$^1/_2$ cup sugar
$^1/_4$ cup egg substitute
   or 2 egg whites
1 cup unsweetened applesauce
2 cups buttermilk
$^1/_2$ teaspoon baking soda
1 to 2 tablespoons caraway seed
   (optional)

$^3/_4$ cup raisins
$^1/_2$ cup Grape-nuts cereal
$2^1/_2$ cups white flour
1 cup whole wheat flour
$^1/_2$ cup wheat germ
1 tablespoon baking powder

Preheat oven to 350°. Spray a Bundt or 10-inch tube pan with nonstick cooking spray and then lightly flour it. Mix oil and sugar together. Add egg substitute or egg whites and applesauce; stir. Combine buttermilk, baking soda, caraway seeds, if using, raisins, and cereal. Add to sugar-applesauce mixture and stir well. Combine flours, wheat germ, and baking powder; stir into rest of mixture and spoon batter into prepared pan. Bake 55 to 65 minutes or until a wooden pick inserted in the center comes out clean. Cool in pan 10 minutes, remove, and cool on wire rack. Slice when cool.

·- Per Slice ~	
Calories:	158
Sodium:	153 mg
Fiber:	2 gm
Total fat:	2 gm
Saturated fat:	Trace gm
Cholesterol:	1 mg
Cholesterol–saturated fat index:	Trace

Round Rye Bread

- Makes two 8-inch round loaves (16 wedges).

This whole grain bread is easy to make. It is great to serve with soups and stews. We like the flavor of rye, but white flour works equally well.

1 cup whole wheat flour	1 tablespoon sugar
1 cup light rye *or* white flour	2 cups buttermilk
2 teaspoons baking soda	1/4 to 1/2 cup whole wheat flour
1 cup uncooked oatmeal	for preparing dough, divided
1/2 teaspoon (or less) Lite Salt	

Preheat oven to 425°. In a large bowl, mix flours, baking soda, oatmeal, Lite Salt, and sugar together. Add buttermilk and stir to make dough the consistency of cooked oatmeal. Sprinkle 1/4 cup whole wheat flour on a baking sheet that has been sprayed with nonstick cooking spray. Divide dough in half and place both pieces on the baking sheet. Sprinkle a small amount of the remaining flour over the *sticky* top of the dough. Press dough flat with palm of hand, adding flour if necessary, to make 2 round flat loaves (each about 8 inches in diameter). Leave excess flour on top of loaves. Bake 18 to 22 minutes or until lightly golden. Cover warm loaves with kitchen towels or wax paper to keep moist. Cut into wedges and serve warm.

- Per Wedge -	
Calories:	91
Sodium:	221 mg
Fiber:	3 gm
Total fat:	1 gm
Saturated fat:	Trace gm
Cholesterol:	1 mg
Cholesterol–saturated fat index:	Trace

Sour Cream Prune Bread

1/4 cup margarine
1 cup sugar
3/4 cup egg substitute
2 1/3 cups flour
1 teaspoon allspice
1 teaspoon cinnamon
1 teaspoon baking powder

1/2 teaspoon baking soda
1/2 teaspoon (or less) Lite Salt
1/2 teaspoon cloves
1/2 cup nonfat sour cream
1 tablespoon freshly squeezed
   lemon juice
1 cup chopped pitted prunes

Preheat oven to 350°. Cream margarine and sugar until light and fluffy. Gradually beat in egg substitute. Mix together flour, allspice, cinnamon, baking powder, baking soda, Lite Salt, and cloves. Add dry ingredients to creamed mixture alternately with the sour cream. Mix just until blended. Combine lemon juice with prunes and add to batter. Spray a 9-by-5-inch loaf pan with nonstick cooking spray. Bake for 50 to 60 minutes, or until a wooden pick inserted in the center comes out clean. Cool on a wire rack for 10 minutes; remove from pan.

~ Per Slice ~	
Calories:	174
Sodium:	161 mg
Fiber:	2 gm
Total fat:	3 gm
Saturated fat:	Trace gm
Cholesterol:	Trace mg
Cholesterol–saturated fat index:	Trace

Tipsy Prunes and Pecan Bread

·‿ Makes 1 loaf (16 slices).

A delicious and hearty bread that keeps well when wrapped tightly in foil. The sherry gives it a special flavor, but fruit juice works well, also.

1¹/₂ cups chopped pitted prunes

¹/₄ cup sherry *or* orange juice

2 tablespoons grated orange peel

1 cup white flour

1 cup whole wheat flour

¹/₂ cup sugar

¹/₄ teaspoon baking soda

2 teaspoons baking powder

¹/₂ teaspoon ground ginger

¹/₂ teaspoon (or less) Lite Salt

¹/₂ cup egg substitute
    or 3 egg whites

¹/₂ cup skim milk

2 tablespoons vegetable oil

¹/₄ cup chopped pecans

Preheat oven to 350°. Combine prunes, sherry or juice, and orange peel, and set aside. In a separate bowl, combine flours, sugar, baking soda, baking powder, ginger, and Lite Salt. In a large mixing bowl, beat egg substitute or egg whites until foamy; add milk and oil. Add prune-sherry mixture and then the dry ingredients. Stir just until combined and fold in chopped pecans. Spoon batter into a 9-by-5-inch loaf pan that has been sprayed with nonstick cooking spray. Bake 35 to 45 minutes or until a wooden pick inserted in the center comes out clean. Let cool in pan 10 minutes, then remove from pan and place on a wire rack to finish cooling.

·‿ Per Slice ·‿	
Calories:	151
Sodium:	127 mg
Fiber:	2 gm
Total fat:	3 gm
Saturated fat:	Trace gm
Cholesterol:	Trace mg
Cholesterol–saturated fat index:	Trace

Blackberry Muffins

The Pacific Northwest is loaded with these wonderful berries, but you can find them in other parts of the country as well.

1¼ cups fresh *or* frozen blackberries, washed and well drained
1 cup white flour
¾ cup whole wheat flour
¾ cup sugar
2½ teaspoons baking powder
½ teaspoon (or less) Lite Salt
¼ cup egg substitute

3 tablespoons margarine, melted
¼ cup freshly squeezed lemon juice
½ cup skim milk

Cinnamon Sugar Topping
½ teaspoon cinnamon
1 teaspoon sugar

Preheat oven to 375°. In a large mixing bowl, gently toss blackberries with 1 tablespoon white flour; set aside.

In a second mixing bowl, combine remaining white flour, whole wheat flour, sugar, baking powder, and Lite Salt. Combine egg substitute, margarine, lemon juice, and milk; add to dry ingredients, stirring just until all ingredients are moistened. Carefully fold in coated blackberries, adding any excess flour from bowl. Spoon batter into muffin tins that have been sprayed with nonstick cooking spray or lined with papers. Mix cinnamon and sugar and sprinkle on top of each muffin. Bake about 20 minutes or until a wooden pick inserted in the center comes out clean and muffins are slightly brown.

Per Muffin	
Calories:	154
Sodium:	194 mg
Fiber:	2 gm
Total fat:	3 gm
Saturated fat:	Trace gm
Cholesterol:	Trace mg
Cholesterol—saturated fat index:	Trace

Chile Cheese Dinner Muffins

— Makes 12 muffins.

We like to serve these muffins with one of our black bean soups.

1 cup white flour

1 cup whole wheat flour

$^1/_4$ cup sugar

2 teaspoons baking powder

$^1/_2$ teaspoon baking soda

$^1/_2$ teaspoon (or less) Lite Salt

2 egg whites

1 cup buttermilk

3 tablespoons vegetable oil

$^1/_4$ cup diced green chiles, drained

$^1/_4$ cup finely diced red *or*
   green bell pepper

2 tablespoons finely diced onion

$^1/_2$ cup grated Jarlsberg Lite Reduced
   Fat Swiss Cheese

3–6 drops Tabasco sauce

Preheat oven to 400°. Combine flours, sugar, baking powder, baking soda, and Lite Salt. Lightly beat egg whites and mix with buttermilk, oil, chiles, bell pepper, onion, cheese, and Tabasco sauce. Add to dry ingredients and stir just until moistened. Put in muffin tins that have been sprayed with nonstick cooking spray or lined with papers. Bake 20 to 25 minutes or just until a wooden pick inserted in the center comes out clean.

·– Per Muffin ·–	
Calories:	144
Sodium:	257 mg
Fiber:	2 gm
Total fat:	5 gm
Saturated fat:	1 gm
Cholesterol:	2 mg
Cholesterol–saturated fat index:	1

Cinnamon Applesauce Bran Muffins

$^1/_2$ cup white flour

$^1/_2$ cup whole wheat flour

2 teaspoons baking powder

$^1/_2$ teaspoon baking soda

$^1/_2$ teaspoon cinnamon

2 cups All-Bran cereal

$1^1/_4$ cups skim milk

$^1/_4$ cup brown sugar

1 egg white

$^1/_2$ cup unsweetened applesauce

Preheat oven to 400°. Mix flours, baking powder, baking soda, and cinnamon in a small bowl. Mix cereal, milk, and sugar in a large bowl. Let stand 5 minutes. Stir in egg white and applesauce. Add flour mixture and stir just until moistened (batter will be lumpy). Spoon batter into muffin tins that have been sprayed with nonstick cooking spray or lined with papers. Bake 15 to 18 minutes, or until golden brown and wooden pick inserted in the center comes out clean. Serve warm.

·~ Per Muffin ~·	
Calories:	104
Sodium:	284 mg
Fiber:	6 gm
Total fat:	1 gm
Saturated fat:	Trace gm
Cholesterol:	Trace mg
Cholesterol—saturated fat index:	Trace

Fresh Apple and
Pumpkin Spice Muffins

∙⤳ Makes 24 muffins.

This is a popular snack, especially during the fall.

¹/₂ cup skim milk
¹/₂ cup egg substitute
   or 4 egg whites, lightly beaten
1 can (16 ounces) pumpkin
3 tablespoons vegetable oil
2 cups finely diced unpeeled
   green apple

1 cup white flour
1¹/₂ cups whole wheat flour
1¹/₄ cups sugar
4 teaspoons pumpkin pie spice
1 teaspoon baking soda

Preheat oven to 350°. Combine milk, egg substitute or whites, pumpkin, oil, and diced apple. Mix flours, sugar, pumpkin pie spice, and baking soda together and add to other ingredients. Stir just until moistened. Spoon into muffin tins that have been sprayed with nonstick cooking spray or lined with papers. Bake for 20 minutes or until a wooden pick inserted in the center comes out clean.

∙⤳ Per Muffin ⤳∙	
Calories:	117
Sodium:	64 mg
Fiber:	2 gm
Total fat:	2 gm
Saturated fat:	Trace gm
Cholesterol:	Trace mg
Cholesterol–saturated fat index:	Trace

Lemon Blueberry Muffins

⌐ Makes 12 muffins.

Blueberry muffins with an added twist!

1³/₄ cups flour	³/₄ cup nonfat plain yogurt
²/₃ cup sugar	3 tablespoons vegetable oil
2 teaspoons baking powder	1 tablespoon fresh grated lemon peel
¹/₄ teaspoon (or less) Lite Salt	¹/₄ cup freshly squeezed lemon juice
¹/₂ cup egg substitute	1 cup fresh or frozen blueberries

Preheat oven to 400°. In a large bowl, combine flour, sugar, baking powder, and Lite Salt. In a small bowl, beat egg substitute well. Add yogurt, oil, lemon peel and juice. Stir into dry ingredients just until moistened (batter should be lumpy). Carefully fold in berries. Put in muffin tins that have been sprayed with nonstick cooking spray or lined with papers. Bake 20 to 25 minutes or until a wooden pick inserted in the center comes out clean and muffins are lightly browned.

⌐ Per Muffin ⌐	
Calories:	161
Sodium:	130 mg
Fiber:	1 gm
Total fat:	4 gm
Saturated fat:	Trace gm
Cholesterol:	Trace mg
Cholesterol–saturated fat index:	Trace

Pear Almond Muffins

Serve warm with Lemon Cheese Spread *(page 134) for a delicious breakfast or snack.*

1 cup white flour

3/4 cup whole wheat flour

1/2 cup sugar

2 1/2 teaspoons baking powder

1/4 cup egg substitute

3/4 cup skim milk

1/4 cup vegetable oil

1/2 teaspoon almond extract

1 cup finely chopped fresh

  or canned pears

1 tablespoon chopped almonds

Preheat oven to 400°. Mix together flours, sugar, and baking powder. In a separate bowl, combine egg substitute, milk, oil, and almond extract. Add all at once to flour mixture. Stir just until moistened. Carefully fold in chopped pears. Spoon into muffin tins that have been sprayed with nonstick cooking spray or lined with papers. Sprinkle chopped almonds on top. Bake 20 to 25 minutes or until wooden pick inserted in the center comes out clean.

~ Per Muffin ~	
Calories:	156
Sodium:	117 mg
Fiber:	2 gm
Total fat:	5 gm
Saturated fat:	Trace gm
Cholesterol:	Trace mg
Cholesterol–saturated fat index:	Trace

Pie Cherry Muffins

With canned pie cherries, these muffins can be made all year round.

1 can (16 ounces) tart pie cherries,
    drained and pitted
1 cup white flour
¹/₂ cup whole wheat flour
¹/₃ cup sugar
¹/₄ teaspoon (or less) Lite Salt

¹/₂ teaspoon cinnamon
1 teaspoon baking powder
3 egg whites
¹/₂ cup skim milk
¹/₄ cup vegetable oil
¹/₂ teaspoon almond *or* vanilla extract

Preheat oven to 375°. Cut pitted cherries into chunks. Combine flours, sugar, Lite Salt, cinnamon, and baking powder. In a separate bowl, beat egg whites until frothy; add milk, oil, and almond or vanilla extract. Combine egg mixture with the dry ingredients and stir just until moistened (batter should be somewhat lumpy). Fold in cherries; put batter in muffin tins that have been sprayed with nonstick cooking spray or lined with papers. Bake 20 to 25 minutes or until a wooden pick inserted in the center comes out clean.

·⁓ Per Muffin ⁓·	
Calories:	140
Sodium:	79 mg
Fiber:	1 gm
Total fat:	5 gm
Saturated fat:	Trace gm
Cholesterol:	Trace mg
Cholesterol–saturated fat index:	Trace

Raisin Bran Muffins

– Makes 60 muffins.

Here's a "convenience plus" recipe—the batter may be stored in the refrigerator up to 6 weeks, allowing you to produce fresh-baked muffins with minimal fuss. A similar recipe was very popular twenty years ago in our community study, The Family Heart Study, in which 233 families spent 5 years trying low-fat recipes and products.

10 cups raisin bran cereal	1 teaspoon nutmeg
1 cup sugar	1 cup egg substitute
3 cups white flour	$1/2$ cup vegetable oil
2 cups whole wheat flour	$1/2$ cup water
5 teaspoons baking soda	1 quart buttermilk
1 teaspoon (or less) Lite Salt	

In a large mixing bowl, stir together cereal, sugar, flours, baking soda, Lite Salt, and nutmeg. Add egg substitute, oil, water, and buttermilk. Mix just until dry ingredients are moistened. Put in a container with a tight lid and store in the refrigerator; remove batter and bake as needed.

Preheat oven to 375°. Spoon batter into muffin tins that have been lined with papers or sprayed with nonstick cooking spray. Bake 25 to 30 minutes or until a wooden pick inserted in the center comes out clean.

– Per Muffin –	
Calories:	100
Sodium:	193 mg
Fiber:	2 gm
Total fat:	2 gm
Saturated fat:	Trace gm
Cholesterol:	1 mg
Cholesterol–saturated fat index:	Trace

Sweet Potato Muffins

A sweet and colorful muffin that tastes great any time of the day. One visit to Williamsburg, Virginia, is all it took to develop this all-time favorite.

1 medium sweet potato (large
   enough to make ²/₃ cup mashed)
¹/₄ cup margarine
¹/₂ cup sugar
¹/₄ cup egg substitute
1 teaspoon grated fresh lemon peel
1 cup flour
2 teaspoons baking powder
¹/₂ teaspoon baking soda
¹/₂ teaspoon (or less) Lite Salt

¹/₂ teaspoon cinnamon
¹/₄ teaspoon nutmeg
¹/₂ cup skim milk
2 tablespoons chopped walnuts
¹/₄ cup chopped raisins

Topping
1 teaspoon cinnamon
1 teaspoon sugar

Preheat oven to 375°. Wash sweet potato and pierce with a fork in several places. Bake 45 minutes or until tender. *Bake in the microwave oven if you wish to speed up process.* Cool potato to room temperature. Peel potato; mash with a fork and reserve ²/₃ cup.

Preheat oven to 400°. In a large mixing bowl, cream margarine and sugar until light and fluffy. Beat in ²/₃ cup of sweet potato, egg substitute, and lemon peel. In another bowl, combine flour, baking powder, baking soda, Lite Salt, cinnamon, and nutmeg. Add the dry ingredients and milk to the potato mixture and stir just until blended. Fold in nuts and raisins. Spoon into muffin tins that have been sprayed with nonstick cooking spray. Bake 20 minutes or until a wooden pick inserted in the center comes out clean. Mix cinnamon and sugar together and sprinkle over the tops of the muffins.

·— Per Muffin ·—	
Calories:	145
Sodium:	240 mg
Fiber:	1 gm
Total fat:	5 gm
Saturated fat:	1 gm
Cholesterol:	Trace mg
Cholesterol—saturated fat index:	1

Tiny Pineapple Muffins
with Orange Glaze

⁓ Makes 44 tiny muffins.

¼ cup margarine, softened

½ cup sugar

¼ cup egg substitute

¾ cup nonfat sour cream

1 teaspoon orange *or* lemon extract

1 cup white flour

1 cup whole wheat flour

½ teaspoon (or less) Lite Salt

1 teaspoon baking soda

1 tablespoon grated orange peel

1 can (8 ounces) juice-packed
   crushed pineapple, well drained

¼ cup chopped walnuts

Topping

3 tablespoons sugar

2 tablespoons orange juice

Preheat oven to 375°. In a bowl, cream margarine and sugar until fluffy. Add egg substitute, sour cream, and orange or lemon extract and mix well. Add flours, Lite Salt, baking soda, orange peel, pineapple, and walnuts; stir just until all ingredients are moistened. Spoon batter into small muffin tins that have been sprayed with nonstick cooking spray. Bake 10 to 12 minutes or until a wooden pick inserted in the center comes out clean.

While muffins are baking, make topping by combining sugar and orange juice; set aside. Remove muffins while still warm and dip tops in the orange juice mixture.

⁓ Per 3 Tiny Muffins ⁓	
Calories:	150
Sodium:	177 mg
Fiber:	1 gm
Total fat:	5 gm
Saturated fat:	1 gm
Cholesterol:	Trace mg
Cholesterol–saturated fat index:	1

Apricot Prune Coffee Cake

~ Makes 16 servings.

Streusel

1/4 cup brown sugar

2 tablespoons margarine, softened

2 tablespoons flour

1 teaspoon cinnamon

Coffee Cake

3 cups flour

1 1/2 teaspoons baking powder

3/4 teaspoon baking soda

1/4 teaspoon (or less) Lite Salt

1/4 cup margarine, softened

1 cup sugar

1 cup egg substitute

1 1/2 teaspoons vanilla

1 1/2 cups nonfat plain yogurt

3/4 cup pitted prunes, cut in
    small pieces

3/4 cup dried apricots, cut in
    small pieces

1 tablespoon powdered sugar

Preheat oven to 350°. In a small bowl, combine brown sugar, margarine, flour, and cinnamon. Mix with a fork until crumbly. Set aside. Spray a 10-inch tube pan with nonstick cooking spray. In a small bowl, combine flour, baking powder, baking soda, and Lite Salt. In a separate mixing bowl, cream margarine and sugar. Add egg substitute and vanilla. Mix until fluffy. Add dry ingredients alternately with yogurt. Beat for 1 minute. Gently fold in prunes and apricots and mix just until combined.

Put 1/3 of the coffee cake batter in the prepared pan and spread evenly. Sprinkle with 1/3 of the streusel mixture. Repeat layering of the coffee cake batter and the streusel mixture. Bake 55 to 60 minutes or until a wooden pick inserted in the center comes out clean.

Let cake cool in pan on wire rack 20 minutes. With a spatula, carefully loosen the edge of the cake from the side of pan. Remove from pan and dust with powdered sugar. Cut into wedges and serve warm.

~ Per Serving ~	
Calories:	243
Sodium:	218 mg
Fiber:	2 gm
Total fat:	5 gm
Saturated fat:	1 gm
Cholesterol:	Trace mg
Cholesterol–saturated fat index:	1

Baked Chicken Sandwich

This party dish comes from one of Joyce's friends who serves it at all "Ten-Star" occasions such as a baptism, a special birthday lunch, or a Mother's Day brunch. It should be assembled the day before, refrigerated overnight, and baked just before serving. Fresh fruit goes very nicely with it.

12 to 16 slices white bread, crusts removed (generally takes 12 slices)

2 tablespoons chopped onion
1½ cups sliced fresh mushrooms
2 cups chopped cooked chicken*
¼ cup sliced ripe olives, drained
⅓ cup nonfat mayonnaise
5 hard-cooked egg whites, cut in half and thinly sliced
1 can (10¾ ounces) Campbell's Healthy Request Cream of Chicken Soup

½ cup nonfat sour cream
2 tablespoons dry sherry (*not* cooking sherry), optional

¾ cup grated low-fat Cheddar cheese
Paprika
Chopped fresh parsley for garnish

To assemble sandwich: Spray a 9-by-13-inch baking dish with nonstick cooking spray. Trim sides of 6 to 8 slices of bread so they lie flat and cover the bottom of the dish. In a nonstick skillet, sauté onions and mushrooms, stirring frequently. In a large mixing bowl, combine onions and mushrooms, including liquid, with chicken, olives, and mayonnaise. Carefully fold in hard-cooked egg whites so they won't break up. Spread all of this mixture over the layer of bread. Place remaining 6 to 8 slices of trimmed bread on top of the chicken mixture. In a small bowl, combine cream of chicken soup, sour cream, and sherry, if using. Spread over bread. Cover and refrigerate overnight.

One hour and 45 minutes before serving time, remove dish from refrigerator and let stand 1 hour. Preheat oven to 325°. Remove cover and spread grated cheese evenly over the top. Sprinkle with paprika. Bake 40 minutes, uncovered. Check to be sure center is heated through. Remove from oven and sprinkle with chopped parsley. Let stand 5 minutes; cut into squares. Serve warm.

⸭ Per Serving ⸭	
Calories:	204
Sodium:	531 mg
Fiber:	1 gm
Total fat:	5 gm
Saturated fat:	2 gm
Cholesterol:	29 mg
Cholesterol–saturated fat index:	3

* Cook skinned breasts in the microwave oven for about 10 minutes or use canned chicken.

Calico Strata

8 ounces French bread (¹/₂ loaf)

³/₄ cup grated low-fat
  Cheddar cheese

³/₄ cup grated low-fat Swiss cheese
  (Jarlsberg Lite is a good choice)

1 teaspoon olive oil

2 cups sliced mushrooms

1 cup chopped onion

2 cloves garlic, minced

1 teaspoon dried oregano leaves

1 teaspoon dried basil leaves

2 cups chopped fresh spinach

¹/₂ cup chopped green bell pepper

¹/₂ cup chopped red bell pepper

2 cups egg substitute

1 cup skim milk

Spray a 9-by-13-inch baking dish with nonstick cooking spray. Cut bread in small cubes, place in baking dish, top with ¹/₂ of the cheeses and set aside. Heat olive oil in a nonstick skillet over medium heat. Add mushrooms, onion, and garlic and sauté until the liquid has cooked away. Add oregano, basil, spinach, and bell peppers; mix well and spread over bread.

Beat together egg substitute and milk and pour over bread cubes and vegetables. Sprinkle with remaining cheeses. Cover with foil and refrigerate at least 1 hour. Preheat oven to 350° and bake, covered, 50 minutes. Remove cover and bake 10 minutes to brown the top. Remove from oven and let stand 5 minutes; cut into squares and serve warm.

·- Per Serving -·	
Calories:	171
Sodium:	337 mg
Fiber:	2 gm
Total fat:	4 gm
Saturated fat:	2 gm
Cholesterol:	8 mg
Cholesterol—saturated fat index:	3

Cranapple Dutch Baby

The Dutch Baby is a great "show-off" treat that can be made by the beginning cook (it's fun to make with young people). We've added the fruit topping to make it special, but any fresh fruit or syrup can be used.

Cranapple Topping
1 teaspoon vegetable oil
3 medium tart apples (Granny
    Smith, McIntosh, Gravenstein)
    peeled, cored, and sliced
1/4 cup sugar
1/2 cup fresh cranberries
1/4 teaspoon vanilla

Dutch Baby
1 tablespoon margarine
1/2 cup flour

1 tablespoon sugar
1/2 cup skim milk
3/4 cup egg substitute (we like
    Nulaid*)
1 teaspoon grated orange peel
Pinch of nutmeg

4 teaspoons powdered sugar,
    for garnish

In a large skillet, heat 1 teaspoon oil. Sauté apples and sugar 10 minutes or until apples are tender and lightly caramelized. Add cranberries and vanilla; cook until berries pop. Keep warm.

Preheat oven to 425°. Select a 10-inch skillet or cake pan and spray with nonstick cooking spray. Put margarine in the skillet and place in the oven while it is heating to melt the margarine. In a medium bowl, mix flour, sugar, milk, egg substitute, orange peel, and nutmeg. Tilt the skillet so margarine coats the bottom. Pour flour and milk mixture into the skillet and place in oven. Bake 15 minutes or until light brown. The Dutch Baby will be light and puffy at this point, so serve immediately. Cut into 4 pieces, top with 1/2 cup fruit topping, and sprinkle with 1 teaspoon powdered sugar.

* Found in the dairy section of most supermarkets.

Per Serving (Including Topping)	
Calories:	249
Sodium:	116 mg
Fiber:	4 gm
Total fat:	5 gm
Saturated fat:	1 gm
Cholesterol:	1 mg
Cholesterol–saturated fat index:	1

Cranberry Apricot Scones

Be careful not to overbake these scones—low-fat baked goods tend to dry out quickly.
Eat them within a day or two; otherwise, freeze them.

2 cups Reduced Fat Bisquick
$1/2$ cup oatmeal
$1/4$ cup sugar
1 teaspoon cinnamon
$1/3$ cup chopped dried apricots

$1/3$ cup chopped dried cranberries
$1/2$ cup unsweetened applesauce
$1/4$ cup water
1 tablespoon vegetable oil

Preheat oven to 400°. In a medium bowl, combine Bisquick, oatmeal, sugar, cinnamon, apricots, and cranberries; mix well. Add applesauce, water, and oil. Stir until a soft dough forms. Drop $1/4$ cup dough onto an ungreased baking sheet, making 12 scones. Bake 12 to 16 minutes, just until golden brown. Serve warm.

~ Per Scone ~	
Calories:	141
Sodium:	219 mg
Fiber:	2 gm
Total fat:	3 gm
Saturated fat:	Trace gm
Cholesterol:	0 mg
Cholesterol—saturated fat index:	Trace

Fruit Slush Cups

A slightly different version of this recipe was served by Sonja's sister, Sandra, at a brunch following her daughter's wedding. Some of us prefer them as a refreshing snack or dessert. Actually, these delicious treats are great anytime.

1 can (16 ounces) lite apricots
1 can (20 ounces) juice-packed
    crushed pineapple
1 cup liquid drained from fruit
1/2 cup (or less) sugar
2 packages (16 ounces each)
    frozen mixed whole raspberries
    and blackberries

1 can (6 ounces) frozen
    orange-banana-pineapple juice
    concentrate, thawed
2 tablespoons freshly squeezed
    lemon juice
3 bananas, diced

Drain apricots and pineapple, reserving liquid; add water as necessary to reserved liquid to make 1 cup. In a saucepan, combine liquid from fruit and sugar; heat and stir until sugar dissolves. Add berries (include juice if berries have thawed), juice concentrate, and lemon juice. Dice apricots and add to mixture along with pineapple and bananas. Spoon into paper-lined muffin tins. Freeze until solid. Remove from tins and discard paper liners. Store frozen fruit cups in plastic bags. Thirty minutes before serving, remove from freezer and put in small dessert bowls or cups. Soften to a slushy state and serve.

➤ Per Serving ➤	
Calories:	69
Sodium:	1 mg
Fiber:	2 gm
Total fat:	Trace gm
Saturated fat:	Trace gm
Cholesterol:	0 mg
Cholesterol–saturated fat index:	Trace

Oatmeal
Buttermilk Waffles

⁓ Makes 7 waffles (7 inches each).

What a great way to start off your day—having waffles. The Cranberry Maple Syrup (page 91) makes a very nice addition.

1 cup uncooked old-fashioned oatmeal	2 tablespoons vegetable oil
2 cups buttermilk	2 teaspoons baking powder
1/2 cup white flour	1 teaspoon baking soda
1/2 cup whole wheat flour	3 egg whites

Soak oatmeal in buttermilk 1/2 hour to 24 hours in refrigerator. Add flours, oil, baking powder, and baking soda, and mix well. In a separate bowl, beat egg whites until stiff; fold into the oatmeal-flour mixture.

Preheat waffle iron. Pour scant 2/3 cup batter onto center of hot waffle iron. Bake 5 minutes or until steaming stops. Remove waffle carefully. Serve with warm syrup, jam, or fresh fruit.

⁓ Per Waffle (Without Topping) ⁓	
Calories:	177
Sodium:	417 mg
Fiber:	3 gm
Total fat:	5 gm
Saturated fat:	1 gm
Cholesterol:	2 mg
Cholesterol–saturated fat index:	1

Oven-Baked French Toast with Cranberry Maple Syrup

Makes 8 servings.

We were pleased to find a new product, Nulaid French Toast Mix,* which makes this day-ahead breakfast dish go together very quickly. We have also given an option for you to make your own mix.

1 loaf (15 to 16 ounces) French bread
1 cup fresh *or* frozen cranberries

EITHER
2 cups Nulaid French Toast Mix
1/2 cup skim milk

OR
2 tablespoons sugar
1 teaspoon vanilla

1/4 teaspoon cinnamon
2 cups egg substitute
1/2 cup skim milk

Cranberry Maple Syrup
(makes 1 2/3 cups)
1 1/2 cups maple syrup
1 cup fresh cranberries

Day before serving: Choose baking sheet with sides and spray with nonstick cooking spray. Slice bread into 3/4-inch slices. Arrange bread so slices do not overlap and pour 1 cup cranberries over the bread. If using French Toast Mix, add milk. *If you wish to make your own mix, combine sugar, vanilla, cinnamon, egg substitute, and milk.* Beat until well mixed. Pour egg mixture over bread and cranberries and let stand 15 minutes. Lift bread slices so egg mixture will moisten the bottoms. Cover baking sheet and refrigerate overnight.

One hour before serving time, preheat oven to 350°. Remove bread mixture from refrigerator and bake, uncovered, 40 minutes. Prepare syrup while toast is baking.

To prepare syrup: Bring maple syrup to a boil and add 1 cup cranberries. Cook over low heat 10 minutes, stirring occasionally. Serve warm or at room temperature.

* Found in the dairy section of most supermarkets.

Per Serving (Including Syrup)	
Calories:	361
Sodium:	419 mg
Fiber:	3 gm
Total fat:	2 gm
Saturated fat:	Trace gm
Cholesterol:	Trace mg
Cholesterol–saturated fat index:	Trace

Poppy Seed Pancakes

Fresh strawberries or hot maple syrup (or both) are very good with these breakfast treats.

2 cups whole wheat flour	$3/4$ cup egg substitute
2 tablespoons brown sugar	$1/4$ cup mashed ripe banana
3 tablespoons poppy seeds	2 teaspoons vanilla
$2^1/4$ teaspoons baking powder	2 tablespoons vegetable oil
2 cups skim milk	

Preheat nonstick griddle or skillet. Combine flour, brown sugar, poppy seeds, and baking powder in a bowl and set aside. In another bowl, mix milk, egg substitute, mashed banana, vanilla, and oil. Beat with a mixer until frothy. Add banana mixture to dry ingredients and stir just until combined. If batter is too thick, add a small amount of water. Cook pancakes on griddle for 3 minutes or until done. Keep warm or serve immediately.

- Per Serving -	
Calories:	201
Sodium:	203 mg
Fiber:	4 gm
Total fat:	6 gm
Saturated fat:	1 gm
Cholesterol:	1 mg
Cholesterol—saturated fat index:	1

Raap-Wal-O
(Great Hot Cereal)

One of the points Sonja makes when she gives public presentations is that, when we develop recipes, we first test them over and over and over—to make sure they work. One evening following a presentation, a lovely lady asked Sonja if she would like a recipe that had been made at least 200 times. Of course! Since then Raap-Wal-O *has become a breakfast favorite and is requested on the average of twice a week by some of our staff's family members. It's a microwave recipe that is appealing to a busy cook.*

2 unpeeled cooking apples, chopped,
   or 2 cups chopped bananas,
   peaches, *or* pears
2¼ cups water
¾ cup uncooked old-fashioned
   oatmeal
¼ cup dried cranberries, raisins,
   dates, *or* chopped prunes

2 tablespoons chopped walnuts
   or almonds
1 teaspoon cinnamon
¼ teaspoon nutmeg
1½ teaspoons freshly grated orange
   or lemon peel

Combine all ingredients in a 2-quart glass dish; cover tightly. Cook in the microwave oven on high for 5 minutes. Stir, cover and continue cooking for another 5 minutes. Serve warm with skim milk.

⁓ Per Serving ⁓	
Calories:	155
Sodium:	3 mg
Fiber:	4 gm
Total fat:	4 gm
Saturated fat:	Trace gm
Cholesterol:	0 mg
Cholesterol—saturated fat index:	Trace

Sweet Potato Pancakes

1¼ cups flour

¼ cup brown sugar

1¼ teaspoons baking powder

½ teaspoon cinnamon

¼ teaspoon nutmeg

¾ cup skim milk

½ cup water

½ cup mashed sweet potatoes

¼ cup egg substitute

1 tablespoon vegetable oil

1 teaspoon vanilla

1 tablespoon grated lemon peel

In a large mixing bowl, combine flour, brown sugar, baking powder, cinnamon, and nutmeg. In a separate bowl, combine milk, water, sweet potatoes, egg substitute, oil, vanilla, and lemon peel; mix well. Add to flour mixture and stir just until moistened. Lightly spray a griddle with nonstick cooking spray and heat to medium. Spread about ¼ cup batter on griddle and cook until bubbles form on the surface and begin to break. Turn pancake over and cook until bottom is golden brown. Repeat with remaining batter. Serve immediately with fruit or warm maple syrup.

·‿ Per Serving ·‿	
Calories:	285
Sodium:	207 mg
Fiber:	2 gm
Total fat:	4 gm
Saturated fat:	Trace gm
Cholesterol:	1 mg
Cholesterol–saturated fat index:	Trace

Green Salads

Allison's Caesar Salad
Apples and Greens with Toasted Walnuts
Cranberry Spinach Salad
Greens and Apple Salad with Garlic Dijon Dressing
Greens with Strawberries and Poppy Seed Dressing
Megan's Tossed Green Salad with Mango,
Red Pepper, and Cucumber
Molly's Spinach Salad

Bean and Vegetable Salads

Barbecued Bean Salad with Chips
Blackeye Pea Salad
Cindy's Potato Salad
Green Pea Salad
Japanese Slaw
Marinated Asparagus or Broccoli
Roasted Eggplant and Bean Salad
Sourdough Bread Salad with Roasted Vegetables
Southwestern Salad
Spinach Couscous Salad
Tangy Cucumber Salad
Thai Black Bean Salad
Thai Cucumber Salad

Pasta Salads

Greek Pasta Salad with Tomato Vinaigrette
Indonesian Pasta Salad
Jane's Asian Pasta Salad
Pasta Salad with White Beans and Rosemary
Southwestern Couscous and Black Bean Salad

Chicken and Fruit Salads

Chicken Couscous Salad with Lemon Dressing
Curried Chicken and Rice Salad with Grapes
Family Favorite Fruit Salad
Flying Farmer Chicken Salad
Summer Salad with Chicken and Blueberries

Allison's Caesar Salad

A medical student who works with us gave us this tasty recipe. She was skeptical about our ability to reduce the fat content without affecting the flavor, but this is the version she now serves to company.

Caesar Dressing
2 cloves garlic, minced
1 teaspoon anchovy paste
1 tablespoon egg substitute
1 tablespoon olive oil
2 teaspoons Dijon-style mustard
1 tablespoon freshly squeezed
   lemon juice
$1/2$ teaspoon Worcestershire sauce

$1/8$ teaspoon Tabasco sauce
$1/4$ teaspoon balsamic *or*
   red wine vinegar
$1/4$ cup nonfat plain yogurt

Salad
12 cups romaine (1 medium head),
   torn into bite-size pieces
$1/4$ cup grated Parmesan cheese

Prepare dressing by combining garlic, anchovy paste, egg substitute, oil, mustard, lemon juice, Worcestershire sauce, Tabasco sauce, vinegar, and yogurt. Mix well and chill until serving time. When ready to serve, toss with romaine. Sprinkle with Parmesan cheese.

⤳ Per Serving ⤳	
Calories:	60
Sodium:	121 mg
Fiber:	2 gm
Total fat:	4 gm
Saturated fat:	1 gm
Cholesterol:	4 mg
Cholesterol–saturated fat index:	1

Apples and Greens with Tousled Walnuts

`~ Makes 14 cups.`

If you like blue cheese, you will love this salad. Make it whenever you see beautiful red apples or need a special treat.

2 tablespoons coarsely
   chopped walnuts

$^1/_4$ teaspoon (or less) Lite Salt
$^1/_4$ teaspoon freshly ground pepper

Oil and Vinegar Dressing
2 tablespoons vegetable oil
3 tablespoons rice *or*
   red wine vinegar
2 tablespoons freshly squeezed
   lemon juice
2 tablespoons minced shallots
1 tablespoon maple syrup

Salad
2 Red Delicious apples, unpeeled
4 cups red leaf lettuce
8 cups greens of choice such as
   Bibb, watercress leaves, *or*
   butter lettuce
2 tablespoons crumbled blue cheese

To roast walnuts: Preheat oven to 350°. Spread walnuts on a baking sheet and bake for 10 to 12 minutes, stirring occasionally. Watch closely as walnuts burn easily. Set aside.

In a small jar with a tight-fitting lid, combine oil, vinegar, lemon juice, shallots, syrup, Lite Salt, and pepper. Shake until well mixed. Cut half of one apple into thin slices and reserve for use as a garnish. Chop remaining apples into small pieces. Place all apples in the dressing to prevent darkening. Tear red leaf lettuce and other greens into bite-sized pieces and place in a large salad bowl. Sprinkle walnuts and chopped apple over salad. Pour dressing over salad and toss gently but thoroughly. Decorate top with sliced apples and crumbled blue cheese. Serve immediately.

~ Per Cup ~	
Calories:	52
Sodium:	41 mg
Fiber:	1 gm
Total fat:	3 gm
Saturated fat:	Trace gm
Cholesterol:	1 mg
Cholesterol–saturated fat index:	Trace

Cranberry Spinach Salad

Cranberry Dressing

1 tablespoon vegetable oil

1/4 cup cranberry juice concentrate, thawed

2 tablespoons rice wine vinegar

1 teaspoon Dijon-style mustard

1/4 teaspoon pepper

Salad

1/2 cup thinly sliced red onion

8 cups fresh spinach leaves, torn into bite-sized pieces

1/2 cup dried cranberries

Combine oil, cranberry juice concentrate, vinegar, mustard, and pepper, and set aside. Cut onion slices in half. Place spinach in a large salad bowl. Add onion slices, dried cranberries, and dressing. Toss gently but mix thoroughly. Serve immediately. Save some of the cranberries to sprinkle on top, if desired.

- Per Cup -	
Calories:	78
Sodium:	54 mg
Fiber:	2 gm
Total fat:	2 gm
Saturated fat:	Trace gm
Cholesterol:	0 mg
Cholesterol—saturated fat index:	Trace

Greens and Apple Salad with Garlic Dijon Dressing

Makes 12 cups.

For low-fat salads generally, it's important to mix dressing and greens very well to distribute the flavor throughout. This is particularly true for this salad.

Garlic Dijon Dressing
2 tablespoons freshly squeezed
   lemon juice
2 tablespoons rice vinegar
1 teaspoon Dijon-style mustard
2 tablespoons olive oil
1/4 teaspoon pepper
3 cloves garlic, minced

Salad
4 cups romaine, torn into
   small pieces

4 cups red lettuce, torn into
   small pieces
2 red apples, chopped
1/2 cup sliced red onion
1 1/2 cups chopped yellow *or*
   red bell pepper
3 tablespoons chopped filberts *or*
   slivered almonds

3 tablespoons grated
   Parmesan cheese

Combine dressing ingredients and mix well with a wire whisk until smooth. Set aside while salad is assembled.

Place romaine and red leaf lettuce in a salad bowl. Add apple, onion slices, bell peppers, and nuts. Toss thoroughly with dressing and sprinkle with Parmesan cheese.

Per Cup	
Calories:	63
Sodium:	32 mg
Fiber:	1 gm
Total fat:	4 gm
Saturated fat:	1 gm
Cholesterol:	1 mg
Cholesterol—saturated fat index:	1

Greens with Strawberries and Poppy Seed Dressing

·~ Makes 10 cups.

One of the most unusual and GORGEOUS salads we've tasted! If strawberries are not available, use canned mandarin oranges.

3 tablespoons pecan pieces
2 tablespoons sugar

Poppy Seed Dressing
3 tablespoons vinegar (strawberry vinegar is great)
1 tablespoon sugar
$1/8$ teaspoon (or less) Lite Salt
1 teaspoon dry mustard
2 tablespoons vegetable oil
1 tablespoon poppy seeds

Salad
8 cups torn fresh spinach *or* other salad greens (packed loosely)
1 cup sliced celery
2 tablespoons finely sliced green onions
1 pint fresh strawberries, cleaned and sliced

To caramelize pecans (these can be prepared ahead): Combine sugar and pecans in a heavy skillet. Cook slowly, stirring often, until all the sugar has melted onto the pecans and they are brown. Quickly remove from hot pan and cool on waxed paper. If prepared ahead, store in a tight container.

Prepare dressing by combining vinegar, sugar, Lite Salt, and mustard powder in a blender or mix with wire whisk. Add oil slowly and then stir in poppy seeds. Refrigerate until ready to serve the salad.

To assemble salad: Combine prepared greens, celery, onions, strawberries, and caramelized pecans. Toss gently with dressing and serve immediately.

·~ Per Cup ~·	
Calories:	81
Sodium:	59 mg
Fiber:	2 gm
Total fat:	5 gm
Saturated fat:	Trace gm
Cholesterol:	0 mg
Cholesterol—saturated fat index:	Trace

Megan's Tossed Green Salad with Mango, Red Pepper, and Cucumber

Makes 12 cups.

The creative and enterprising developer of this beautiful salad has catered many fine meals for her friends. We are appreciative that she generously shared her innovative idea with us.

Dressing

2 tablespoons rice vinegar

1 clove garlic, minced

2 teaspoons lower-sodium
  soy sauce*

1/4 teaspoon sugar

2 teaspoons grated fresh gingeroot

1 tablespoon freshly squeezed
  lime juice

1 tablespoon chopped fresh cilantro

1 tablespoon olive oil

1 tablespoon fish sauce (optional)

Salad

2 cups fresh *or* frozen diced mango

2 red bell peppers, seeded and
  thinly sliced

2 cups diced cucumber

1/2 cup chopped green onions

1/2 cup matchstick-size jicama

8 cups romaine, torn into
  bite-size pieces

1/4 cup chopped fresh mint leaves
  (optional)

1/4 cup chopped fresh cilantro

2 tablespoons toasted sliced *or*
  slivered almonds

Prepare dressing by combining vinegar, garlic, soy sauce, sugar, ginger, lime juice, cilantro, olive oil, and fish sauce, if using. Add mangoes, bell peppers, cucumber, green onions, and jicama to the dressing and marinate for at least 2 hours. When ready to serve, combine romaine, mint leaves, if using, cilantro, and almonds in a large salad bowl. Add dressing mixture and toss to mix thoroughly.

* Kikkoman Lite Soy Sauce is available.

~ Per Cup ~	
Calories:	49
Sodium:	38 mg
Fiber:	2 gm
Total fat:	2 gm
Saturated fat:	Trace gm
Cholesterol:	0 mg
Cholesterol–saturated fat index:	Trace

Molly's Spinach Salad

Molly is a lucky lady who lives on picturesque Puget Sound in western Washington State and is a terrific cook. Her house is built on stilts, and when the tide comes in, she must feel she is living on top of a lake.

^{1}/2 package low-fat ramen noodle
    soup (do not use the seasoning
    packet)
2 tablespoons sliced almonds
1 tablespoon sesame seeds

Molly's Balsamic Vinegar Dressing
1 tablespoon olive oil *or* 2 teaspoons
    olive oil and 1 teaspoon sesame oil

2 tablespoons balsamic vinegar
^{1}/8 teaspoon (or less) Lite Salt
Dash white pepper

8 cups fresh spinach

Heat a nonstick skillet over medium heat. Break up ramen noodles and toast with almonds and sesame seeds in skillet. Stir often and watch closely so they do not burn. *Guess how we learned this!* Remove from pan and cool. Mix dressing ingredients together and set aside.

Just before serving: Tear spinach into bite-sized pieces and toss lightly with toasted noodles, nuts, and seeds. Add dressing, toss again, and serve immediately to keep the toasted noodles and almonds crunchy.

~ Per Cup ~	
Calories:	64
Sodium:	85 mg
Fiber:	2 gm
Total fat:	3 gm
Saturated fat:	Trace gm
Cholesterol:	0 mg
Cholesterol–saturated fat index:	Trace

Barbecued Bean Salad with Chips

With the arrival of baked corn chips, we can recommend this festive salad. If the Barbecue Sauce is made ahead of time, the salad is quick to assemble.

Barbecue Sauce

1/4 cup ketchup

1/4 cup vinegar

1 tablespoon olive oil

1 tablespoon Worcestershire sauce

3 tablespoons brown sugar

1 teaspoon chili powder

1 teaspoon cumin

1/4 teaspoon pepper

1/4 teaspoon Tabasco sauce

1 1/2 teaspoons Dijon-style mustard

Salad

2 cans (16 ounces each) kidney beans, drained and rinsed*

1 can (16 ounces) unsalted whole-kernel corn, drained

3/4 cup diced green bell pepper

3/4 cup diced red bell pepper

3/4 cup diced onion

4 cups baked tortilla chips

Combine Barbecue Sauce ingredients and heat until boiling in the microwave oven on high or on the stovetop. Cool. Combine drained beans, corn, bell peppers, and onions. Add Barbecue Sauce and mix well. Just before serving, break tortilla chips into smaller pieces, add to salad and carefully toss. Serve at room temperature.

* S&W has a 50% Less Salt product available.

~ Per Serving ~	
Calories:	239
Sodium:	174 mg
Fiber:	8 gm
Total fat:	3 gm
Saturated fat:	Trace gm
Cholesterol:	0 mg
Cholesterol—saturated fat index:	Trace

Blackeye Pea Salad

Simple, easy to fix, and very colorful.

2 cans (15 ounces each) blackeye
    peas, drained and rinsed
1 cup finely diced carrots
1 cup frozen corn, thawed
1/2 cup chopped celery
1/2 cup chopped red onion

1 large red *or* green bell pepper,
    chopped
1/4 cup finely chopped fresh parsley
    (broad leaf parsley has great
    flavor)
1/4 cup seasoned rice vinegar

Combine all ingredients, cover, and chill. Allow salad to sit 2 hours in refrigerator, if possible, to develop flavors. Serve cold or at room temperature.

~ Per Cup ~	
Calories:	127
Sodium:	379 mg
Fiber:	7 gm
Total fat:	1 gm
Saturated fat:	Trace gm
Cholesterol:	0 mg
Cholesterol–saturated fat index:	Trace

Cindy's Potato Salad

·– Makes 6 cups.

This delicious salad has a light oil and vinegar dressing and can be served warm or cold (we prefer cold). The flavors blend well when made the day before serving.

6 cups cubed red potatoes, unpeeled	3 tablespoons chopped fresh chives
6 tablespoons chopped green onions	3/4 teaspoon (or less) Lite Salt
1/4 cup red wine vinegar	3/4 teaspoon pepper
1 tablespoon olive oil	3/4 teaspoon sugar

Bring cubed potatoes to a boil and simmer for about 10 minutes or until potatoes are tender but not mushy. Drain well. Add chopped green onions while potatoes are still warm. In a separate bowl, mix vinegar, oil, chives, Lite Salt, pepper, and sugar. Add to potato and onion mixture. Cover well and refrigerate until ready to serve.

·– Per Cup ~·	
Calories:	163
Sodium:	133 mg
Fiber:	3 gm
Total fat:	2 gm
Saturated fat:	Trace gm
Cholesterol:	0 mg
Cholesterol—saturated fat index:	Trace

Green Pea Salad

Need a simple dish for a picnic? This is a good choice.

Creamy Mustard Dressing

¹/₃ cup nonfat mayonnaise
  or Miracle Whip
1 to 2 tablespoons Dijon-style
  mustard
¹/₂ teaspoon (or less) Lite Salt
1 clove garlic, minced
¹/₄ teaspoon pepper

Salad

1 package (16 ounces) frozen peas
4 hard-cooked egg whites, chopped
1 can (5 ounces) sliced water
  chestnuts, drained
2 tablespoons chopped pimiento
¹/₃ cup chopped green onions
¹/₂ cup chopped celery

Combine mayonnaise, mustard, Lite Salt, garlic, and pepper to make dressing; mix well and set aside. Cook peas a few minutes until barely tender. Rinse in cold water immediately to stop cooking and drain well. Combine peas, egg whites, water chestnuts, pimiento, green onions, celery, and the dressing. Stir carefully to avoid crushing egg whites and peas. Cover and chill 24 hours.

⁓ Per Serving ⁓	
Calories:	70
Sodium:	305 mg
Fiber:	4 gm
Total fat:	Trace gm
Saturated fat:	Trace gm
Cholesterol:	0 mg
Cholesterol–saturated fat index:	Trace

Japanese Slaw

Low-fat ramen noodles are now available, so this favorite salad can be prepared in a low-fat manner with great results.

1 package (3 ounces) low-fat ramen
    noodle soup (do not use seasoning
    packet)
1 tablespoon sesame seeds
2 tablespoons sliced almonds

Rice Vinegar Dressing
2 tablespoons sugar
$^1/_2$ teaspoon pepper
$^1/_2$ teaspoon (or less) Lite Salt
$^1/_3$ cup rice vinegar
2 tablespoons sesame oil

7 cups finely shredded red cabbage
$^1/_3$ cup thinly sliced green onions

    Preheat oven to 350°. Discard seasoning packet from ramen noodles and break uncooked noodles into small pieces. Spread broken noodles, sesame seeds, and sliced almonds on a baking sheet. Bake approximately 3 minutes until lightly browned. Watch carefully, as they burn easily. Cool on a paper towel. Mix dressing ingredients together in a small jar and shake to mix well.

    Just before serving, toss cabbage and green onions with the toasted noodles, sesame seeds, and almonds. Pour dressing over salad and toss.

·- Per Cup -·	
Calories:	115
Sodium:	124 mg
Fiber:	2 gm
Total fat:	5 gm
Saturated fat:	1 gm
Cholesterol:	0 mg
Cholesterol—saturated fat index:	1

Marinated Asparagus
or Broccoli

This recipe is a must when fresh asparagus is available. Serve as a side dish or salad with anything.

1 pound asparagus *or* broccoli
1 clove garlic, minced
2 teaspoons lower-sodium
   soy sauce*
2 teaspoons sesame oil

1½ tablespoons grated fresh
   gingerroot
½ cup rice vinegar
2 tablespoons sugar

Steam asparagus or broccoli 5 to 7 minutes or cook in the microwave oven on high for 5 minutes. Immediately cool by plunging in cold water. Drain and gently pat dry with paper towels. Combine garlic, soy sauce, sesame oil, ginger, vinegar, and sugar and pour over asparagus or broccoli. Gently toss to thoroughly coat asparagus or broccoli. Cover and refrigerate 1 hour or longer. Serve at room temperature.

* Kikkoman Lite Soy Sauce is available.

•~ Per Serving ~•	
Calories:	110
Sodium:	140 mg
Fiber:	3 gm
Total fat:	4 gm
Saturated fat:	1 gm
Cholesterol:	0 mg
Cholesterol—saturated fat index:	1

Roasted Eggplant and Bean Salad

Makes 6 cups.

A hearty salad with colorful roasted vegetables combined with fresh tomatoes and herbs.

4 cups unpeeled eggplant, cut in
$^1/_2$- to 1-inch pieces (use Japanese
eggplant *or* the firm part from a
larger eggplant)

2 cups red *or* yellow bell pepper, cut
in $^1/_2$- to 1-inch pieces

2 cups onion, cut in $^1/_2$- to 1-inch
pieces

4 cloves garlic, minced

1 tablespoon olive oil

2 cups plum tomato, cut in $^1/_2$- to
1-inch cubes

2 cups chopped fresh basil
or 2 teaspoons dried basil leaves

2 tablespoons chopped fresh oregano
or $^1/_2$ teaspoon dried oregano
leaves

$^1/_2$ teaspoon (or less) Lite Salt

$^1/_4$ teaspoon pepper

2 cans (15 ounces each) large white
beans, drained and rinsed

2 tablespoons rice vinegar

Fresh basil for garnish

To roast vegetables: Preheat oven to 400°. Combine eggplant, bell pepper, onion, and garlic in a large bowl. Toss with oil. Spread onto a nonstick baking sheet with edges. Bake 30 minutes, stirring every 10 minutes. Remove from oven and set aside.

In a large bowl, combine tomatoes, basil, oregano, Lite Salt, pepper, beans, and vinegar. Add roasted vegetables and toss gently so as not to break up the beans and vegetables. Garnish with fresh basil. Serve at room temperature.

Per Cup	
Calories:	242
Sodium:	340 mg
Fiber:	10 gm
Total fat:	3 gm
Saturated fat:	Trace gm
Cholesterol:	0 mg
Cholesterol–saturated fat index:	Trace

Sourdough Bread Salad with Roasted Vegetables

~ Makes 9 servings (a generous 1½ cups each).

This wonderful salad requires some time to prepare, but it's fun to do and definitely worth the effort. It's the kind of do-ahead salad that many of us prefer.

5 thick slices rustic sourdough bread,
    day-old or lightly toasted
1 teaspoon olive oil

1 red bell pepper, cut into
    ½-inch strips
1 medium red onion, cut into eighths
1 medium zucchini, halved
    lengthwise and sliced into
    ¼-inch-thick half circles
½ pound red potatoes, scrubbed,
    halved and cut into ¼-inch-thick
    half circles
1 small eggplant, cubed

2 teaspoons olive oil
3 cloves garlic, minced
2 cups ripe cherry tomatoes,
    cut in halves

Bread Salad Dressing
1 tablespoon olive oil
3 tablespoons balsamic vinegar
¼ teaspoon (or less) Lite Salt
¼ teaspoon freshly ground pepper
2 tablespoons minced fresh basil
    or 2 teaspoons dried basil leaves
1 clove garlic, minced

Brush both sides of the bread with 1 teaspoon olive oil. Toast both sides of the bread under broiler until golden brown. Cut into 1-inch cubes. Set aside.

Early in the day: Preheat oven to 375°. Spray 2 baking sheets with nonstick cooking spray. Combine bell peppers, onion, zucchini, potatoes, and eggplant, and toss with 2 teaspoons olive oil and 3 cloves minced garlic. Assemble vegetables on baking sheets. Bake for 15 minutes. Turn vegetables and add tomatoes. Continue baking for 10 minutes or until potatoes are done. Remove from oven and allow the vegetables to cool.

Prepare dressing by combining oil, vinegar, Lite Salt, pepper, basil, and garlic. Mix the cooled, roasted vegetables and toasted bread cubes in a large bowl. Drizzle the dressing over the vegetable-bread mixture. Toss well. Chill in refrigerator for 2 to 3 hours or overnight. Toss twice while salad is chilling.

~ Per Serving ~	
Calories:	232
Sodium:	353 mg
Fiber:	4 gm
Total fat:	5 gm
Saturated fat:	1 gm
Cholesterol:	0 mg
Cholesterol–saturated fat index:	1

Southwestern Salad

We named this salad for all the colorful and slightly unusual ingredients it contains—beans, corn, peppers, and bulgur.

½ cup uncooked bulgur

1 cup lower-salt chicken broth*
  or vegetable broth

¼ teaspoon cumin

1 tablespoon olive oil

2 tablespoons freshly squeezed
  lime juice

¼ teaspoon (or less) Lite Salt

⅛ teaspoon pepper

1 cup cooked black beans (if using
  canned beans, drain and rinse) †

1 cup frozen whole-kernel corn,
  thawed

1 cup chopped tomato

½ cup chopped red, yellow, *or* green
  bell pepper

¼ cup chopped green onions

¼ cup chopped fresh cilantro

2 tablespoons chopped fresh parsley

2 cups torn salad greens

In a small skillet, heat bulgur about 5 minutes, stirring until toasted. Stir in chicken broth or vegetable broth and cumin. Bring to a boil, reduce heat to low, cover, and simmer 15 minutes. Remove from heat; let stand 5 minutes. Fluff bulgur with a fork and set aside.

In a mixing bowl, stir together olive oil, lime juice, Lite Salt, and pepper. Add black beans, corn, tomato, bell pepper, green onions, cilantro, parsley, and toasted bulgur. To serve, place greens on individual plates and spoon bean mixture over the greens. Serve at room temperature or chilled.

* Swanson Natural Goodness with ⅓ less sodium is available.
† S&W has a 50% Less Salt product available.

⌐ Per Serving ⌐	
Calories:	212
Sodium:	344 mg
Fiber:	9 gm
Total fat:	5 gm
Saturated fat:	Trace gm
Cholesterol:	0 mg
Cholesterol–saturated fat index:	Trace

Spinach Couscous Salad

A colorful, fresh spinach salad. It has the unusual addition of couscous that has been marinated in a purchased dressing.

³/₄ cup lower-salt chicken broth*
³/₄ cup uncooked couscous
¹/₂ cup S&W Vintage Lites Red Wine & Herb Vinegar Dressing *or* ²/₃ cup Good Seasons Fat Free Italian Dressing

2 cups shredded fresh spinach
12 cherry tomatoes, halved
¹/₂ cup sliced water chestnuts, cut into slivers
6 whole spinach leaves, to garnish

Several hours before serving: Bring chicken broth to a boil. Remove from heat and add couscous. Cover and let sit 5 minutes. Put couscous into salad bowl and fluff with a fork; add salad dressing. Mix well, cover, and refrigerate about 3 hours or until completely cold.

Near serving time: Combine shredded spinach, tomatoes, and water chestnuts. Add dressing and couscous; toss well. Serve on spinach leaves.

* Swanson Natural Goodness with ¹/₃ less sodium is available.

◟ Per Serving ◞	
Calories:	162
Sodium:	484 mg
Fiber:	3 gm
Total fat:	1 gm
Saturated fat:	Trace gm
Cholesterol:	0 mg
Cholesterol–saturated fat index:	Trace

Tangy Cucumber Salad

3 cucumbers

1 tablespoon vinegar

1 clove garlic, minced

¹/₄ teaspoon (or less) Lite Salt

¹/₈ teaspoon pepper

1 teaspoon dillweed

2 tablespoons water

1 cup nonfat plain yogurt

1 tablespoon olive oil

1 tablespoon chopped fresh mint leaves
or 1 teaspoon dried mint leaves
(optional)

Peel cucumbers and dice (about 3¹/₂ cups after dicing). In a bowl, combine vinegar, garlic, Lite Salt, pepper, dillweed, water, yogurt, and oil. Stir in cucumber. Garnish with mint, if desired. Serve chilled.

~ Per Serving ~	
Calories:	39
Sodium:	55 mg
Fiber:	Trace gm
Total fat:	2 gm
Saturated fat:	Trace gm
Cholesterol:	1 mg
Cholesterol–saturated fat index:	Trace

Thai Black Bean Salad

1 can (15 ounces) black beans,
   drained and rinsed*
1 cup frozen whole-kernel corn,
   thawed
$1/2$ cup diced celery
$1/2$ cup diced red onion
$1/2$ cup diced red bell pepper
$1/4$ cup chopped fresh cilantro
1 jalapeño pepper, diced
2 cloves garlic, minced

1 teaspoon grated fresh gingerroot
1 tablespoon sesame oil
2 tablespoons rice vinegar
1 tablespoon freshly squeezed
   lime juice
$1/2$ teaspoon (or less) Lite Salt

Garnishes
Lime wedges
Red bell pepper rings

In a large bowl, combine black beans, corn, celery, onion, bell pepper, cilantro, jalapeños, garlic, and ginger. In a small bowl, whisk together sesame oil, vinegar, lime juice, and Lite Salt; pour over bean mixture and toss to combine. Chill until ready to serve. Garnish with lime wedges and bell pepper rings.

* S&W has a 50% Less Salt product available.

·~ Per Cup ~·	
Calories:	191
Sodium:	331 mg
Fiber:	7 gm
Total fat:	4 gm
Saturated fat:	1 gm
Cholesterol:	0 mg
Cholesterol–saturated fat index:	1

Thai Cucumber Salad

1 large English cucumber, unpeeled
1/4 cup minced onion
2 tablespoons rice vinegar
1 teaspoon sugar

1 teaspoon chopped fresh cilantro
3 tablespoons shredded carrot
2 tablespoons chopped peanuts (dry
   roasted and unsalted)

Two or 3 hours before serving: Slice cucumber into thin rounds. In a separate bowl, combine onion, vinegar, sugar, cilantro, and carrot, and add the sliced cucumber. Toss together and sprinkle top with peanuts. Cover and refrigerate. Serve cold.

→ Per Serving →	
Calories:	45
Sodium:	4 mg
Fiber:	1 gm
Total fat:	2 gm
Saturated fat:	Trace gm
Cholesterol:	0 mg
Cholesterol–saturated fat index:	Trace

Greek Pasta Salad with Tomato Vinaigrette

*~ Makes 9 cups.

How can a Greek salad be low in fat? By using sun-dried tomatoes and artichoke hearts not packed in oil, and by using small amounts of olives and feta cheese, you get a low-fat Greek salad that is delicious!

Greek Pasta Salad

8 ounces uncooked shell macaroni

$1/2$ cup chopped sun-dried tomatoes (not packed in oil)

1 cup boiling water

4 cups fresh spinach leaves, torn into bite-sized pieces

$1/4$ cup chopped red onion

$3/4$ cup quartered frozen artichoke hearts, thawed

$1/4$ cup chopped Kalamata olives

Tomato Vinaigrette

$2/3$ cup Consorzio Tomato Flavored Vinegar* (see page 132 for homemade option)

1 teaspoon olive oil

2 teaspoons minced garlic

2 teaspoons Dijon-style mustard

$1/4$ teaspoon Spicy Pepper Seasoning (Spice Islands) *or* your favorite seasoned pepper

$1/4$ cup crumbled feta cheese

Cook pasta in unsalted water according to package directions. Meanwhile, combine sun-dried tomatoes and boiling water in a bowl; let stand 20 minutes and drain.

In a large bowl, combine cooked pasta, sun-dried tomatoes, spinach, onion, artichoke hearts, and olives. In a separate bowl, prepare Tomato Vinaigrette by combining vinegar, olive oil, garlic, mustard, and pepper. When ready to serve, toss vinaigrette with pasta salad. Top with feta cheese. Chill before serving.

* Available in specialty food shops.

~ Per Cup ~	
Calories:	144
Sodium:	248 mg
Fiber:	3 gm
Total fat:	3 gm
Saturated fat:	1 gm
Cholesterol:	4 mg
Cholerterol—Saturated Fat Index:	1

Indonesian Pasta Salad

From the Far East comes a delightful spicy dish that can be served as a main dish or a salad.

Peanut Sauce
3 tablespoons peanut butter
  (any style)
1/2 cup lower-salt chicken broth*
2 tablespoons vinegar
2 tablespoons corn syrup
1 tablespoon lower-sodium
  soy sauce †
1 teaspoon hot chili oil (available in
  Asian grocery stores)
1 teaspoon sesame seeds

Salad
3 cups uncooked pasta swirls (or
  choose any shape you wish)

1 teaspoon hot chili oil
2 teaspoons grated fresh gingerroot
1 teaspoon minced garlic
1 1/2 cups matchstick-size carrot strips
1 1/2 cups matchstick-size snow
  pea strips
1/2 cup matchstick-size red *or* green
  bell pepper strips
1/4 cup lower-salt chicken broth*
1/2 cup sliced green onions

Red cabbage leaves

To make Peanut Sauce: Combine peanut butter, chicken broth, vinegar, corn syrup, soy sauce, and chili oil. Heat, stirring constantly with wire whisk, just until sauce is smooth and begins to boil. Remove from heat. Add sesame seeds and set aside until serving time.

To make Salad: Cook pasta in unsalted water until tender. Drain well. In a large skillet, heat chili oil over medium heat. Add ginger and garlic; sauté 30 seconds. Add carrots, snow peas, and bell peppers; stir-fry 2 to 3 minutes or until crisp-tender. Add chicken broth and stir. Remove from heat. Add green onions and cooked pasta; toss until broth is absorbed. Chill until serving time. Place red cabbage leaves on a platter. Spoon salad over the cabbage and drizzle salad with Peanut Sauce.

* Swanson Natural Goodness with 1/3 less sodium is available.
† Kikkoman Lite Soy Sauce is available.

~ Per Cup ~	
Calories:	280
Sodium:	184 mg
Fiber:	4 gm
Total fat:	6 gm
Saturated fat:	1 gm
Cholesterol:	0 mg
Cholesterol–saturated fat index:	1

Jane's Asian Pasta Salad

•⁓ Makes 8 servings (1½ cups each).

This recipe came from one of our dietitian friends. It was a big hit when served at a salmon barbecue we held in conjunction with a bridal shower for one of our staff members. We made this salad ahead of time, putting each of the ingredients in a separate package. At serving time, we put the noodles in a colander, rinsed them with cold water to separate the noodles, and drained them well before putting the salad together. This is a large salad that could easily be cut in half for a small group.

1 package (12 ounces) somen (Japanese noodles)*

Sesame Seed Dressing
2 teaspoons toasted sesame seeds
2 tablespoons sugar
¼ cup lower-sodium soy sauce†
1 tablespoon sesame oil
¼ cup rice vinegar
1 teaspoon grated fresh gingerroot

1½ cups shredded Chinese cabbage
   or other greens
1½ cups chopped tomatoes
1 cucumber, peeled and chopped
½ cup chopped green onions
2 cups broccoli, cut into small pieces
1 cup grated carrots

Break somen noodles in half and cook 2 or 3 minutes in unsalted boiling water. Drain and rinse with cold water. Place noodles in a large bowl and set aside. *If made ahead, store in refrigerator.* Prepare dressing by combining sesame seeds, sugar, soy sauce, oil, vinegar, and ginger; shake well to mix.

When ready to serve, pour half of the dressing over the cooked noodles and mix well. Add shredded cabbage or greens, tomatoes, cucumber, green onions, broccoli, and carrots. Pour remaining dressing over the salad and mix well just before serving.

* Somen can be found in the Asian-food section of most supermarkets.
† Kikkoman Lite Soy Sauce is available.

⁓ Per Serving ⁓	
Calories:	231
Sodium:	325 mg
Fiber:	4 gm
Total fat:	3 gm
Saturated fat:	Trace gm
Cholesterol:	0 mg
Cholesterol–saturated fat index:	Trace

Pasta Salad with White Beans and Rosemary

16 ounces uncooked rotini pasta

1 tablespoon olive oil

3 cloves garlic, minced

1 cup chopped onion

1 bunch fresh spinach,
   stems removed

1 teaspoon chopped fresh rosemary

1 cup lower-salt chicken broth*

$^3/_4$ teaspoon (or less) Lite Salt

$^1/_2$ teaspoon pepper

3 tablespoons chopped fresh parsley

4 cups cooked white beans *or* 2 cans
   (15 ounces each) large white
   beans, drained and rinsed

$^1/_4$ cup grated Parmesan cheese

Cook pasta in unsalted water according to package directions. Drain and set aside. Meanwhile, heat oil in nonstick skillet and sauté garlic, onion, and spinach, stirring frequently, until spinach is wilted and onions are browned, about 10 minutes. Add rosemary and sauté 1 minute. Add chicken broth, Lite Salt, and pepper, and simmer 5 minutes. Toss pasta with the spinach mixture, fresh parsley, and beans. Serve chilled. Garnish with Parmesan cheese.

* Swanson Natural Goodness with $^1/_3$ less sodium is available.

~ Per Cup ~	
Calories:	268
Sodium:	181 mg
Fiber:	6 gm
Total fat:	3 gm
Saturated fat:	1 gm
Cholesterol:	2 mg
Cholesterol–saturated fat index:	1

Southwestern Couscous and Black Bean Salad

·⁓ Makes 10 cups.

A colorful and great-tasting salad that works well as a main dish or a side dish.

2¹/₄ cups water	I cup frozen corn, thawed
I box (10 ounces) couscous	¹/₂ cup diced celery
I tablespoon olive oil	2 cans (15 ounces each) black beans,
¹/₃ cup freshly squeezed lime juice	drained and rinsed*
2 tablespoons vinegar	I teaspoon (or less) Lite Salt
I teaspoon cumin	¹/₈ teaspoon pepper
I teaspoon chili powder	¹/₄ cup chopped fresh cilantro *or*
³/₄ cup chopped green onions	Italian parsley
I cup chopped red bell pepper	

In a medium saucepan, bring the 2¹/₄ cups water to a boil and stir in the couscous. Cover and remove from heat. Let stand 5 minutes.

Meanwhile, in a large serving bowl, combine oil, lime juice, vinegar, cumin, and chili powder. Add green onions, bell pepper, corn, celery, and black beans. Stir to combine. Fluff the couscous with a fork and add to the mixture. Stir to mix the couscous with the dressing and vegetables. Add Lite Salt and pepper and mix. Garnish with chopped cilantro. Chill until ready to serve.

* S&W has a 50% Less Salt product available.

·⁓ Per Cup ⁓·	
Calories:	262
Sodium:	314 mg
Fiber:	8 gm
Total fat:	2 gm
Saturated fat:	Trace gm
Cholesterol:	0 mg
Cholesterol–saturated fat index:	Trace

Chicken Couscous Salad
with Lemon Dressing
⤳ Makes 8 servings (1½ cups each).

We really like this attractive main dish salad. If you have leftover turkey, it could be used in place of the chicken.

1 can (14½ ounces) lower-salt
   chicken broth*
½ cup water
½ teaspoon (or less) Lite Salt
1¾ cups uncooked couscous
2 cups diced, cooked chicken
   (use white meat)
1 tomato, chopped
3 green onions, thinly sliced
1 can (16 ounces) garbanzo beans,
   drained and rinsed†
½ cup diced red bell pepper
½ cup chopped carrots
½ cup golden raisins *or* currants
¼ cup chopped dried apricots
¼ cup minced fresh parsley

Lemon Dressing
½ cup freshly squeezed lemon juice
2 tablespoons olive oil
1 clove garlic, minced
¼ teaspoon turmeric
¼ teaspoon cumin
¼ to ½ teaspoon curry powder
¼ teaspoon Tabasco sauce
¼ teaspoon pepper (to taste)

¼ cup slivered almonds *or* roasted
   pine nuts

In a medium-sized saucepan, bring chicken broth, water, and Lite Salt to a boil and slowly stir in couscous. Mix thoroughly with a fork; cover and remove from heat. Let stand until broth is absorbed, about 15 minutes. Fluff couscous with a fork and transfer to a large bowl. Place in refrigerator about 10 minutes to cool. Cut cooked chicken into bite-sized pieces. Add to bowl with couscous. Mix in tomato, green onions, garbanzo beans, bell pepper, carrots, raisins or currants, apricots, and parsley.

Blend together lemon juice, olive oil, garlic, turmeric, cumin, curry powder, Tabasco sauce, and pepper in a small bowl. Add to couscous mixture and toss well. Chill at least 1 hour or up to 1 day. Sprinkle with nuts before serving.

⤳ Per Serving ⤳	
Calories:	381
Sodium:	336 mg
Fiber:	5 gm
Total fat:	8 gm
Saturated fat:	1 gm
Cholesterol:	27 mg
Cholesterol–saturated fat index:	3

* Swanson Natural Goodness with ⅓ less sodium is available.
† S&W has a 50% Less Salt product available.

Curried Chicken and Rice Salad with Grapes

At a neighborhood gathering for a birthday celebration, we all loved this main dish salad. It would be perfect for a potluck of any kind.

Curried Rice
1 to 2 tablespoons curry powder
1 tablespoon olive oil
2 large cloves garlic, minced
½ teaspoon grated fresh gingerroot
½ cup chopped onion
2 cups uncooked basmati rice
2 cans (14½ ounces each) lower-salt
   chicken broth*
½ teaspoon (or less) Lite Salt

Curry Dressing
½ cup nonfat mayonnaise
½ cup nonfat plain yogurt

½ cup mango chutney
½ teaspoon curry powder
⅛ teaspoon cayenne pepper
2 cups diced, cooked chicken
   (use white meat)
1 tart unpeeled apple, diced

Garnishes
2 tablespoons raisins
2 tablespoons sliced *or* slivered
   almonds
½ cup red seedless grapes

Early in the day: In a large saucepan or skillet with a tight-fitting lid, brown curry powder in olive oil over medium-high heat for 1 minute, just long enough to "toast" the spices and bring out their flavor. Add garlic, ginger, and onion; sauté until tender and onion is translucent, 4 to 5 minutes. Add rice, broth, and Lite Salt. Bring to a boil, cover, reduce heat to low, and simmer 15 minutes. Remove from heat and let stand 10 minutes, covered. Transfer to a large mixing bowl and cool to room temperature.

Prepare dressing by mixing together mayonnaise, yogurt, chutney, curry powder, and cayenne. (For a smoother dressing, pulse briefly in blender or food processor.) Stir in chicken and apple.

When rice is cooled, combine with dressing. Sprinkle with raisins, almonds, and grapes. Cover well and chill. Serve cold.

⌐ Per Serving ⌐	
Calories:	354
Sodium:	591 mg
Fiber:	2 gm
Total fat:	5 gm
Saturated fat:	1 gm
Cholesterol:	28 mg
Cholesterol–saturated fat index:	2

* Swanson Natural Goodness with ⅓ less sodium is available.

Family Favorite Fruit Salad

This recipe was passed down from Cindy's grandmother and is still served at many special family gatherings—holidays, showers, birthdays, etc.

4 oranges
1 large can (20 ounces) juice-packed
    pineapple tidbits, undrained
¼ cup sugar
1 tablespoon cornstarch

1 tablespoon freshly squeezed
    lemon juice
4 large bananas, sliced

Peel oranges, remove membranes, and dice. In a bowl, combine diced oranges, undrained pineapple tidbits and sugar; refrigerate overnight. The following day, drain liquid into saucepan and put fruit in a serving bowl. Add cornstarch and lemon juice to saucepan. Stir and bring to a boil; remove from heat and cool.

When ready to serve, pour cooled fruit juice mixture over the fruit and add bananas. Mix carefully and serve immediately.

~ Per Cup ~	
Calories:	215
Sodium:	3 mg
Fiber:	5 gm
Total fat:	1 gm
Saturated fat:	Trace gm
Cholesterol:	0 mg
Cholesterol–saturated fat index:	Trace

Flying Farmer
Chicken Salad

Sonja got this recipe from her mother, Ollie, who lives in Kansas. She and her friends, all good cooks, have made this recipe for years. In fact, Sonja has copied the recipe several times when she has been visiting her mother. The original was in the Farm Journal *in the late 1970s. We hope you like this version.*

Flying Farmer Dressing
³/₄ cup nonfat mayonnaise
2 tablespoons orange juice
2 tablespoons vinegar
1½ teaspoons (or less) Lite Salt

4 cups cooked white *or* brown rice
   (chilled overnight)
4 cups diced, cooked chicken
   (use white meat)

1 can (8 ounces) pineapple
   tidbits, drained
2 cans (11 ounces each) mandarin
   oranges, drained
1 cup chopped celery
½ cup chopped green onions
¼ cup sliced almonds

Combine mayonnaise, orange juice, vinegar, and Lite Salt; set aside. Mix together rice, chicken, pineapple, oranges, celery, green onions, and nuts. Add dressing and mix well. Serve cold on lettuce leaves.

⸺ Per Serving: ⸚	
Calories:	321
Sodium:	534 mg
Fiber:	2 gm
Total fat:	5 gm
Saturated fat:	1 gm
Cholesterol:	52 mg
Cholesterol–saturated fat index:	4

Summer Salad with Chicken and Blueberries

Honey Ginger Dressing
$\frac{1}{2}$ cup nonfat lemon yogurt
2 tablespoons honey
$\frac{1}{4}$ teaspoon ground ginger

Salad
3 cups diced, cooked chicken
   (use white meat)
1 cup seedless grapes
1 cup sliced celery

1 cup chopped unpeeled apple
1 cup sliced fresh peaches *or*
   nectarines
3 cups cantaloupe chunks *or* other
   melon
$\frac{1}{4}$ cup coarsely chopped walnuts
2 cups fresh blueberries,
   strawberries, *or* a combination of
   your favorites

Mix yogurt, honey, and ginger to make dressing; set aside. Combine chicken, grapes, celery, apple, peaches, cantaloupe, and walnuts. Pour dressing over chicken mixture and stir. Gently fold in blueberries or strawberries. Serve cold on a plate lined with lettuce.

~ Per Serving ~	
Calories:	280
Sodium:	85 mg
Fiber:	4 gm
Total fat:	6 gm
Saturated fat:	1 gm
Cholesterol:	52 mg
Cholesterol–saturated fat index:	4

Salad Dressings

Ginger Vinaigrette Dressing
Honey Dijon Dressing
Salad Dressing à la Mango
Spicy Tomato Vinaigrette Salad Dressing

Spreads

Aioli (Garlic Mayonnaise)
Lemon Cheese Spread

Salad Dressings Included with Recipes

(see Index for page numbers)

Bread Salad Dressing
Caesar Dressing
Cranberry Dressing
Creamy Mustard Dressing
Curry Dressing
Flying Farmer Dressing
Garlic Dijon Dressing
Honey Ginger Dressing
Lemon Dressing
Molly's Balsamic Vinegar Dressing
Oil and Vinegar Dressing
Poppy Seed Dressing
Rice Vinegar Dressing
Sesame Seed Dressing

Spread Included with Recipes

Garlic Mayonnaise

Ginger Vinaigrette Dressing

3 tablespoons rice vinegar

2 tablespoons olive oil

2 cloves garlic, minced

2 teaspoons grated fresh gingerroot

1 tablespoon lower-sodium
   soy sauce*

⅛ teaspoon seasoned pepper

Combine all ingredients and place in a container with a tight lid. Store in refrigerator at least 24 hours to develop flavors. Use up to 3 tablespoons dressing for 6 cups of greens.

* Kikkoman Lite Soy Sauce is available.

~ Per Tablespoon ~	
Calories:	33
Sodium:	75 mg
Fiber:	Trace gm
Total fat:	3 gm
Saturated fat:	Trace gm
Cholesterol:	0 mg
Cholesterol saturated fat index:	Trace

Honey Dijon Dressing

Try this on spinach salad, mixed greens, or fresh vegetables.

¹/₄ cup freshly squeezed lemon juice	1¹/₂ teaspoons dried basil leaves
¹/₄ cup balsamic vinegar	¹/₄ cup chopped green onions
2 cloves garlic, minced	¹/₂ teaspoon (or less) Lite Salt
1 tablespoon chopped fresh parsley	¹/₂ teaspoon pepper
1¹/₂ tablespoons Dijon-style mustard	¹/₄ cup vegetable oil
1¹/₂ tablespoons honey	

Mix all ingredients in a food processor or shake in a tightly sealed jar. Store in refrigerator. Use up to 3 tablespoons dressing for 6 cups of greens.

·‿ Per Tablespoon ‿·	
Calories:	40
Sodium:	49 mg
Fiber:	Trace gm
Total fat:	3 gm
Saturated fat:	Trace gm
Cholesterol:	0 mg
Cholesterol–saturated fat index:	Trace

Salad Dressing à la Mango

·– Makes 1 cup.

We love the Consorzio Vignettes (flavored vinegars) that are made in California. Mango vinegar makes this one very special. Raspberry or passion fruit vinegar is great, too. In case you cannot find mango vinegar, we've provided a homemade option.

EITHER
3/4 cup Consorzio Mango Flavored
    Vinegar*

OR
1/4 cup diced mango
1/4 cup champagne vinegar *or* white
    wine vinegar
3 to 4 tablespoons sugar
1/4 cup water
1/8 teaspoon vanilla

AND
3 tablespoons olive oil
2 teaspoons finely chopped garlic
2 teaspoons Dijon-style mustard
1/4 teaspoon seasoned pepper

Combine selected ingredients and mix well. Chill until serving time. When ready to serve, toss with mixed greens. Use up to 3 tablespoons dressing for 6 cups of greens.

* Available in specialty food shops.

·– Per Tablespoon ·–	
Calories:	25
Sodium:	8 mg
Fiber:	Trace gm
Total fat:	3 gm
Saturated fat:	Trace gm
Cholesterol:	0 mg
Cholesterol—saturated fat index:	Trace

Spicy Tomato Vinaigrette Salad Dressing

EITHER

²/₃ cup Consorzio Tomato Flavored
   Vinegar*

OR

3 tablespoons tomato paste

¹/₄ cup champagne vinegar *or* white
   wine vinegar

1 teaspoon finely minced garlic

2 tablespoons fresh basil
   or 1 teaspoon dried basil leaves

¹/₄ cup water

AND

2 tablespoons olive oil

2 teaspoons finely minced garlic

2 teaspoons Dijon-style mustard

¹/₄ teaspoon (or less) Lite Salt

¹/₄ teaspoon Spicy Pepper Seasoning
   (Spice Islands) *or* your favorite
   seasoned pepper

Combine selected ingredients and mix well. Chill until serving time. When ready to serve, toss with mixed greens. Three tablespoons of dressing is enough for 6 cups of greens.

* Available in specialty food shops.

⟶ Per Tablespoon ⟵	
Calories:	26
Sodium:	67 mg
Fiber:	Trace gm
Total fat:	2 gm
Saturated fat:	Trace gm
Cholesterol:	0 mg
Cholesterol–saturated fat index:	Trace

Aioli (Garlic Mayonnaise)

Makes ½ cup (24 teaspoons).

This is a topping that can be served with many things such as Grilled Pepper, Eggplant, and Zucchini Sandwiches *(page 171) and* Herb Tomato Soup *(page 152). It can be made 24 hours ahead, so it is ready to go when needed.*

2 cloves garlic, peeled and left whole
⅓ cup coarsely chopped fresh basil
   or 1 teaspoon dried basil leaves

1 teaspoon freshly squeezed lemon
   juice
¼ cup nonfat mayonnaise

Purée garlic, basil, and lemon juice in a food processor or blender until smooth. Add mayonnaise and blend. Place in a covered container and store in refrigerator.

∙ Per Teaspoon ∙	
Calories:	3
Sodium:	32 mg
Fiber:	Trace gm
Total fat:	Trace gm
Saturated fat:	0 gm
Cholesterol:	0 mg
Cholesterol–saturated fat index:	0

Lemon Cheese Spread

This is definitely worth the time it takes to mix a few ingredients together. It is a terrific topping for any type of muffin.

4 ounces fat-free cream cheese, at
  room temperature
1 tablespoon honey

1 teaspoon grated fresh lemon peel
1½ teaspoons freshly squeezed
  lemon juice

Beat all ingredients together, cover, and let stand 1 hour to better develop its flavor.

Per Teaspoon	
Calories:	13
Sodium:	57 mg
Fiber:	Trace gm
Total fat:	Trace gm
Saturated fat:	Trace gm
Cholesterol:	Trace mg
Cholesterol–saturated fat index:	Trace

Soups and Stews

African Peanut Soup with Rice Balls
Amazing Chili
Black and White Bean Chili
Black Bean Picante Soup
Chilled Creamy Red Pepper Soup
Chilled Garden Gazpacho
Cold Cucumber Yogurt Soup
Colorful Hot and Sour Soup
Corn and Chicken Chowder (With a Bite!)
Curried Apple Soup
Curried Pumpkin Soup
Donna's Easy Bean Soup
Em's Black Bean Soup
Fresh Corn and Zucchini Chowder
Good Old Vegetable Soup
Herb Tomato Soup
Marie's Seafood Vegetable Soup
Minestrone Clam Soup
Moroccan Stew
Nancy's Puerto Rican Rice and Chicken Stew
Salmon Bisque
Sorrel and Red Potato Soup
Special Minestrone Soup
Spicy Peanut Soup
Tortilla Seafood Soup

Broths

Vegetable Broth (Using Summer Vegetables)
Vegetable Broth (Using Winter Vegetables)

African Peanut Soup with Rice Balls

·— Makes 6 servings.

This dish is very popular in Ghana, West Africa. It is usually eaten at the big Sunday brunch with the soup served over "rice balls."

Soup

1 pound chicken breast meat, cut into 1½-inch cubes
1 cup finely diced onion
1 large ripe tomato
2 tablespoons unsalted tomato paste
1 tablespoon grated fresh gingerroot
⅛ teaspoon dried oregano leaves
⅛ teaspoon paprika
1 teaspoon (or less) Lite Salt
1 cup lower-salt chicken broth *
¼ to ½ teaspoon cayenne pepper *or* red pepper flakes
½ cup reduced-fat peanut butter
1 cup water
2 tablespoons chopped fresh cilantro

Rice Balls

2½ cups water, divided
2 cups uncooked pearl (sticky) rice

To prepare Soup: Put chicken in a soup pot. Add onions, whole tomato, tomato paste, ginger, oregano, paprika, and Lite Salt. Cover and cook on medium heat 10 minutes, stirring occasionally. Add chicken broth and cayenne pepper to steamed chicken. Remove the fresh tomato, blend it, and return tomato to broth. Continue cooking on medium heat for about 5 minutes. While the soup is cooking, blend peanut butter in 1 cup of water and add to the soup. Simmer for 20 minutes on low heat. Add cilantro just before serving.

To prepare Rice Balls: While the soup is cooking, boil 2 cups of water in a separate pan and add 2 cups of rice. Return to boiling, cover, and cook rice on simmer for 15 minutes. Add ½ cup of water very slowly to the rice and stir with a wooden spoon to get the rice to stick together. Let the rice cook for about 5 more minutes on very low heat.

To serve: Scoop up rice with ice cream scoop and form into balls. Place "rice balls" in a serving bowl or put in individual large soup bowls and ladle the peanut soup over the rice.

* Swanson Natural Goodness with ⅓ less sodium is available.

·— Per Serving (Including Rice) ·—	
Calories:	485
Sodium:	451 mg
Fiber:	3 gm
Total fat:	11 gm
Saturated fat:	2 gm
Cholesterol:	41 mg
Cholesterol–saturated fat index:	4

Amazing Chili

A meatless bean chili full of flavor.

$^1/_2$ cup uncooked bulgur
4 cups V-8 juice, divided
1 tablespoon olive oil
1 large onion, chopped
2 large cloves garlic, minced
1 to 2 tablespoons chili powder
2 to 4 teaspoons cumin
$^1/_2$ teaspoon coriander
$^1/_2$ teaspoon dried oregano leaves
$^1/_2$ teaspoon dried thyme leaves
$^1/_4$ to $^1/_2$ teaspoon cayenne pepper
$^1/_8$ teaspoon cinnamon
2 cans (16 ounces each) unsalted
    tomatoes

$^1/_2$ cup chopped bell pepper
1 package (10 ounces) frozen
    blackeye peas, thawed
1 package (10 ounces) frozen lima
    beans, thawed
1 package (10 ounces) frozen corn,
    thawed
1 to 2 cups water

1 tablespoon chopped fresh cilantro,
    for garnish

Place bulgur in a bowl and cover with 1 cup V-8 juice. Let stand 2 hours. Heat olive oil in a large soup pot. Add chopped onion and sauté until well cooked. Add garlic and cook 5 to 10 minutes.

Combine chili powder, cumin, coriander, oregano, thyme, cayenne pepper, and cinnamon, and add to onions; cook 5 minutes. Add tomatoes, bell pepper, and remaining 3 cups V-8 juice. Heat to boiling, reduce heat to medium-low, cover, and cook 20 to 30 minutes. Add bulgur and blackeye peas. Cook, stirring often, 25 minutes. Add lima beans, corn, and 1 to 2 cups water, as needed. Finish cooking, uncovered, 10 minutes or until lima beans are tender. Just before serving, sprinkle with cilantro.

– Per Cup –	
Calories:	166
Sodium:	400 mg
Fiber:	7 gm
Total fat:	2 gm
Saturated fat:	Trace gm
Cholesterol:	0 mg
Cholesterol–saturated fat index:	Trace

Black and White Bean Chili

·⁓ Makes 10 cups.

Chili with turkey chunks makes a great one-pot meal. This recipe can be cut in half easily for a smaller group.

1 teaspoon vegetable oil
1 pound uncooked, boneless, skinless
 turkey breast, cut into bite-size
 pieces
1 cup chopped onion
1 can (14½ ounces) lower-salt
 chicken broth*
2 cups water
2 cans (15 ounces each) black beans,
 drained and rinsed†
2 cans (15 ounces each) white
 beans, drained and rinsed

1 can (6 ounces) unsalted tomato
 paste
2 cans (4 ounces each) chopped
 green chiles, undrained,
 or 1 jalapeño pepper, chopped
1 teaspoon cumin
3 tablespoons chili powder or to
 taste

10 teaspoons grated Parmesan
 cheese

In a large soup kettle, heat oil over medium heat. Add turkey pieces and chopped onion; cook and stir about 5 minutes until turkey is no longer pink and onions are soft. Stir in chicken broth, water, beans, tomato paste, chiles or jalapeño pepper, cumin, and chili powder, and bring to a boil. Reduce heat to low and simmer 10 to 15 minutes, stirring occasionally. Serve hot with 1 teaspoon grated Parmesan cheese on top of each serving.

* Swanson Natural Goodness with ⅓ less sodium is available.
† S&W has a 50% Less Salt product available.

·⁓ Per Cup ⁓·	
Calories:	284
Sodium:	596 mg
Fiber:	10 gm
Total fat:	4 gm
Saturated fat:	1 gm
Cholesterol:	28 mg
Cholesterol—saturated fat index:	2

Black Bean Picante Soup

·⤳ Makes 6 cups.

Simple and good!

2 teaspoons vegetable oil
1 cup chopped onion
1 clove garlic, minced
2 cans (15 ounces each) black beans, undrained *
1 can (16 ounces) unsalted tomatoes
1/2 cup picante sauce

1/8 to 1/4 teaspoon red pepper flakes *or* 1/4 teaspoon Spicy Pepper Seasoning (Spice Islands)
1/2 teaspoon dried oregano leaves

Nonfat sour cream *or* nonfat plain yogurt, for garnish

Heat oil in a skillet. Sauté onions and garlic until onions are soft. Add undrained beans, tomatoes, picante sauce, pepper flakes, and oregano. Heat and serve with dollop of sour cream or yogurt on top of each serving.

* S&W has a 50% Less Salt product available.

·⤳ Per Cup ·⤳	
Calories:	198
Sodium:	400 mg
Fiber:	10 gm
Total fat:	3 gm
Saturated fat:	Trace gm
Cholesterol:	0 mg
Cholesterol–saturated fat index:	Trace

Chilled Creamy Red Pepper Soup

·‿ Makes 11 cups.

The idea for this beautiful cold soup came to us from California. Just to show off a little, we sometimes serve it in hollowed-out red, green, or yellow bell peppers.

1 tablespoon vegetable oil
4 cups chopped leeks *or* green onions
¹/₈ to ¹/₄ teaspoon red pepper flakes
   (optional)
6 large red bell peppers, sliced

3 cups lower-salt chicken broth*
6 cups buttermilk
Garnish ideas: Lemon slices, nonfat
   plain yogurt, or chopped chives

Heat oil and sauté leeks or green onions. Add red pepper flakes, if using. Cook until tender, stirring often, about 20 minutes. Add bell pepper and chicken broth and simmer, partially covered, over low heat for 30 minutes. Purée in blender and cool. When the soup base has cooled, add buttermilk; stir to mix and chill. Serve cold with any of the garnishes that strike your fancy.

* Swanson Natural Goodness with ¹/₃ less sodium is available.

·‿ Per Cup ·‿	
Calories:	96
Sodium:	321 mg
Fiber:	2 gm
Total fat:	3 gm
Saturated fat:	1 gm
Cholesterol:	5 mg
Cholesterol–saturated fat index:	1

Chilled Garden Gazpacho

Great to serve on a warm day, either at home or on a picnic.

3 cans (14$\frac{1}{2}$ ounces each) unsalted
   stewed tomatoes
$\frac{1}{4}$ cup wine vinegar
$\frac{1}{4}$ to $\frac{1}{2}$ teaspoon garlic powder
$\frac{1}{8}$ teaspoon cayenne pepper or to
   taste
1 can (14$\frac{1}{2}$ ounces) lower-salt
   chicken broth*

1 small avocado, peeled and sliced
2 cups chopped fresh tomato
1$\frac{1}{2}$ cups chopped cucumber
$\frac{1}{4}$ cup chopped green onions
$\frac{1}{4}$ cup sliced black olives, drained

In a blender or food processor, mix stewed tomatoes, vinegar, garlic powder, cayenne, and chicken broth. Blend until smooth. Add remaining ingredients and chill at least 4 hours. Serve cold.

*Swanson Natural Goodness with $\frac{1}{3}$ less sodium is available.

·– Per Cup ·–	
Calories:	69
Sodium:	246 mg
Fiber:	3 gm
Total fat:	2 gm
Saturated fat:	Trace gm
Cholesterol:	0 mg
Cholesterol–saturated fat index:	Trace

Cold Cucumber Yogurt Soup

Makes 4-plus cups.

$^3/_4$ pound cucumber, peeled and chopped

2 cups nonfat plain yogurt

1 cup lower-salt chicken broth *

2 tablespoons freshly squeezed lemon juice

2 tablespoons freshly squeezed orange juice

2 teaspoons chopped fresh oregano leaves

or $^1/_2$ teaspoon dried oregano leaves

$^1/_2$ teaspoon (or less) Lite Salt

$^1/_4$ teaspoon pepper

4 fresh parsley sprigs for garnish

Peel and chop cucumber (enough to make about 3 cups). In a medium bowl, stir together all the ingredients, leaving the parsley for garnish. Chill at least 1 hour or overnight. Garnish each serving with parsley.

* Swanson Natural Goodness with $^1/_3$ less sodium is available.

~ Per Cup ~	
Calories:	90
Sodium:	379 mg
Fiber:	1 gm
Total fat:	1 gm
Saturated fat:	Trace gm
Cholesterol:	2 mg
Cholesterol–saturated fat index:	Trace

Colorful Hot and Sour Soup

·~ *Makes 9 cups.*

Most of the preparation for this soup can be done the day before serving. For Mandarin Soup, *omit the pepper and vinegar.*

4 dried black mushrooms
1 cup boiling water
12 ounces tofu, drained
2 tablespoons cornstarch
1¼ cups water, divided
2 cans (14½ ounces each) vegetable broth
¼ cup celery, cut into matchstick-size pieces
¼ cup carrots, cut into matchstick-size pieces

1 tablespoon sherry
2 tablespoons white vinegar
1 teaspoon lower-sodium soy sauce*
¼ teaspoon white pepper
2 tablespoons egg substitute
½ cup frozen peas
⅛ teaspoon sesame oil
1 green onion, minced

Soak dried mushrooms in 1 cup boiling water for 30 minutes. After soaking, save the liquid by draining well and squeezing liquid out of mushrooms; set liquid aside. Remove stems and slice mushrooms into thin strips. Slice tofu into strips about 1½ by ¼ by ¼ inches. Dissolve cornstarch in ¼ cup water.

Bring remaining 1 cup water, vegetable broth, and mushroom soaking liquid to a boil. Add mushrooms, celery, and carrots and simmer, covered, for 10 minutes. Stir in sherry, vinegar, soy sauce, and pepper. Add cornstarch-water mixture and stir constantly until thickened. *The soup may be prepared to this point and refrigerated. If refrigerated, additional pepper and vinegar may need to be added at serving time.*

When ready to serve: Heat soup and slowly add egg substitute. Add tofu and frozen peas. Cook 1 minute or until peas are hot. Remove from heat. Sprinkle with a few drops sesame oil and green onion.

* Kikkoman Lite Soy Sauce is available.

·~ Per Cup ~·	
Calories:	63
Sodium:	472 mg
Fiber:	1 gm
Total fat:	2 gm
Saturated fat:	Trace gm
Cholesterol:	0 mg
Cholesterol–saturated fat index:	Trace

Corn and Chicken Chowder (With a Bite!)

This spicy chowder is a special treat when served with "extra" garnishes that are put in small bowls to pass at the table.

1 tablespoon vegetable oil

1 cup chopped onion

1 clove garlic, minced

1 can (17 ounces) cream-style corn

2 cans (17 ounces each) unsalted whole-kernel corn, drained

1 can (14^1/2 ounces) lower-salt chicken broth* *or* vegetable broth *or* water

1^1/2 cups skim milk

1 can (4 ounces) diced green chiles, drained

1 teaspoon cumin

^{1}/2 to 1 teaspoon white pepper (choose for yourself how spicy)

^{1}/4 teaspoon Tabasco sauce

1^1/2 cups cooked chicken, cut into ^{1}/2-inch cubes

Garnishes: Chopped red bell peppers, nonfat sour cream, salsa, crumbled baked tortilla chips

Heat oil in a heavy soup pot. Sauté onion and garlic over medium heat until onion is soft but not brown, about 6 minutes. In a blender, purée cream-style corn, 1 can drained whole-kernel corn, and chicken broth (mixture will be creamy but not completely smooth). Add puréed corn mixture and remaining can of whole-kernel corn to onions in soup pot. Simmer gently over medium heat 10 to 15 minutes. Add milk, chiles, cumin, pepper, Tabasco sauce, and chicken. Heat through. Serve garnishes in small bowls so guests can choose their favorites.

* Swanson Natural Goodness with ^{1}/3 less sodium is available.

- Per Cup -	
Calories:	182
Sodium:	416 mg
Fiber:	4 gm
Total fat:	3 gm
Saturated fat:	1 gm
Cholesterol:	19 mg
Cholesterol—saturated fat index:	2

Curried Apple Soup

This is a delightful soup. It was first tasted at a restaurant on the Oregon coast. We came home and immediately started cooking. Hope you like our version.

1 teaspoon vegetable oil
$1/2$ teaspoon grated fresh gingerroot
2 cloves garlic, minced
$3/4$ cup chopped onion
$2^1/2$ cups apple juice
$2^1/2$ cups unsweetened applesauce
1 cup apple butter

1 tablespoon curry powder (we like
Sharwood's Mild Curry)
$1/8$ to $1/4$ teaspoon cayenne pepper
1 cup nonfat plain yogurt
1 tablespoon freshly squeezed lemon
juice

Heat oil in a heavy 3-quart pan. Add ginger and garlic and stir for 1 minute. Add onion and cook, while stirring, until onions are golden brown. Add apple juice, bring to a boil, reduce heat, cover, and cook 15 minutes. Add applesauce, apple butter, curry powder, and cayenne pepper. Bring to a boil, reduce heat, cover, and cook 15 minutes. Whisk or stir small amounts of hot soup slowly into yogurt (if yogurt is stirred into the hot soup it will curdle); add lemon juice. Heat slowly over low heat to avoid any curdling. Serve hot.

Per Cup	
Calories:	226
Sodium:	40 mg
Fiber:	4 gm
Total fat:	2 gm
Saturated fat:	Trace gm
Cholesterol:	1 mg
Cholesterol–saturated fat index:	Trace

Curried Pumpkin Soup

A great lunch idea for a cold day.

1 tablespoon vegetable oil
1/2 pound fresh mushrooms, sliced
1/2 cup chopped onion
2 tablespoons flour
1 tablespoon curry powder
   (Sharwood's Mild Curry is our
   favorite)

1 can (14 1/2 ounces) vegetable broth
1 cup water
1 can (16 ounces) pumpkin
1 tablespoon honey
1/8 teaspoon nutmeg
1/4 teaspoon pepper
1 cup evaporated skim milk

Heat oil in a heavy saucepan. Sauté mushrooms and onions until onions are softened, about 3 minutes. Add flour and curry powder and cook, stirring constantly, 5 minutes. Remove pan from heat and, stirring constantly, add vegetable broth and water. Stir in pumpkin, honey, nutmeg, and pepper. Simmer 15 minutes, stirring occasionally. Stir in evaporated skim milk near serving time and heat through; do not boil.

-- Per Cup --	
Calories:	110
Sodium:	315 mg
Fiber:	2 gm
Total fat:	3 gm
Saturated fat:	Trace gm
Cholesterol:	1 mg
Cholesterol–saturated fat index:	Trace

Donna's Easy Bean Soup

This came from a camping trip, but is so good and so quickly prepared that it is now an all-time favorite at home, too. If you keep all the ingredients on hand, it can be put together in 15 minutes.

1 tablespoon vegetable oil
$1/2$ cup chopped green bell pepper
$1/2$ cup chopped onion
1 can (15 ounces) black beans,
   drained and rinsed*
1 can (16 ounces) large white beans,
   drained and rinsed
2 cups frozen corn
   or 1 can (16 ounces) whole-kernel
   corn, drained and rinsed

2 cups salsa (canned S&W Salsa
   with Cilantro is handy)
1 can ($14^1/2$ ounces) unsalted diced
   tomatoes
$1/4$ teaspoon (or less) Lite Salt (omit
   if using canned corn)
$2^1/2$ cups water

Heat oil in a large nonstick skillet. Sauté bell pepper and onion until wilted, about 5 minutes. Add beans to soup along with corn, salsa, tomatoes, Lite Salt, and water. Serve when hot.

* S&W has a 50% Less Salt product available.

⤳ Per Cup ⤳	
Calories:	193
Sodium:	493 mg
Fiber:	9 gm
Total fat:	3 gm
Saturated fat:	Trace gm
Cholesterol:	0 mg
Cholesterol–saturated fat index:	Trace

Em's Black Bean Soup

Our friend Jo has been a helpful recipe critic and has, on more than one occasion, shared some of her family's favorites. This is one her daughter, Emilie, really likes.

¹/₃ cup (10 pieces) sun-dried
  tomatoes (not packed in oil)
1 cup boiling water
1¹/₂ cups finely chopped onion
3 cloves garlic, minced
¹/₄ to ¹/₂ teaspoon cayenne pepper
  or 1 teaspoon Tabasco sauce *or* to
  taste
1 tablespoon vegetable oil
1 teaspoon cumin

1 teaspoon (or less) Lite Salt
2 cans (14¹/₂ ounces each) unsalted
  diced tomatoes (we like S&W
  Ready-Cut Peeled Tomatoes)
2 cans (15 ounces each) black beans,
  undrained*
¹/₄ cup chopped fresh cilantro

Nonfat yogurt *or* nonfat sour cream,
  for garnish

In a small bowl, cover sun-dried tomatoes with 1 cup boiling water and set aside.

In a soup pot, sauté the onions, garlic, and cayenne in the oil for 5 minutes, stirring frequently until onions are translucent. Add cumin, Lite Salt, tomatoes (including the liquid), and black beans. Bring to a boil; reduce heat to low and cover. Simmer 20 minutes stirring occasionally to prevent sticking.

Drain and chop the softened sun-dried tomatoes. Add them to the soup and cook 10 minutes. Stir in the cilantro and remove soup from heat. Purée half of the soup in a blender or food processor and return it to the pot. If the soup is too thick, add water. Heat soup and serve with a dollop of yogurt or sour cream.

* S&W has a 50% Less Salt product available.

⁓ Per Cup ⁓	
Calories:	208
Sodium:	186 mg
Fiber:	10 gm
Total fat:	3 gm
Saturated fat:	Trace gm
Cholesterol:	0 mg
Cholesterol–saturated fat index:	Trace

Fresh Corn and
Zucchini Chowder

1½ cups chopped onion

2 cloves garlic, minced

2 tablespoons chopped jalapeño
pepper (remove seeds)

2 cups chopped zucchini (remove
seeds before chopping)

½ teaspoon cumin

¼ teaspoon chili powder

¾ teaspoon (or less) Lite Salt

¼ teaspoon pepper

4 cups cubed red potatoes

2 cups fresh or frozen corn

1 can (12 ounces) evaporated skim
milk

2 tablespoons chopped fresh cilantro,
for garnish

Spray a large nonstick skillet with nonstick cooking spray. Sauté onion, garlic, and jalapeño pepper until onion turns golden brown, about 5 minutes. Add zucchini and sauté until crisp-tender. Add cumin, chili powder, Lite Salt, and pepper.

Put potatoes in a soup pot and cover with water. Bring to a boil, reduce heat, cover, and simmer 20 minutes, or until potatoes are soft. Drain well. Add zucchini mixture, corn, and milk, and heat through. Remove 2 cups and purée in a blender (to give it the thick chowder consistency). Add the purée to the chowder and heat thoroughly. Garnish with cilantro.

·~ Per Serving ~·	
Calories:	320
Sodium:	323 mg
Fiber:	8 gm
Total fat:	1 gm
Saturated fat:	Trace gm
Cholesterol:	4 mg
Cholesterol–saturated fat index:	Trace

Good Old Vegetable Soup

Good soup requires time to cook, but you do not have to be in constant attendance. So fix your soup when you are home but have other chores. Combine ingredients in this order and just keep an eye on the pot as you breeze through the kitchen. Just getting a whiff of the aroma makes everyone smile in anticipation. This soup keeps well for a future dinner if that fits your schedule. Be sure to have a nice loaf of whole grain bread to warm and serve with it.

1 tablespoon olive oil
5 cloves garlic, minced
3/4 cup chopped onion
1 cup chopped celery
2 cups finely chopped carrots
2 cans (16 ounces each) unsalted
   tomatoes, chopped
3/4 cup chopped fresh parsley
2 teaspoons dried basil leaves
1 teaspoon dried rosemary leaves
1 teaspoon (or less) Lite Salt

1/2 teaspoon pepper
2 cups diced red potatoes
1 cup diced parsnips, turnips, *or*
   rutabagas
5 cups chopped cabbage
3 cans (14 1/2 ounces each) lower-salt
   chicken broth*
4 cups water
1 tablespoon vinegar
1/2 cup grated Parmesan cheese, for
   garnish

Heat oil in a large kettle and sauté garlic, onions, celery, and carrots until the onions are transparent. Add tomatoes, parsley, basil, rosemary, Lite Salt, and pepper. Cook on low for a few minutes to heat through. Add potatoes, parsnips, cabbage, chicken broth, and water. Bring to a boil, reduce heat and cook, uncovered, for 2 hours. *At this point the soup can be refrigerated up to 2 days.*

When ready to serve, heat soup and then add vinegar. Ladle into warm bowls and top with a small amount of Parmesan cheese (1 tablespoon per 1 1/2 cups soup).

* Swanson Natural Goodness with 1/3 less sodium is available.

·~ Per Cup ~·	
Calories:	111
Sodium:	473 mg
Fiber:	5 gm
Total fat:	3 gm
Saturated fat:	1 gm
Cholesterol:	3 mg
Cholesterol—saturated fat index:	1

Herb Tomato Soup

⁓ Makes 5 servings (1 generous cup each).

*We especially like to have this soup when the garden tomatoes are at their prime.
Garlic lovers will want to spoon Aioli (Garlic Mayonnaise) (page 133) on top of
this fragrant soup.*

1 tablespoon olive oil
2 cups chopped onion (3 medium)
1/3 cup chopped celery
4 cups chopped tomatoes
   (6 medium)
3 cloves garlic, minced
1 bay leaf
2 large sprigs fresh basil, chopped
   or 1 teaspoon dried basil leaves

3/4 teaspoon dried marjoram leaves
1/4 teaspoon pepper
1/2 cup dry sherry
2 cups water
1 1/2 teaspoons (or less) Lite Salt

5 small slices French bread, toasted
   in oven

Heat olive oil in a large skillet or soup pot over medium heat. Sauté onions and celery until lightly cooked. Add chopped tomatoes and cook for 5 minutes. Add garlic, bay leaf, basil, marjoram, pepper, sherry, water, and Lite Salt. Bring to a boil, reduce heat to low, cover, and cook for 20 minutes. Purée soup, 2 to 3 cups at a time, in a blender or food processor. Return soup to cooking pot and heat to boiling.

Toast French bread in oven under broiler. Place 1 slice toasted bread in each soup bowl and ladle hot soup over top. Drizzle with Aioli, if desired.

⁓ Per Serving (Including Bread) ⁓	
Calories:	161
Sodium:	405 mg
Fiber:	3 gm
Total fat:	4 gm
Saturated fat:	1 gm
Cholesterol:	0 mg
Cholesterol–saturated fat index:	1

Marie's Seafood
Vegetable Soup

*For something different, use unshelled seafood such as clams, mussels, crab, shrimp, etc.
It's messy to eat, but that's part of the fun.*

1 tablespoon olive oil

1½ cups carrots, sliced into ¼-inch
    coins

1 cup sliced celery

1 medium onion, chopped

1 red bell pepper, chopped

1 green bell pepper, chopped

2 cans (8 ounces each) unsalted
    tomato sauce

1 can (16 ounces) unsalted stewed
    tomatoes

1 bottle (8 ounces) mild green taco
    sauce *or* green chili salsa

1 cup clam juice

1½ teaspoons (or less) Lite Salt

2 cups water

1 can (8 ounces) clams, undrained

½ pound halibut, cut into chunks

½ pound peeled shrimp

Heat oil in a large pot. Sauté carrots for 5 minutes. Add celery, onions, and bell peppers, and continue cooking until tender. Add tomato sauce, tomatoes, green taco sauce or green chili salsa, clam juice, Lite Salt, and water. Simmer 30 minutes. Add clams, halibut, and shrimp. Simmer until fish is cooked, 5 to 7 minutes. Serve hot.

·— Per Cup ·—	
Calories:	74
Sodium:	323 mg
Fiber:	2 gm
Total fat:	2 gm
Saturated fat:	Trace gm
Cholesterol:	36 mg
Cholesterol—saturated fat index:	2

Minestrone Clam Soup

A hearty, tasty soup; good for a cold evening at the beach or mountains.

1 tablespoon olive oil

2 cups chopped onion

4 cloves garlic, minced

1 teaspoon dried thyme leaves

1 teaspoon dried basil leaves

1/4 teaspoon dried marjoram leaves

1 can (15 ounces) white beans, drained and rinsed

4 cans (14 1/2 ounces each) lower-salt chicken broth*

1 zucchini, cut in half lengthwise and sliced

1/2 cup diagonally sliced carrots

1/2 cup diagonally sliced celery

1 1/2 cups uncooked small seashell macaroni

1/2 cup chopped fresh parsley

1 teaspoon grated lemon peel

1/2 teaspoon (or less) Lite Salt

1/4 to 1/2 teaspoon crushed red pepper flakes

3 cans (6 1/2 ounces each) minced clams, drained

1/4 cup grated Parmesan cheese

Heat oil in a soup pot over medium heat. Add onion, garlic, thyme, basil, and marjoram, and sauté 5 minutes. Add beans and broth; bring to a boil, reduce heat, cover, and simmer 15 minutes. Add zucchini, carrots, celery, macaroni, parsley, lemon peel, Lite Salt, pepper flakes, and clams. Cook 15 minutes or until pasta is done. Serve warm with Parmesan cheese to sprinkle over top.

* Swanson Natural Goodness with 1/3 less sodium is available.

·~ Per Cup ·~	
Calories:	181
Sodium:	402 mg
Fiber:	3 gm
Total fat:	3 gm
Saturated fat:	1 gm
Cholesterol:	16 mg
Cholesterol–saturated fat index:	2

Moroccan Stew

If you like squash and curry, you will enjoy this tasty vegetable stew. It is definitely worth the preparation time. Serve hot in deep bowls over couscous or steamed rice.

1 tablespoon olive oil
1 medium onion, diced
3 cloves garlic, minced
1 medium eggplant, unpeeled and cubed
3 cups vegetable broth
2 sticks cinnamon
2 teaspoons curry powder
1 teaspoon cumin
¹/₄ teaspoon turmeric
¹/₄ teaspoon (or less) Lite Salt
¹/₄ teaspoon pepper
1 large carrot, cut into ¹/₂-inch slices
¹/₂ medium acorn squash, cut into large wedges and peeled, then cut into 1-inch cubes*

2 medium parsnips, peeled and cut into 1-inch slices
¹/₂ green bell pepper, cut into 1-inch pieces
1 can (16 ounces) unsalted diced tomatoes
1 medium zucchini, cut into 1-inch pieces
¹/₂ cup golden raisins
2 tablespoons chopped fresh cilantro

Hot steamed couscous or rice

Heat olive oil in a large, heavy kettle. Add onion, garlic, and eggplant and sauté about 10 minutes over low heat until onion is tender. Add vegetable broth, cinnamon sticks, curry powder, cumin, turmeric, Lite Salt, and pepper. Mix well, bring to a boil, and reduce heat and simmer, covered, for about 10 minutes. Add carrots, squash, parsnips, and bell pepper. Simmer, uncovered, for 10 minutes.

Add tomatoes, zucchini, raisins, and 1 tablespoon chopped cilantro. Continue to simmer, covered, for 10 minutes or until zucchini is just tender. Remove cinnamon sticks, if desired.

Serve over couscous or steamed rice with remaining chopped cilantro sprinkled on top.

·— Per Serving (Not Including Rice or Couscous) —·	
Calories:	203
Sodium:	576 mg
Fiber:	8 gm
Total fat:	4 gm
Saturated fat:	1 gm
Cholesterol:	0 mg
Cholesterol—saturated fat index:	1

* For easier peeling, place whole squash in microwave oven and cook it on high heat for 2 minutes. Then allow squash to sit for a couple of minutes before peeling. Slice off the top and bottom of squash first; then you will be better able to handle it when peeling.

Nancy's Puerto Rican Rice and Chicken Stew

⌐ Makes 6 servings.

A one-pot dish that smells wonderful when cooking; your dinner crowd will come to the table eagerly.

2 chicken breast halves, skinned	1 quart water
4 chicken thighs, skinned	1 1/2 teaspoons dried oregano leaves
1 large onion, chopped	1/2 teaspoon cumin
3 cloves garlic, minced	1 teaspoon (or less) Lite Salt
2 cans (16 ounces each) unsalted tomatoes, crushed (reserve liquid)	Pepper, to taste
	3 drops Tabasco sauce
1 bay leaf, bent in half	1 cup uncooked white rice

In a large pot, combine chicken, onion, garlic, tomatoes and liquid, bay leaf, water, oregano, cumin, Lite Salt, pepper, and Tabasco sauce. Bring to a boil. Reduce heat to medium, cover, and cook 20 minutes. Add rice, bring to a boil, reduce heat to simmer, cover, and cook 20 minutes. Serve in warm bowls immediately or rice will absorb all the liquid.

⌐ Per Serving ⌐	
Calories:	289
Sodium:	239 mg
Fiber:	3 gm
Total fat:	5 gm
Saturated fat:	1 gm
Cholesterol:	55 mg
Cholesterol–saturated fat index:	4

Salmon Bisque

2 cans (14$\frac{1}{2}$ ounces each) lower-salt
   chicken broth*
1 cup water
1 fresh salmon fillet (8 ounces)
$\frac{1}{2}$ cup chopped celery
2 tablespoons chopped fresh chives
   or green onions
1 can (6 ounces) unsalted tomato
   paste

$\frac{1}{3}$ cup sherry *or* water
$\frac{1}{4}$ cup flour
2 cans (12 ounces each) evaporated
   skim milk
$\frac{1}{4}$ teaspoon pepper
$\frac{1}{2}$ teaspoon (or less) Lite Salt

Chopped green onions, for garnish

Heat chicken broth and water in a large saucepan. Remove any bones and skin from salmon. Combine uncooked salmon fillet, celery, and chives or green onions and add to hot chicken broth. Bring to a boil, reduce heat to simmer, cover and cook 8 minutes. Remove salmon fillet from broth with slotted spoon, separate into pieces and set aside. Add tomato paste and sherry or water to broth. Bring to a boil, reduce heat, and simmer 10 minutes, mixing thoroughly with a whisk.

In a separate small dish, mix flour and milk until there are no lumps, add to broth and stir with whisk. Add salmon pieces, pepper, and Lite Salt. Continue heating just until bisque comes to a boil and is thickened. Serve hot. Top bisque with chopped green onions.

* Swanson Natural Goodness with $\frac{1}{3}$ less sodium is available.

Per Cup	
Calories:	184
Sodium:	386 mg
Fiber:	1 gm
Total fat:	4 gm
Saturated fat:	1 gm
Cholesterol:	25 mg
Cholesterol–saturated fat index:	2

Sorrel and Red Potato Soup

Makes 10 cups.

Sorrel, fresh from the garden, makes a delicious soup.

1 teaspoon olive oil

3 cups water, divided

3 leeks, white part only, cut into
   1/4-inch rounds

7 cups loosely packed sorrel leaves,
   stems removed and coarsely sliced
   or chopped

1 teaspoon (or less) Lite Salt

6 cups red potatoes, cut in quarters
   and thinly sliced

1/8 teaspoon pepper

2 cans (14 1/2 ounces each) lower-salt
   chicken broth*

For Garnish

Nonfat sour cream *or* nonfat plain
   yogurt

1 tablespoon chopped fresh chives

Put olive oil in a large pot with 1/2 cup water. Add leeks, sorrel, and Lite Salt. Cover and cook 5 minutes over medium-low heat. Add potatoes, pepper, chicken broth, and 2 1/2 cups water. Bring to a boil, lower heat, cover, and simmer until potatoes are tender, about 30 minutes.

Ladle soup into bowls and top with a spoonful of sour cream or yogurt and chives, if desired.

* Swanson Natural Goodness with 1/3 less sodium is available.

~ Per Cup ~	
Calories:	84
Sodium:	508 mg
Fiber:	3 gm
Total fat:	1 gm
Saturated fat:	Trace gm
Cholesterol:	0 mg
Cholesterol–saturated fat index:	Trace

Special Minestrone Soup

This is a favorite among our staff.

½ cup chopped onion

3 cloves garlic, minced

4½ cups lower-salt chicken broth *

¾ teaspoon dried oregano leaves

½ teaspoon dried thyme leaves

¾ teaspoon dried basil leaves

½ teaspoon (or less) Lite Salt

¼ teaspoon pepper

2 tablespoons red wine

1 can (14½ ounces) unsalted diced tomatoes, undrained

1 can (6 ounces) unsalted tomato paste

5 ounces (½ package) frozen chopped spinach, thawed and drained

1 can (15 ounces) garbanzo beans, drained and rinsed †

2 cups uncooked tiny bow tie pasta *or* your favorite shape

2 tablespoons grated Parmesan cheese, for garnish

Spray a large saucepan with nonstick cooking spray and warm over medium heat. Sauté onion, garlic, and 2 tablespoons of the broth 3 to 4 minutes. Add oregano, thyme, basil, Lite Salt, pepper, and wine. Add remaining broth, tomatoes, tomato paste, spinach, and garbanzo beans. *Soup can be refrigerated or frozen at this point, if desired.* Bring soup to a boil, add pasta, reduce heat and simmer; cook 10 minutes or until pasta is done. Top each serving with grated Parmesan cheese.

* Swanson Natural Goodness with ⅓ less sodium is available.
† S&W has a 50% Less Salt product available.

·– Per Cup ·–	
Calories:	272
Sodium:	486 mg
Fiber:	6 gm
Total fat:	3 gm
Saturated fat:	1 gm
Cholesterol:	1 mg
Cholesterol–saturated fat index:	1

Spicy Peanut Soup

Peanuts play a prominent role in the cuisine of Southeast Asia. We were pleased to discover how well coconut extract works when combined with evaporated skim milk as a replacement for the high-fat coconut milk. We've made the serving size of this soup somewhat small, as it is usually served with other things, such as a stir-fry dish and rice.

1 teaspoon vegetable oil
2 cloves garlic, minced
1 tablespoon grated fresh gingerroot
2 cups finely diced onion
2 cups finely diced green bell pepper
1 can (14¹/2 ounces) vegetable broth
¹/4 cup creamy peanut butter
1 can (12 ounces) evaporated skim
   milk

³/4 teaspoon coriander
¹/8 to ¹/4 teaspoon cayenne pepper
1 teaspoon lemongrass (optional)*
2 tablespoons freshly squeezed
   lemon juice
¹/4 teaspoon coconut extract

Heat oil in a 3-quart pan. Sauté garlic and ginger, stirring until garlic is tender. Add diced onions, bell pepper, and vegetable broth and bring to a boil. Lower heat, cover, and simmer for 20 minutes. Pour into a blender or food processor. Add peanut butter and blend until smooth. *Be careful, as hot liquid can come out around the cover and cause a painful burn!* Return to pan. Using a whisk, mix evaporated skim milk, coriander, cayenne, and lemongrass, if using, into the soup. Simmer 15 minutes longer. Just before serving, remove soup from heat and stir in lemon juice and coconut extract. Serve immediately.

* Lemongrass is dried and can be found in supermarkets or Asian grocery stores.

~ Per Serving ~	
Calories:	88
Sodium:	246 mg
Fiber:	1 gm
Total fat:	4 gm
Saturated fat:	1 gm
Cholesterol:	1 mg
Cholesterol–saturated fat index:	1

Tortilla Seafood Soup *⌐ Makes 5 servings (a generous 1½ cups each).*

A spicy, chili-flavored soup with corn and peppers. We've given suggestions for condiments to serve on the side to add pizzazz to your meal.

1 teaspoon vegetable oil
3 cloves garlic, minced
2 to 4 teaspoons finely minced jalapeño peppers (you select the degree of "fire")
1 cup chopped onion
2 cans (14½ ounces each) lower-salt chicken broth*
2 cans (16 ounces each) unsalted tomatoes
1 can (8 ounces) unsalted tomato sauce
2 teaspoons chili powder

2 teaspoons cumin
1 tablespoon freshly squeezed lime juice
1 bag (12 ounces) frozen corn
8 ounces cooked shrimpmeat, crabmeat, *or* a combination of both

Condiments
5 corn tortillas
1 cup chopped fresh cilantro
2 small tomatoes, coarsely chopped
Fresh lime wedges

Heat oil in a large cooking pot. Sauté garlic, jalapeño peppers, and onion for 1 minute. Stir in chicken broth. Cover, reduce heat to low, and simmer 5 minutes or until onion is well cooked. Coarsely chop tomatoes, reserving liquid. Add tomatoes plus liquid to cooking pot along with tomato sauce, chili powder, cumin, and lime juice. Bring to a boil, reduce heat, and simmer, uncovered, 15 minutes. Stir in corn and cook 5 minutes. *Soup can be refrigerated up to 2 days at this point or frozen.*

While soup simmers, prepare tortilla strips: Preheat oven to 350°. Stack tortillas and cut into ½-inch strips; cut strips in half. Place in a single layer on a baking sheet that has been sprayed with nonstick cooking spray. Bake 15 to 18 minutes or until dry and crisp. After baking, strips can be stored in an airtight container for several days or frozen.

When ready to serve, place condiments in small serving dishes. Heat soup to boiling, put seafood in serving bowls, and pour hot soup over top. Pass condiments, including tortilla strips.

⌐ Per Serving (Including Condiments) ⌐	
Calories:	249
Sodium:	641 mg
Fiber:	8 gm
Total fat:	4 gm
Saturated fat:	1 gm
Cholesterol:	65 mg
Cholesterol–saturated fat index:	4

* Swanson Natural Goodness with ⅓ less sodium is available.

Vegetable Broth
(Using Summer Vegetables)

— Makes 8 cups.

Use 2 cups of this broth in place of 1 can vegetable or chicken broth in any of our recipes. There are definite advantages in making your own broth for use in recipes or for poaching fish or chicken. It contains less than half the sodium of canned vegetable broth, costs much less, and has a fresh flavor, especially if you have a vegetable garden. Frozen in 1-cup quantities, this broth can be very handy. Also, as the vegetables can be cut into large chunks, since they will not be eaten, it's easy to prepare.

4 cloves	2 cups cubed red potatoes
1 unpeeled onion, halved	1 cup chopped tomato
10 cups water	1/2 teaspoon dillweed
2 ribs celery, chopped	1 bay leaf, bent in half
7 mushrooms, halved	1/2 teaspoon pepper
2 carrots, chopped	1 tablespoon (or less) Lite Salt
2 cloves garlic, quartered	

Stick 2 cloves into each onion half. Place all ingredients in a large pot. Bring to a boil. Reduce heat, cover, and simmer 2 hours. Strain broth, measure, and add water to make 8 cups of broth.

— Per Cup —	
Calories:	60
Sodium:	389 mg
Fiber:	2 gm
Total fat:	Trace gm
Saturated fat:	Trace gm
Cholesterol:	0 mg
Cholesterol–saturated fat index:	Trace

Vegetable Broth
(Using Winter Vegetables)

~ Makes 8 cups.

Use 2 cups of this broth in place of 1 can vegetable or chicken broth in any of our recipes. The same advantages in making homemade broth apply here as with the previous recipe. Since many of us spend more time cooking in the colder months, we have developed a recipe using some of the wintertime vegetables. Even though this broth needs to simmer a long time, once you have cut up a few vegetables into large chunks, you only need to look at it every now and then. It's also handy to have something to do with those "extras" in the refrigerator that need to be used up.

10 cups water
2 leeks, chopped
1 fennel bulb, chopped
9 cloves garlic, quartered
2 unpeeled onions, halved
1 unpeeled parsnip, chopped
2 unpeeled carrots, chopped
10 mushrooms, halved

2 ribs celery, chopped
2 cups cubed new potatoes
1 bay leaf
8 black peppercorns
4 sprigs fresh thyme
    or ¼ teaspoon dried thyme leaves
1 tablespoon (or less) Lite Salt

Place all ingredients in a large pot. Bring to a boil. Reduce heat, cover, and simmer 2 hours. Strain broth, measure, and add water to make 8 cups of broth.

~ Per Cup ~	
Calories:	101
Sodium:	409 mg
Fiber:	5 gm
Total fat:	Trace gm
Saturated fat:	Trace gm
Cholesterol:	0 mg
Cholesterol–saturated fat index:	Trace

Vegetables

Acorn Squash with Apple Filling
Butternut Squash Enchiladas with Spicy Peanut Sauce
Cheese Enchiladas with Spicy Green Sauce
Fresh Asparagus with Tahini Sauce
Grilled Pepper, Eggplant, and Zucchini Sandwiches
Italian Marinara Sauce
Mediterranean-Style Spaghetti Squash
Mushroom, Bok Choy, and Tomato Stir-Fry
Paula's Italian Eggplant, Pepper, and Potato Casserole
Roasted Veggie Pizza
Spicy Thai Pizza
Spicy Tomato Sauce
Stir-Fried Bean Sprouts and Onions
Stir-Fried Vegetables with Tahini Sauce
Sweet Onion Bake
Vegetables Middle Eastern Style
Yam and Parsnip Sauté
Zucchini Pancakes with Green Chile Salsa
Zucchini Pie

Potatoes

Bangon Aloo (Eggplant and Potatoes)
Barbecued Yams
Cheese-Stuffed Potatoes
Curried Potatoes, Cauliflower, and Peas
Garlic Mashed Potatoes
Kate Aloo (Cut Potatoes)
Parmesan Potatoes
Party Mashed Potatoes
Potatoes Bhaji
Potato Latkes
Roasted Potatoes and Mushrooms with Fennel
Santa Fe Potatoes
Thai Sweet Potatoes over Rice

Grains (pasta and other noodles)

Angel Hair Pasta with Tomatoes and Basil
Angry Penne
Pad Thai
Pasta with Fresh Vegetable Sauce

(continued)

(continued)

Grains (pasta and other noodles)

Roasted Vegetable Lasagna
Savory Eggplant Sauce with Pasta
Spicy Si-Cuan Noodles
Thai Fusilli
Yakisoba Stir-Fry

Grains (rice)

Cranberry Rice Pilaf
Gobi Pilaf
Golden Risotto Cakes (Grilled Rice Cakes)
Jollof Rice
Rice and Currant Pilaf
Rice with Sweet Onions, Red Pepper, and Broccoli
Spiced Fruit Pilaf
Thai Sandwiches
Tropical Rice
Wild Mushroom Risotto

Grains (other)

Apple and Dried Fruit Bread Dressing
Baked Barley Pilaf
Baked Corn Casserole
Holiday Corn Bread Dressing
Polenta with Late Summer Garden Vegetables
Polenta with Tomato Sauce and GardenSausage

Lentils

Peppers Stuffed with Red Lentils and Drizzled with "Fire"
Syrian Lentils with Tomatoes

Beans

Beans and Tomatoes Provençale
Best Ever Black Beans
Black Bean Enchiladas
Black Bean Pizza
Blackeye Peas and Plantains (Red Red)
Chickpea Masala
Kung Pao Vegetarian Style
"Pile-Ons" (Our Favorite Tostada)

Acorn Squash with Apple Filling

⁓ Makes 4 servings.

1 small acorn squash

1 large Granny Smith apple, peeled, cored, and thinly sliced

1/8 cup brown sugar

1/2 teaspoon grated fresh gingerroot

1/4 teaspoon cinnamon

1/8 teaspoon nutmeg

1/8 teaspoon allspice

1/4 cup nonfat vanilla yogurt

1/2 teaspoon grated lemon peel

Pierce squash with fork in several places. Cook in the microwave oven on high for 6 minutes. Turn over and cook 8 to 10 minutes longer, or until squash is tender. Set aside.

In a microwave-safe bowl, combine apple, brown sugar, ginger, cinnamon, nutmeg, and allspice; cover with waxed paper and microwave on high 8 to 10 minutes, stirring every 3 minutes.

Cut squash in quarters; remove seeds. Spoon apple mixture into squash. In a small bowl, combine yogurt and lemon peel. Spoon on top of apple mixture and serve immediately.

⁓ Per Serving ⁓	
Calories:	129
Sodium:	14 mg
Fiber:	5 gm
Total fat:	Trace gm
Saturated fat:	Trace gm
Cholesterol:	Trace mg
Cholesterol–saturated fat index:	Trace

Butternut Squash Enchiladas with Spicy Peanut Sauce

˙⁓ Makes 6 servings (2 enchiladas each).

This recipe tastes similar to a unique enchilada dish served at one of our favorite local Mexican restaurants.

Filling
1 teaspoon vegetable oil
1/2 cup diced carrots
1 1/4 cups sliced mushrooms
1/2 cup diced onion
3/4 cup diced jicama
3/4 cup diced Granny Smith apple
1 package (12 ounces) frozen
   butternut squash, thawed
1 tablespoon vinegar
1/4 cup chopped fresh cilantro

Spicy Peanut Sauce
1 can (14 1/2 ounces) lower-salt
   chicken broth*

1/2 teaspoon cumin
1 clove garlic, minced
1 tablespoon flour
3 tablespoons chili powder
1/2 teaspoon dried oregano leaves
1 tablespoon minced onion
1/4 cup reduced-fat peanut butter

12 corn tortillas
1/2 cup grated fat-free Cheddar
   cheese

To prepare Filling: Heat oil in skillet and sauté carrots, mushrooms, onions, jicama, and apple until tender. Add squash, vinegar, and 2 tablespoons cilantro. Mix well and set aside.

To prepare Spicy Peanut Sauce: In a medium saucepan, combine broth, cumin, garlic, flour, chili powder, oregano, and onion. Bring to a boil and cook 2 minutes. Reduce heat to low, add peanut butter, and stir until smooth. Set aside.

⁓ Per Serving: ⁓	
Calories:	272
Sodium:	453 mg
Fiber:	9 gm
Total fat:	8 gm
Saturated fat:	1 gm
Cholesterol:	Trace mg
Cholesterol–saturated fat index:	1

To assemble: Preheat oven to 350°. Soften tortillas by wrapping in a damp paper towel and heating in the microwave oven 1/2 to 2 minutes, or by wrapping in foil and warming in the conventional oven 10 minutes. Place 1/4 cup squash mixture down the center of each tortilla. Roll up tortilla and place seam side down in a 9-by-13-inch baking pan coated with nonstick cooking spray. Pour peanut sauce over rolled tortillas and sprinkle with Cheddar cheese.

   Cover with foil and bake 20 to 25 minutes or until cheese is melted. Garnish with remaining cilantro.

* Swanson Natural Goodness with 1/3 less sodium is available.

Cheese Enchiladas with Spicy Green Sauce

~ Makes 6 servings (2 enchiladas each).

Spicy Green Sauce
1 can (10³/₄ ounces) Campbell's
   Healthy Request Cream of
   Mushroom Soup
2 tablespoons chopped jalapeño
   peppers
1 package (10 ounces) chopped
   frozen spinach, thawed (not
   drained)
¹/₂ cup finely chopped onion
1 clove garlic, minced
1 cup water
1 tablespoon flour
1 tablespoon water

Enchiladas
¹/₂ cup chopped onion
1 cup nonfat sour cream
1 cup nonfat cottage cheese
1 cup grated low-fat Cheddar cheese
2 tablespoons chopped jalapeño
   peppers
1 teaspoon cumin
12 corn tortillas

Garnishes
Nonfat sour cream
Chopped tomatoes
Chopped green onions

To prepare Spicy Green Sauce: In a blender or food processor, mix soup, jalapeño peppers, spinach, onion, and garlic until smooth. Pour 1 cup of water in a saucepan. Add soup mixture and bring to a boil. Simmer 10 to 15 minutes. Mix flour and 1 tablespoon water until smooth; add to sauce and cook until thickened, stirring constantly. Pour 1 cup of mixture in the bottom of a 9-by-13-inch baking dish that has been coated with nonstick cooking spray.

To prepare Enchiladas: Steam onions in the microwave oven until cooked. Combine onion with sour cream, cottage cheese, Cheddar cheese, jalapeño peppers, and cumin. Soften tortillas by wrapping in damp paper towels and heating in the microwave oven ¹/₂ to 2 minutes, or by wrapping in foil and warming in the conventional oven for 10 minutes.

Preheat oven to 350°. Place ¹/₄ cup cheese filling in the center of each warm tortilla and roll up. Place seam-side-down in the baking dish. Pour remaining green sauce over enchiladas and bake 25 to 30 minutes. Top with the garnishes (nonfat sour cream, tomatoes, and green onions) before serving.

~ Per Serving ~	
(Not Including Garnishes)	
Calories:	264
Sodium:	586 mg
Fiber:	5 gm
Total fat:	6 gm
Saturated fat:	3 gm
Cholesterol:	14 mg
Cholesterol–saturated fat index:	4

Fresh Asparagus with Tahini Sauce

You've seen this Tahini Sauce in other recipes, but we especially like it with fresh, tender asparagus. It's great on broccoli, too. When you make the sauce, it is nice to double the amounts so you'll have enough for 2 meals.

Tahini Sauce
2 tablespoons tahini*
2 medium cloves garlic, minced
1/2 teaspoon (or less) Lite Salt
1/4 cup warm water

1 tablespoon freshly squeezed
  lemon juice

2 pounds fresh asparagus
1/2 teaspoon toasted sesame seeds

Prepare Tahini Sauce by placing tahini, garlic, Lite Salt, and water in a blender and processing until smooth. Pour into a container, add lemon juice, and stir. Cover and store in refrigerator. To serve, remove from refrigerator, bring to room temperature, and stir.

Clean asparagus and cook it (steam or microwave in a small amount of water) until crisp-tender. Drain and place in a shallow serving bowl. Spoon Tahini Sauce over asparagus and sprinkle with sesame seeds.

* Tahini (sesame seed butter) is available in most supermarkets.

•– Per Serving •–	
Calories:	81
Sodium:	136 mg
Fiber:	3 gm
Total fat:	5 gm
Saturated fat:	1 gm
Cholesterol:	0 mg
Cholesterol–saturated fat index:	1

Grilled Pepper, Eggplant, and Zucchini Sandwiches

~ Makes 4 servings.

We first tasted these sandwiches at the Hilton Hotel in San Francisco. They were served with a high-fat roasted red pepper Aioli that contained a lot of oil, red pepper, and garlic. We chose to just use the roasted red pepper in the sandwich. If you wish, add some of our Aioli (page 133) to the toasted roll.

1 sweet onion, cut into 8 slices
2 red bell peppers, each cut into
   4 pieces
1 small zucchini, cut into 8 pieces
   (cut in half crosswise; then cut in
   half lengthwise)
2 Japanese eggplants, each cut into
   4 pieces

4 sourdough rolls, each 3 by 7 inches
   (cut each roll in half crosswise;
   then cut in half lengthwise)
4 teaspoons margarine
1 clove garlic, minced

2 tablespoons balsamic vinegar
1/4 teaspoon seasoned pepper

Cut and slice vegetables and rolls as described above. Combine margarine and garlic and spread on cut sides of rolls. Spray grill with nonstick cooking spray and heat. Brush vegetables with balsamic vinegar and place on grill. Sprinkle with seasoned pepper. Grill vegetables 3 to 5 minutes. Brush with vinegar and turn. Grill second side of vegetables for another 3 to 5 minutes. Brush with remaining vinegar and sprinkle with seasoned pepper.

Place vegetables to one side of grill or remove to a warm serving platter. Place rolls cut-side-down on grill and cook 1 to 2 minutes or until golden brown. Fill toasted rolls with vegetables and serve.

~ Per Serving ~	
Calories:	365
Sodium:	685 mg
Fiber:	6 gm
Total fat:	8 gm
Saturated fat:	2 gm
Cholesterol:	0 mg
Cholesterol–saturated fat index:	2

Italian Marinara Sauce

We got the idea for this recipe at a medical meeting in Hawaii. Eighty-five Italian cardiologists attended this meeting. One of them described in meticulous, mouthwatering detail how his mother made what he called "real" Italian marinara sauce. This is the recipe we developed based on his description. Our Italian staff member, Paula, says this is how her mother always made marinara sauce, too.

1 tablespoon olive oil	1/2 cup finely chopped fresh basil
1 tablespoon minced garlic	*or* 2 tablespoons dried basil leaves
2 cups chopped onion	2 teaspoons sugar
1 can (28 ounces) peeled tomatoes (Italian style with basil is great)	1 teaspoon (or less) Lite Salt
	1/8 teaspoon pepper
2 cans (14 1/2 ounces each) unsalted tomatoes	1/4 cup chopped fresh basil for garnish

Heat oil in a 3-quart pan. Add garlic and onions, reduce heat to medium and cook, while stirring, 8 to 10 minutes. Do not let onions get brown around the edges; they should be golden throughout and well cooked. Add canned tomatoes, basil, sugar, Lite Salt, and pepper. Bring to a boil, reduce heat so mixture bubbles lightly, and cook, uncovered, 1 1/2 to 2 hours. Break up tomatoes as the sauce cooks. Serve over pasta or in any dish that calls for a flavored tomato sauce. When serving, sprinkle with chopped fresh basil.

~ Per Cup ~	
Calories:	185
Sodium:	444 mg
Fiber:	6 gm
Total fat:	3 gm
Saturated fat:	Trace gm
Cholesterol:	0 mg
Cholesterol–saturated fat index:	Trace

Mediterranean-Style Spaghetti Squash

‣ Makes 2 servings (2 cups each).

The idea for this recipe came from a potluck dinner during our community study, The Family Heart Study. Jack, a psychologist on our staff, arrived with an uncooked spaghetti squash and a jar of marinara sauce. He cooked the squash whole in the microwave, and then heated the marinara sauce in the microwave. He removed the squash to a serving platter, topped it with marinara sauce, dusted it with Parmesan cheese, and served it. The dish was new to everyone and was very popular. Here is our version using Mediterranean Spaghetti Sauce,* developed by two of our staff members, Paula and Fay.

1 spaghetti squash, 7 inches long (yields about 3 cups of squash)

1 cup Mediterranean Spaghetti Sauce* or use your favorite spaghetti or marinara sauce

1 tablespoon grated Parmesan cheese

2 tablespoons finely chopped fresh basil or finely chopped fresh parsley

Using a sharp knife, score the skin of the squash from top to bottom several times. Place squash in microwave oven and cook 5 minutes. Turn squash and cook 5 minutes. Turn squash again and cook another 5 minutes. Heat sauce in the microwave oven on high for 2 minutes. While sauce is heating, cut squash in half lengthwise. Remove seeds and discard. Using a fork, dig squash loose from rind (it will come loose in strings and look like spaghetti) and place in a shallow serving dish. Spoon the sauce over the squash. Sprinkle Parmesan cheese and basil over the top.

* Mediterranean Spaghetti Sauce is sold under the brand name *Diomonde Foods*. Outside the Portland, Oregon, area, it may be obtained by writing to Diomonde Foods, P.O. Box 69351, Portland, OR 97201–0351.

‣ Per Serving ‣	
Calories:	112
Sodium:	484 mg
Fiber:	4 gm
Total fat:	5 gm
Saturated fat:	1 gm
Cholesterol:	2 mg
Cholesterol–saturated fat index:	2

Mushroom, Bok Choy, and Tomato Stir-Fry

– Makes 3 cups.

2 cups sliced bok choy (see
   directions below)
1 teaspoon olive oil
2 cups sliced fresh mushrooms

2/3 cup chopped tomato
2 teaspoons lower-sodium soy
   sauce*

Prepare bok choy by chopping 1½ cups of the white part into 3/8-inch slices and coarsely chopping the leaves (½ cup). Heat oil in skillet. Add mushrooms and white slices of bok choy. Stir-fry until mushrooms are golden brown and bok choy is crisp-tender. Add bok choy leaves and tomato. Stir until heated through. Add soy sauce and serve.

* Kikkoman Lite Soy Sauce is available.

– Per Cup –	
Calories:	42
Sodium:	169 mg
Fiber:	1 gm
Total fat:	2 gm
Saturated fat:	Trace gm
Cholesterol:	0 mg
Cholesterol–saturated fat index:	Trace

Paula's Italian Eggplant, Pepper, and Potato Casserole

·~ Makes 6 servings.

This is another wonderful recipe from Paula. It is both visually and aromatically appealing.

2 medium eggplants (8 inches long each)

2 teaspoons olive oil, divided

2 medium (3-inch diameter) potatoes (we like Yukon Gold), scrubbed and eyes removed

1 large green bell pepper, sliced

1 large red bell pepper, sliced

2$^{1}/_{2}$ cups Italian Marinara Sauce (page 172) *or* 2$^{1}/_{2}$ cups of your favorite marinara sauce

1$^{1}/_{4}$ teaspoons (or less) Lite Salt

8 tablespoons chopped fresh basil

Preheat oven to 400°. Slice eggplants into $^{3}/_{8}$-inch thick rounds. Place on 2 baking sheets that have been sprayed with nonstick cooking spray. Using 1 teaspoon olive oil, brush the tops of the eggplant rounds. Bake 15 minutes, turn, and bake 10 minutes or until eggplant is soft and lightly browned. Remove from oven and set aside. Reduce heat to 350°. Slice potatoes into $^{1}/_{8}$-inch pieces. Heat a large skillet to medium. Add 1 teaspoon olive oil and spread to coat skillet. Add potatoes, cover, and sauté 10 minutes, turn, add $^{1}/_{3}$ cup water, and cook 10 minutes or until potatoes are tender. Add additional water if needed. Remove potatoes and set aside. Add bell pepper slices and sauté until crisp-tender. Remove from skillet and set aside.

Spray a 10-inch baking dish with nonstick cooking spray. Place $^{1}/_{3}$ of the eggplant in a single layer on the bottom of the baking dish, sprinkle with $^{1}/_{4}$ teaspoon Lite Salt, and 1 tablespoon basil. Spread $^{1}/_{2}$ cup marinara sauce over the eggplant. Add all of the potatoes; sprinkle with $^{1}/_{4}$ teaspoon Lite Salt, and 1 tablespoon basil. Spread $^{1}/_{2}$ cup marinara sauce over the potatoes. Add $^{1}/_{3}$ of the eggplant, sprinkle with $^{1}/_{4}$ teaspoon Lite Salt, and 1 tablespoon basil. Spread $^{1}/_{2}$ cup marinara sauce over the eggplant. Add all of the peppers, sprinkle with $^{1}/_{4}$ teaspoon Lite Salt, and 1 tablespoon basil. Spread $^{1}/_{2}$ cup marinara sauce over the peppers. Add the rest of the eggplant, sprinkle with $^{1}/_{4}$ teaspoon Lite Salt, and 1 tablespoon basil. Top with $^{1}/_{2}$ cup marinara sauce. Bake, uncovered, 30 minutes. Remove from oven, sprinkle with 3 tablespoons basil, and serve.

·~ Per Serving ~·	
Calories:	195
Sodium:	398 mg
Fiber:	9 gm
Total fat:	3 gm
Saturated fat:	Trace gm
Cholesterol:	0 mg
Cholesterol–saturated fat index:	Trace

Roasted Veggie Pizza

This is a nice recipe because any combination of vegetables can be used.
We like the vegetables cut in big chunks.

1 cup chopped onion (Walla Walla or
  Vidalia sweet onions are great)
1 1/2 cups chopped, unpeeled eggplant
1 cup chopped bell pepper (red,
  yellow, *or* green)
1 1/2 cups quartered mushrooms
2 tablespoons vinegar (balsamic,
  rice, etc.)

1 loaf (15 to 16 ounces) unbaked
  focaccia bread
3/4 cup Italian Marinara Sauce (page
  172) *or* commercial pizza sauce
1/4 cup chopped fresh basil
1/4 cup grated Parmesan cheese

Preheat oven to 425°. In a bowl, combine onion, eggplant, bell pepper, mushrooms, and vinegar. Spread on baking sheet and bake 10 to 15 minutes (10 minutes for small pieces and 15 for large pieces). Set aside. Slice unbaked bread horizontally, place cut-side-up on baking sheet and bake 5 minutes. Spread marinara sauce or pizza sauce over bread. Top with roasted vegetables and sprinkle with basil and Parmesan cheese. Bake 15 to 20 minutes or until lightly browned. Remove from oven, cut into wedges, and serve immediately.

Per Serving	
Calories:	268
Sodium:	563 mg
Fiber:	5 gm
Total fat:	4 gm
Saturated fat:	1 gm
Cholesterol:	3 mg
Cholesterol—saturated fat index:	1

Spicy Thai Pizza

This is our version of a popular pizza served at a local gourmet pizza place. You may prefer to roast the bell peppers before baking the pizza.

1 loaf (15 to 16 ounces) unbaked
focaccia bread

Peanut Sauce (makes 2¹/₃ cups)
1³/₄ to 2 cups hot water
³/₄ cup reduced-fat peanut butter
1 tablespoon lower-sodium soy
sauce*
1 teaspoon freshly squeezed lemon
juice

¹/₂ to 1 teaspoon red pepper flakes
1 packet (1 ounce) Dutch Indonesian
Peanut Sauce Mix †

2 tablespoons grated Parmesan
cheese
1 cup thinly sliced red bell pepper
1 cup thinly sliced green bell pepper
¹/₂ cup sliced green onions
2 teaspoons sesame seeds

Preheat oven to 425°. Slice focaccia bread in half horizontally and set aside. Place hot water, peanut butter, soy sauce, lemon juice, pepper flakes, and peanut sauce mix in a small saucepan; heat and stir until smooth. Spread ¹/₄ to ¹/₃ cup peanut sauce on each focaccia bread half. *The remaining peanut sauce can be stored in the refrigerator or freezer for later use.* Top with Parmesan cheese, bell peppers, onions, and sesame seeds. Bake for 10 to 12 minutes. Cut into wedges and serve.

* Kikkoman Lite Soy Sauce is available.
† Available in the Asian-food or spice section of most supermarkets.

·~ Per Serving ~·	
Calories:	254
Sodium:	555 mg
Fiber:	3 gm
Total fat:	5 gm
Saturated fat:	1 gm
Cholesterol:	2 mg
Cholesterol–saturated fat index:	1

Spicy Tomato Sauce

⤳ Makes 3 cups.

*This sauce is great with the Sausage and Mushroom Spaghetti Torta (page 276)
or served over your favorite pasta. Double the recipe when you make it
and freeze the extra.*

1 cup chopped onion

1 teaspoon olive oil

2 cloves garlic, minced

1 tablespoon dried basil leaves

2 teaspoons dried oregano leaves

$^1/_4$ teaspoon red pepper flakes

2 cans ($14^1/_2$ ounces each) unsalted
   diced tomatoes

$^1/_2$ teaspoon sugar

$^1/_2$ teaspoon (or less) Lite Salt

$^1/_4$ teaspoon pepper

In a large saucepan, sauté onion in olive oil until tender, about 5 minutes. Add garlic, basil, oregano,
and red pepper flakes. Sauté about 2 minutes more. Add tomatoes, sugar, Lite Salt, and pepper.
Bring to a boil, lower heat, and simmer, uncovered, for 30 minutes, stirring occasionally.

⤳ Per Cup ⤳	
Calories:	101
Sodium:	203 mg
Fiber:	5 gm
Total fat:	2 gm
Saturated fat:	Trace gm
Cholesterol:	0 mg
Cholesterol—saturated fat index:	Trace

Stir-Fried Bean Sprouts and Onions

‑ Makes 5 cups.

A great side dish that takes 10 to 15 minutes to prepare.

6 cups fresh bean sprouts
1 teaspoon vegetable oil
1 large onion, thinly sliced
1/2 cup thinly sliced red *or* green bell
   pepper *or* snow peas
2 tablespoons vinegar

2 teaspoons lower-sodium
  soy sauce*
1/8 teaspoon (or less) Lite Salt
1/8 teaspoon pepper
1/4 teaspoon sesame oil
3 large green onions, chopped

Place bean sprouts in colander and rinse with cold water. Heat oil in a skillet. Add onions and bell peppers or snow peas. Stir-fry 2 to 3 minutes. Add bean sprouts and stir-fry 2 minutes. Add vinegar, soy sauce, Lite Salt, pepper, and sesame oil. Stir in green onions and serve immediately.

* Kikkoman Lite Soy Sauce is available.

‑ Per Cup ‑	
Calories:	140
Sodium:	120 mg
Fiber:	5 gm
Total fat:	7 gm
Saturated fat:	1 gm
Cholesterol:	0 mg
Cholesterol—saturated fat index:	1

Stir-Fried Vegetables with Tahini Sauce

This is a stir-fry version of Vegetables Middle Eastern Style *that Sonja adapted to serve on the annual family camping trip. You can alter the proportions of the vegetables and substitute cauliflower or Japanese eggplant slices for half of the peppers.*

Tahini Sauce
(It is nice to double the amounts so
    you'll have enough for 2 meals.)
2 tablespoons tahini*
2 cloves garlic, minced
$1/2$ teaspoon (or less) Lite Salt
$1/4$ cup warm water
1 tablespoon freshly squeezed
    lemon juice

1 onion, quartered and sliced
$1^{1}/2$ cups sliced mushrooms
1 small zucchini, cut in half and
    sliced
2 cups sliced green
    or red bell peppers
    or 1 cup peppers and 1 cup sliced
    Japanese eggplant
$1/3$ cup chopped fresh parsley

Place tahini, garlic, Lite Salt, and water in a blender and process until smooth. Pour into a container, add lemon juice, and stir. Cover and store in refrigerator. *Remove from refrigerator and let come to room temperature and stir before using.*

Heat large skillet or wok. Spray with nonstick cooking spray and add onion, mushrooms, and zucchini; stir-fry 1 to 2 minutes. Add bell peppers and stir-fry until crisp-tender. Stir in Tahini Sauce. Place in serving dish and sprinkle with parsley. Serve warm.

* Tahini (sesame seed butter) is available in most supermarkets.

➤ Per Serving ➤	
Calories:	90
Sodium:	139 mg
Fiber:	4 gm
Total fat:	4 gm
Saturated fat:	1 gm
Cholesterol:	0 mg
Cholesterol–saturated fat index:	1

Sweet Onion Bake

A flavorful side dish that is very easy to make. It can be assembled and frozen prior to baking to take advantage of the availability of sweet onions.

6 cups chopped sweet onion (Walla Walla sweet onions from eastern Washington are great)

1 teaspoon vegetable oil

3 cups boiling water

1 cup uncooked rice

1 can (12 ounces) evaporated skim milk

1⅓ cups grated Jarlsberg Lite cheese

¾ teaspoon (or less) Lite Salt

Sauté onions in oil over medium heat 10 to 12 minutes, or until onions are golden brown. Bring unsalted water to a boil, add rice, return to a boil, stir, and cook, uncovered, *5 minutes only.* Drain water from rice and rinse.

Preheat oven to 300°. Lightly spray a 9- or 10-inch square baking dish with nonstick cooking spray. Combine partially cooked rice, onions, milk, cheese, and Lite Salt. Put in baking dish. Cover and bake 1 hour.

~ Per Cup ~	
Calories:	302
Sodium:	318 mg
Fiber:	3 gm
Total fat:	5 gm
Saturated fat:	2 gm
Cholesterol:	10 mg
Cholesterol–saturated fat index:	3

Vegetables Middle Custern Style

This delicious Tahini Sauce *will make a vegetable eater out of anyone!*

Tahini Sauce

2 tablespoons tahini*
2 medium cloves garlic, minced
¹/₂ teaspoon (or less) Lite Salt
¹/₄ cup warm water
1 tablespoon freshly squeezed
  lemon juice

Vegetables Middle Eastern Style

(We often substitute 1 cup eggplant
  or cauliflower in place of 1 cup bell
  peppers)
1 onion, cut in half and then into
  1¹/₂-inch wedges
6 large mushrooms, cut in half
2 cups green *or* red bell peppers, cut
  into 1¹/₂-inch pieces
1 cup zucchini, cut into 1¹/₂-inch
  pieces
¹/₃ cup chopped fresh parsley

To prepare Tahini Sauce: Place tahini, garlic, Lite Salt, and water in a blender and process until smooth. Pour into a container, add lemon juice, and stir. Cover and store in refrigerator. Remove from refrigerator, let come to room temperature, and stir before using.

To prepare Vegetables Middle Eastern Style: Place vegetables in a 9-inch square baking dish suitable for the microwave oven. Cover and cook in the microwave oven on high 5 minutes or until crisp-tender. Drain liquid from vegetables, if needed. Broil 6 inches from coil for 10 minutes or until lightly browned. Spoon sauce over vegetables. Do not stir. Sprinkle parsley over vegetables. Serve.

* Tahini (sesame seed butter) is available in most supermarkets.

⌐ Per Serving ⌐	
Calories:	93
Sodium:	139 mg
Fiber:	4 gm
Total fat:	4 gm
Saturated fat:	1 gm
Cholesterol:	0 mg
Cholesterol–saturated fat index:	1

Yam and Parsnip Sauté

·— Makes 6 cups.

1 tablespoon olive oil
3 cups thinly sliced onion
4 cloves garlic, minced
1½ cups peeled and sliced yams
  (¼-inch slices)
1½ cups peeled and sliced parsnips
  (¼-inch slices)

1 can (14½ ounces) vegetable broth
½ cup nonfat plain yogurt
1 teaspoon dried thyme leaves
½ teaspoon pepper

Heat olive oil in a large nonstick skillet. Add onions and garlic. Stir often and sauté 7 to 8 minutes over medium heat until onions are golden brown. Stir in yam and parsnip slices. Add broth, yogurt, thyme, and pepper. Simmer, uncovered, about 35 minutes or until vegetables are tender and liquid absorbed.

·— Per Cup ·—	
Calories:	139
Sodium:	338 mg
Fiber:	4 gm
Total fat:	3 gm
Saturated fat:	Trace gm
Cholesterol:	Trace mg
Cholesterol–saturated fat index:	Trace

Zucchini Pancakes with Green Chile Salsa

Makes 5 generous servings (2 pancakes each).

The West's most plentiful vegetable can be served in many ways.
This version makes a wonderful meatless summer meal with corn on the cob and fresh fruit.
It is also great with grilled fish.

Green Chile Salsa (makes
1¹/₂ cups)
1 cup chopped fresh tomatoes
¹/₄ cup chopped green onions
¹/₄ cup chopped fresh cilantro
3 tablespoons chopped green chiles
1 tablespoon vinegar
2–3 dashes Tabasco sauce

Pancakes
1¹/₄ cups yellow cornmeal
³/₄ cup flour

2¹/₂ teaspoons baking powder
1 tablespoon sugar
¹/₂ teaspoon (or less) Lite Salt
¹/₄ cup egg substitute
1 cup skim milk
1 tablespoon vegetable oil
1¹/₄ cups grated zucchini
¹/₄ cup chopped onion

Mix together tomatoes, green onions, cilantro, green chiles, vinegar, and Tabasco sauce and set aside for flavors to blend. Stir together cornmeal, flour, baking powder, sugar, and Lite Salt. In a separate bowl, mix egg substitute, milk, and oil. Add dry ingredients to egg mixture and gently stir in zucchini and onion. Stir just until moistened.

Heat griddle or skillet and spray with nonstick cooking spray. Cook pancakes over medium heat until both sides are golden brown and insides are done. Serve warm and pass Salsa to spoon over top.

Per 2 Pancakes (with 5 Tablespoons Salsa)	
Calories:	270
Sodium:	422 mg
Fiber:	4 gm
Total fat:	4 gm
Saturated fat:	Trace gm
Cholesterol:	1 mg
Cholesterol–saturated fat index:	Trace

Zucchini Pie

Looking for another way to use zucchini? Try this light summer recipe. Corn on the cob is a good side dish to serve with it. Leftovers travel well in a brown bag for lunch.

Topping

1 tablespoon margarine
3 cups thinly sliced zucchini
1 cup chopped fresh mushrooms
1 cup coarsely chopped onion
2 tablespoons chopped fresh parsley
1/2 teaspoon (or less) Lite Salt
1/2 teaspoon garlic powder
1/4 teaspoon dried basil leaves
1/4 teaspoon dried oregano leaves
3 egg whites

2 cups grated light part-skim mozzarella cheese (we like Frigo Truly Lite)

Crust

1 round loaf (15 to 16 ounces) unbaked, whole wheat focaccia bread
2 teaspoons Dijon-style *or* prepared mustard

Preheat oven to 375°. In a large skillet, melt margarine. Cook zucchini, mushrooms, and onions until tender, about 10 minutes. Stir in parsley, Lite Salt, garlic powder, basil, and oregano. In a separate bowl, blend egg whites and grated cheese. Add to vegetable mixture, stir, and remove from heat.

Slice unbaked bread horizontally and place cut-sides-up on baking sheets. Spread cut sides of bread with mustard. Spread vegetable mixture evenly over bread.

Bake 25 to 35 minutes or until a knife inserted into the topping near the center comes out clean. If crust becomes too brown, cover with foil during last 10 minutes of baking. Let stand 10 minutes before serving.

↽ Per Serving ↽	
Calories:	256
Sodium:	529 mg
Fiber:	3 gm
Total fat:	9 gm
Saturated fat:	2 gm
Cholesterol:	13 mg
Cholesterol–saturated fat index:	3

Bangon Aloo (Eggplant and Potatoes)

~ Makes 4 servings (1 cup each).

This recipe has a lot of ingredients, but it's mostly spices. You be the judge of the "heat" you add from the jalapeño slices.

$^3/_4$ pound eggplant
$^1/_2$ pound potatoes

Spice Paste
1 tablespoon vegetable oil
1 cup sliced onion
$^1/_2$ teaspoon cumin
$^1/_2$ teaspoon coriander seeds
$^1/_2$ teaspoon curry powder
1 teaspoon grated fresh gingerroot
2 cloves garlic, minced
$^1/_2$ teaspoon chili powder
$^1/_2$ teaspoon (or less) Lite Salt
2 tablespoons water

1 tablespoon nonfat plain yogurt
$^1/_2$ teaspoon sugar
1 to 3 teaspoons chopped jalapeño
  slices (canned)
$^2/_3$ cup water
2 cloves garlic, minced
1 cup chopped tomato
1 tablespoon freshly squeezed lemon
  juice
4 tablespoons chopped fresh cilantro

Wash, but do not peel, eggplant and potatoes and cut both into $^1/_2$-inch chunks. Heat oil in medium saucepan and sauté onion 8 minutes or until golden brown throughout. Add cumin, coriander, and curry, and heat for 1 minute. Add ginger, garlic, chili powder, and Lite Salt. Cook over high heat 2 minutes, adding 2 tablespoons water to prevent the spice paste from sticking.

Add eggplant, yogurt, sugar, and jalapeño slices, mix well, and cook 2 to 3 minutes. Add $^2/_3$ cup water, reduce heat, cover, and simmer 15 minutes. Add potatoes. Cover and simmer 10 minutes, stirring occasionally. If dry, add a little water. Add remaining garlic, tomato, lemon juice, and 2 tablespoons cilantro. Cook until potatoes are done, stirring gently. Just before serving, sprinkle with the remaining 2 tablespoons cilantro.

~ Per Serving ~	
Calories:	144
Sodium:	150 mg
Fiber:	4 gm
Total fat:	4 gm
Saturated fat:	Trace gm
Cholesterol:	Trace mg
Cholesterol–saturated fat index:	Trace

Barbecued Yams

*A simple side dish. Choose your favorite barbecue sauce or the variation we have
suggested with Thai chili sauce.*

2 large yams (8 inches long each)
¼ cup Bull's Eye Honey Smoke
   Barbecue Sauce
   or 1 to 2 teaspoons Thai chili
   sauce* mixed with ¼ cup ketchup

Make a long slit in the skin of the yams. Microwave on high 6 minutes. Turn over and microwave
4 additional minutes, or until yams are cooked but not soft. Remove skin and cut yams into
thick rounds (about ¾ inch thick). Spray grill with nonstick cooking spray. Brush yams with barbecue
sauce and grill 3 minutes. Brush tops with barbecue sauce, turn, brush again with barbecue sauce,
and grill another 3 minutes.

* Thai chili sauce can be found in the Asian-food section of supermarkets *or* in Asian grocery stores.

·~ Per Serving ~·	
Calories:	118
Sodium:	159 mg
Fiber:	3 gm
Total fat:	Trace gm
Saturated fat:	Trace gm
Cholesterol:	0 mg
Cholesterol–saturated fat index:	Trace

Cheese-Stuffed Potatoes   *Makes 6 servings (¹/₂ potato each).*

These potatoes are well worth the effort. They were a real crowd pleaser at Cindy's grandmother's holiday dinner.

4 medium baking potatoes (about
  4¹/₂ inches by 2¹/₄ inches each)
1 teaspoon vegetable oil
¹/₂ cup sliced green onions
1 cup 1 percent low-fat cottage
  cheese

2 tablespoons skim milk
1 teaspoon (or less) Lite Salt
¹/₂ teaspoon pepper
1 cup low-fat sharp Cheddar cheese
Paprika

Preheat oven to 400°. Pierce potatoes with a fork and bake 1 hour or until tender. Allow potatoes to cool for a few minutes. Heat oil in a small skillet and sauté onions until tender. Cut potatoes in half lengthwise; carefully scoop insides into a large bowl. Add sautéed onions to potato along with cottage cheese, milk, Lite Salt, and pepper. Mix well, fold in cheese, and stuff potato mixture into the potato jackets. Place in a 9-by-13-inch baking dish. Sprinkle with paprika. Reduce temperature to 350° and bake 20 to 30 minutes or until heated through.

⁓ Per Serving ⁓	
Calories:	180
Sodium:	425 mg
Fiber:	2 gm
Total fat:	4 gm
Saturated fat:	2 gm
Cholesterol:	12 mg
Cholesterol—saturated fat index:	3

Curried Potatoes, Cauliflower, and Peas

‿ Makes 6 cups.

This is a nice, mild curry dish. If you like your food "hot," use red pepper flakes (the older they are, the more it takes).

1 tablespoon vegetable oil
1¹/₂ pounds red potatoes, eyes removed and cut into 1-inch pieces (about 5 cups)
¹/₂ cup chopped onion
1 cup water
1¹/₂ teaspoons (or less) Lite Salt
¹/₂ teaspoon coriander
¹/₂ teaspoon cumin

¹/₂ teaspoon turmeric
¹/₄ teaspoon black pepper, Spicy Pepper Seasoning (Spice Islands), *or* red pepper flakes
2 cups cauliflower, cut into flowerets
¹/₂ cup chopped tomato
1 cup frozen peas, thawed
2 tablespoons chopped fresh cilantro

Heat oil in a large nonstick skillet. Cook potatoes and onion until edges begin to brown (10 to 15 minutes). Add water, Lite Salt, coriander, cumin, turmeric, and pepper. Bring to boil, reduce heat to low (so mixture will bubble lightly), cover, and cook 10 minutes. Add cauliflower and tomatoes and a small amount of water, if needed. Cook 10 to 15 minutes or until cauliflower and potatoes are tender. Remove cover and, if needed, cook until liquid has evaporated. Add frozen peas and cilantro; stir to combine and heat through.

‿ Per Cup ‿	
Calories:	155
Sodium:	281 mg
Fiber:	5 gm
Total fat:	3 gm
Saturated fat:	Trace gm
Cholesterol:	0 mg
Cholesterol–saturated fat index:	Trace

Garlic Mashed Potatoes

These are definitely the "in" mashed potatoes of the 1990s!

2½ pounds potatoes (we like to use
    Yukon Gold potatoes)
6 cloves garlic
1 teaspoon (or less) Lite Salt

¼ cup skim milk
    or ¼ cup lower-salt chicken broth*
⅛ teaspoon pepper
3 tablespoons chopped fresh parsley

Peel potatoes and garlic; cut potatoes into chunks and rinse. Put potatoes and garlic in a 3-quart pan and cover with water. Bring to a boil, reduce heat, and boil gently until done, about 30 minutes. Drain and mash. Add Lite Salt, milk or chicken broth, pepper, and parsley and mash to desired consistency. Add more liquid if needed.

* Swanson Natura! Goodness with ⅓ less sodium is available.

·~ Per Serving ~·	
Calories:	233
Sodium:	267 mg
Fiber:	5 gm
Total fat:	Trace gm
Saturated fat:	Trace gm
Cholesterol:	Trace mg
Cholesterol—saturated fat index:	Trace

Kate Aloo (Cut Potatoes) *Makes 4 servings (1 ¼ cups each).*

Samina, our friend from Pakistan, brought this wonderful potato dish to a potluck and it was an instant success.

1 tablespoon vegetable oil
1 whole dried chili pepper
1 tablespoon cumin seed
1 tablespoon minced garlic
1 medium chopped tomato
   or 1 can (16 ounces) unsalted
   tomatoes
3 large potatoes, peeled and sliced
   3/8 inch thick

¼ cup chopped fresh cilantro
1 teaspoon (or less) Lite Salt
1 teaspoon cumin
½ teaspoon turmeric
1 teaspoon paprika
2 tablespoons water

Heat oil, add chili pepper and cumin seed and stir until seeds have a red roasted tint (takes only a few minutes). Add garlic and cook 1 minute. Add tomatoes and sliced potatoes. Stir until potatoes are coated with oil. Add cilantro, Lite Salt, cumin, turmeric, and paprika and stir carefully. Reduce heat to low, sprinkle with water, and cover. Cook 30 minutes or until potatoes are done. Add water as needed. Occasionally, stir gently so potatoes do not stick to the bottom and burn.

~ Per Serving ~	
Calories:	218
Sodium:	261 mg
Fiber:	4 gm
Total fat:	4 gm
Saturated fat:	Trace gm
Cholesterol:	0 mg
Cholesterol–saturated fat index:	Trace

Parmesan Potatoes

This dish fills the house with a wonderful aroma.

2 teaspoons olive oil
1 clove garlic, minced
1½ teaspoons dried basil leaves
½ teaspoon paprika
¼ teaspoon (or less) Lite Salt

⅛ teaspoon pepper
2 medium unpeeled potatoes, sliced
  ¼ inch thick
2 tablespoons grated Parmesan
  cheese

In a mixing bowl, combine oil, garlic, basil, paprika, Lite Salt, and pepper. Add potato slices and stir to coat. Lay in single layer on baking sheet that has been sprayed with nonstick cooking spray. Broil for 9 to 10 minutes until light brown. Turn potatoes over with a wide spatula. Sprinkle with Parmesan cheese. Broil for another 2 to 4 minutes until potatoes are tender. Serve warm.

~ Per Serving ~	
Calories:	138
Sodium:	166 mg
Fiber:	2 gm
Total fat:	4 gm
Saturated fat:	1 gm
Cholesterol:	3 mg
Cholesterol–saturated fat index:	1

Party Mashed Potatoes

A very handy and appealing mashed potato dish. It can be prepared ahead and baked at serving time. It is flavorful enough to serve as is or could have gravy added if your menu calls for it as part of a holiday celebration.

9 large potatoes
4 cloves garlic, peeled and left whole
8 ounces fat-free cream cheese
1 cup nonfat sour cream
1 teaspoon onion powder
1 teaspoon (or less) Lite Salt
$1/4$ teaspoon pepper

$1/4$ cup finely chopped green onions
   or 2 tablespoons poppy seeds
1 tablespoon margarine
$1/2$ teaspoon paprika
Chopped fresh parsley, if desired for
   garnish

Peel potatoes and cut into quarters. Cook potatoes and garlic cloves in boiling water until potatoes are done. Drain well and mash until smooth (an electric mixer works well). Add cream cheese, sour cream, onion powder, Lite Salt, and pepper and continue beating until light and fluffy. Cool slightly, add green onions or poppy seeds and put in a 9-by-13-inch baking dish that has been sprayed with nonstick cooking spray. *Cover and refrigerate if making ahead.*

One hour before serving, preheat oven to 350°. Remove cover from potatoes and dot top with 1 tablespoon margarine. Bake, uncovered, 45 to 60 minutes or until heated through and top starts to brown. Remove from oven and garnish with paprika and chopped parsley. Cut into squares and serve warm.

Per Serving	
Calories:	236
Sodium:	347 mg
Fiber:	4 gm
Total fat:	2 gm
Saturated fat:	Trace gm
Cholesterol:	1 mg
Cholesterol–saturated fat index:	Trace

Potatoes Bhaji

This is a spicy dish! One of our staff members, Anu, eats it with sliced tomatoes and cucumbers and rice. Another staff member, Fay, includes grilled chicken breasts when she has guests. The gongura (sorrel leaf paste) adds a special flavor but is not essential. Anu says, instead of the gongura, serve lemon wedges so guests can squeeze a little lemon juice on the potatoes.

2¹/₂ pounds red potatoes
1 tablespoon vegetable oil
1 teaspoon grated fresh gingerroot
1¹/₂ cups chopped onion
1 can (7 ounces) diced green chiles
1 large clove garlic, minced
    or ¹/₄ teaspoon garlic powder
1 tablespoon coriander
2 tablespoons mustard seeds (use
    less if you aren't a fire eater)

1¹/₂ teaspoons (or less) Lite Salt
¹/₄ teaspoon pepper
2–3 teaspoons gongura (optional)*
1¹/₂ cups frozen peas and carrots,
    thawed

¹/₄ cup chopped fresh cilantro, for
    garnish
Lemon wedges, for garnish

Wash potatoes, put in a 3-quart pan and cover with water. Bring to a boil and cook 30 minutes or until potatoes are done. Drain. Peel potatoes and cut into 1- to 2-inch pieces. Set aside.

Heat oil in a large nonstick skillet. Sauté ginger, onions, and green chiles 10 minutes or until onions are well cooked. Add garlic, coriander, mustard seed, Lite Salt, pepper, and gongura, if using, and mix well. Add peas and carrots and potatoes. Stir to thoroughly distribute spices. Heat through and serve. Garnish with cilantro and lemon wedges.

* Available in Indian specialty stores.

⁓ Per Cup ⁓	
Calories:	202
Sodium:	329 mg
Fiber:	5 gm
Total fat:	4 gm
Saturated fat:	Trace gm
Cholesterol:	0 mg
Cholesterol–saturated fat index:	Trace

Potato Latkes

Potato pancakes are great for breakfast or as a side dish for dinner.

$^1/_4$ cup egg substitute

$1^1/_2$ cups peeled, coarsely grated
    potatoes

$^1/_4$ cup finely chopped green onions

$1^1/_2$ tablespoons flour

$^1/_2$ to $^3/_4$ teaspoon (or less) Lite Salt

$^1/_2$ teaspoon dried parsley flakes

$^1/_8$ teaspoon dried rosemary leaves

$^1/_8$ teaspoon dried sage

$^1/_8$ teaspoon pepper

1 cup nonfat sour cream

1 tablespoon chopped fresh chives *or*
    green onions

In a medium bowl, beat egg substitute until foamy. Stir in grated potatoes, green onions, flour, Lite Salt, parsley, rosemary, sage, and pepper. Lightly spray a griddle with nonstick cooking spray and heat to medium. Prepare each pancake by spreading about $^1/_4$ cup of mixture on griddle and cooking each side until golden brown. Drain on paper towels and serve hot with sour cream and chives or green onions.

Per Pancake	
Calories:	59
Sodium:	135 mg
Fiber:	1 gm
Total fat:	Trace gm
Saturated fat:	Trace gm
Cholesterol:	1 mg
Cholesterol–saturated fat index:	Trace

Roasted Potatoes and Mushrooms with Fennel

⁓ Makes 6 servings.

We recently gave a friend several recipes. She reported they were all good but the
Roasted Potatoes and Mushrooms with Fennel *was in the GREAT category. This dish*
works best when all the vegetables are cut about the same size.

2 pounds small red potatoes, cut in
   half or 1-inch chunks
1 bulb fennel, coarsely chopped*
   or ¹/₂ teaspoon fennel seed
¹/₂ pound fresh mushrooms, cut in
   half *or* 1-inch chunks

2 teaspoons minced garlic
1 red bell pepper, cut into thick slices
   or 1-inch chunks
2 teaspoons olive oil
¹/₂ teaspoon (or less) Lite Salt
¹/₄ teaspoon pepper

Preheat oven to 400°. Combine potatoes, fennel, mushrooms, garlic, and bell pepper in a large baking dish with sides. Pour olive oil over vegetables; add Lite Salt and pepper. Toss well to coat vegetables.

Bake 20 to 30 minutes without stirring. Shake vegetables to prevent their sticking to the bottom of the pan; return to the oven and bake 20 minutes, stirring once or twice during the last 10 minutes. Potatoes should be browned and slightly crusty when done. Garnish with some of the fennel leaves and serve warm.

*To prepare fennel, trim a thin slice from the base to loosen the outer leaves and pull apart as you would celery. Cut stalks about 1 inch above the bulb. Discard the stalks, saving some of the leaves for garnish. Chop the bulb as you would an onion.

⁓ Per Serving ⁓	
Calories:	174
Sodium:	114 mg
Fiber:	4 gm
Total fat:	2 gm
Saturated fat:	Trace gm
Cholesterol:	0 mg
Cholesterol–saturated fat index:	Trace

Santa Fe Potatoes

The food in our southwestern states is so tasty. After just one visit, we started looking for ways to have those flavors at home. This is a very attractive and easy way to fix potatoes, and the salsa gives them plenty of zip.

4 medium-sized red potatoes
1 tablespoon olive oil
1½ cups salsa, mild *or* spicy—your
   choice

1 cup frozen corn
1 can (14½ ounces) black beans,
   drained and rinsed*
⅛ cup chopped fresh cilantro

Cut unpeeled potatoes into 1-inch cubes. Put into glass dish, cover with wax paper or plastic wrap and microwave 8 to 10 minutes or until tender. Heat olive oil in nonstick skillet. Add the potatoes, sauté, and toss lightly until potatoes are lightly browned. Add salsa, corn, and beans; stir carefully (the beans are pretty soft at this point and the appearance is better if they don't get crushed) until heated through. Sprinkle with cilantro and serve.

* S&W has a 50% Less Salt product available.

·⁓ Per Serving ⁓·	
Calories:	214
Sodium:	301 mg
Fiber:	7 gm
Total fat:	3 gm
Saturated fat:	Trace gm
Cholesterol:	0 mg
Cholesterol–saturated fat index:	Trace

Thai Sweet Potatoes over Rice

Coconut milk is a popular ingredient in Thai recipes, but it is also high in fat.
We've discovered that evaporated skim milk and coconut extract make
a good lower-fat alternative.

1 1/2 pounds sweet potatoes, peeled
    and cut into 1/2-inch pieces
1 tablespoon vegetable oil
1 onion, chopped
2 cloves garlic, minced
1 1/2 tablespoons grated fresh
    gingerroot
2 teaspoons curry powder
1/8 to 1/4 teaspoon crushed red pepper
    flakes
1 can (12 ounces) evaporated skim
    milk

1/4 teaspoon coconut extract
1/2 cup water
1/2 teaspoon (or less) Lite Salt
1 cup frozen green peas, thawed
1 tablespoon grated lemon peel

4 cups hot cooked basmati *or* other
    white rice
2 tablespoons unsalted peanuts, dry
    roasted
1/4 cup chopped fresh cilantro

In a large saucepan, cover sweet potatoes with water and heat until boiling. Cook 10 minutes; drain and set aside. In large skillet, heat oil; add onion and sauté until tender. Add garlic, ginger, curry powder, and pepper flakes; cook, stirring occasionally, 3 minutes. Add cooked sweet potatoes, evaporated milk, coconut extract, water, and Lite Salt. Heat to boiling. Reduce heat, cover, and simmer 20 minutes or until potatoes are tender. Remove from heat and stir in peas and lemon peel. Place hot cooked rice in a serving dish and top with potato mixture. Sprinkle with peanuts and cilantro and serve.

·– Per Serving ~	
Calories:	343
Sodium:	185 mg
Fiber:	5 gm
Total fat:	4 gm
Saturated fat:	1 gm
Cholesterol:	2 mg
Cholesterol–saturated fat index:	1

Angel Hair Pasta with Tomatoes and Basil

This is a perfect side dish with baked salmon and makes a wonderful light entrée. If you reheat this dish, first add a little wine or water.

8 ounces angel hair pasta

1 teaspoon olive oil

2 cloves garlic, minced

½ cup dry white wine

2 tablespoons freshly squeezed
   lemon juice

2 cups chopped Roma tomatoes

½ cup chopped fresh basil
   or 2 tablespoons dried basil leaves

½ teaspoon (or less) Lite Salt

¼ teaspoon pepper

¼ cup grated Parmesan cheese

Cook pasta in unsalted water according to package directions. Meanwhile, heat olive oil and sauté garlic until golden brown. Add wine and cook 2 minutes. Stir in lemon juice and tomato. When pasta is done, drain and put into serving bowl. Add the tomato mixture, basil, Lite Salt, and pepper. Toss. Sprinkle with Parmesan cheese just before serving.

✎ Per Serving ✎	
Calories:	309
Sodium:	252 mg
Fiber:	3 gm
Total fat:	4 gm
Saturated fat:	2 gm
Cholesterol:	5 mg
Cholesterol–saturated fat index:	2

Angry Penne

1 tablespoon olive oil
2 tablespoons minced garlic
$1/2$ to $1^1/2$ teaspoons crushed dried red
   pepper flakes
   ($1/2$ teaspoon for the wimps, 1 for
   the average, and $1^1/2$ teaspoons for
   the fire eaters)
3 cans ($14^1/2$ ounces each) S&W
   Ready-Cut Italian Peeled
   Tomatoes
   or $5^1/2$ cups Italian Marinara Sauce
   (page 172)

16 ounces penne pasta
   ($1^1/2$-inch tubes)
$1/2$ cup chopped fresh basil
$1/2$ cup chopped fresh parsley (we
   prefer Italian parsley)

Heat oil in 3-quart saucepan or large skillet over low heat. Add garlic and red pepper flakes and stir until garlic turns golden but not brown. Add tomatoes, bring to a boil, reduce heat, and simmer (bubbling slightly) 30 minutes or until sauce is thickened. Purée sauce with a "potato masher" or a fork.

Bring a large pot of water to a boil. Add pasta and stir until it begins to boil. Cook 10 minutes. Remove from heat, drain, and rinse thoroughly. Add tomato sauce, basil, and parsley. Mix well and transfer to a warm serving bowl or platter.

The sauce and pasta can be made ahead of time and stored separately in the refrigerator until serving time. When ready to serve, combine pasta, tomato sauce, basil, and parsley. Transfer to a serving bowl or platter, cover, and heat in the microwave oven on high 4 to 5 minutes.

Per Serving	
Calories:	362
Sodium:	341 mg
Fiber:	5 gm
Total fat:	4 gm
Saturated fat:	1 gm
Cholesterol:	0 mg
Cholesterol–saturated fat index:	1

Pad Thai

Pad Thai is the native dish of Thailand, and is a favorite among our staff. It often contains shrimp, chicken, or beef, but we like it meatless. Soaking the rice noodles in cold water rather than cooking them in boiling water keeps them from becoming sticky.

8 ounces rice noodles
($^1/_8$ inch wide) *

Pad Thai Sauce
2 to 3 tablespoons freshly squeezed
lime juice
3 tablespoons ketchup
1 tablespoon brown sugar
2 tablespoons fish sauce* *or*
lower-sodium soy sauce †
2 cups water

3 to 4 cloves garlic, minced
$^1/_2$ teaspoon red pepper flakes
2 cups grated carrots
$^1/_2$ cup egg substitute
$^1/_4$ cup chopped unsalted peanuts,
divided
6 to 8 sliced green onions, divided
3 cups bean sprouts, rinsed and
drained
$^1/_4$ cup chopped fresh cilantro

1 tablespoon vegetable oil (peanut oil
will give more peanut flavor)

Cover rice noodles with cold water and soak 30 to 60 minutes. Meanwhile, make the sauce by combining lime juice, ketchup, brown sugar, fish sauce or soy sauce, and water. Set aside.

Have remaining ingredients ready before beginning to stir-fry. Heat oil in a wok or large skillet. Add garlic and pepper flakes and heat to bring out the flavor. Add carrots and stir-fry 2 minutes. Push carrots aside to make a hollow space in the center. Add egg substitute and quickly scramble it. When cooked, add the sauce and mix well. Bring to a boil, add rice noodles, and cook until the liquid is almost evaporated and noodles are soft (add water if noodles are not as soft as desired). Stir in peanuts and green onions, reserving 1 tablespoon of each for garnishes. Sprinkle bean sprouts, reserved peanuts and green onions, and cilantro over the top.

Per Serving	
Calories:	314
Sodium:	588 mg
Fiber:	5 gm
Total fat:	8 gm
Saturated fat:	1 gm
Cholesterol:	0 mg
Cholesterol–saturated fat index:	1

* Available in Asian grocery stores; the rice noodles are labeled Rice Stick.
† Kikkoman Lite Soy Sauce is available.

Pasta with Fresh Vegetable Sauce

Makes 6 servings (a generous 1½ cups each).

This pasta sauce can include almost anything from the garden. It is very handy to make this large recipe and have extra sauce to serve again a few days later or keep in the freezer for a rainy day.

³/₄ cup thinly sliced carrots

1 large onion, coarsely chopped

¹/₂ cup thinly sliced radishes

¹/₂ cup coarsely chopped Italian (broad leaf) parsley

¹/₄ cup chopped fresh basil
or 1¹/₂ tablespoons dried basil leaves

3 cloves garlic, minced

2 cups chopped tomatoes

³/₄ cup dry white wine

1¹/₂ teaspoons (or less) Lite Salt

¹/₄ to ¹/₂ teaspoon pepper

1 teaspoon sugar

¹/₂ cup chopped green onions

1¹/₂ cups diced zucchini

¹/₂ large green, red, *or* yellow bell pepper, diced

2 teaspoons margarine

1¹/₂ teaspoons flour

¹/₂ cup skim milk

1 can (8 ounces) unsalted tomato sauce

³/₄ pound uncooked shell-shaped pasta

¹/₄ cup grated Parmesan cheese

Spray a large cooking pot with nonstick cooking spray. Add carrots, onions, radishes, parsley, basil, and garlic. Add a very small amount of water to prevent sticking. Sauté the vegetables, stirring often, until they begin to color, about 10 minutes. Add tomatoes, wine, Lite Salt, pepper, and sugar. Simmer the sauce, uncovered, 30 minutes. Add green onions, zucchini, and bell pepper and cook 10 minutes.

When vegetables are almost done, melt margarine in a separate saucepan. Stir in flour until a smooth paste develops. Slowly add milk, stirring it into the paste with a whisk or wooden spoon. Add tomato sauce and whisk the mixture again until it is smooth. Stir the sauce into the vegetables. Continue simmering the sauce over low heat, stirring often, until it is somewhat thick. Cook pasta in a large kettle of unsalted boiling water until al dente (still firm), drain, and pour into a large serving dish. Add sauce, toss, and sprinkle grated Parmesan over the top. Serve immediately.

~ Per Serving ~	
Calories:	328
Sodium:	368 mg
Fiber:	5 gm
Total fat:	4 gm
Saturated fat:	1 gm
Cholesterol:	3 mg
Cholesterol–saturated fat index:	1

Roasted Vegetable Lasagna

⌐ Makes 8 servings.

Serve with French bread and a green salad for a satisfying meal. Tomato lovers may want to add 1 can of unsalted tomato paste.

³/₄ cup chopped red, yellow, or green bell pepper (cut into 1-inch squares)

1 medium zucchini, halved lengthwise and sliced into ¹/₄-inch-thick half circles

1 medium yellow summer squash *or* Japanese eggplant, halved lengthwise and sliced into ¹/₄-inch half circles

1 cup chopped onion

3 cups mushrooms, each cut into 4 pieces

3 cloves garlic, minced

1 teaspoon olive oil

2 cans (15 ounces each) stewed tomatoes, well chopped

2 cans (8 ounces each) unsalted tomato sauce

2 teaspoons dried oregano leaves

2 teaspoons dried basil leaves

8 ounces fat-free ricotta cheese

2 cups (8 ounces) grated light part-skim mozzarella cheese

1 tablespoon chopped fresh parsley

11 to 12 lasagna noodles (8-ounce package)

Preheat oven to 375°. Spray a baking sheet with nonstick cooking spray. Put peppers, zucchini, squash, onions, mushrooms, and garlic in a bowl. Add oil and mix well to coat vegetables. Place on a baking sheet and cook 15 minutes, turn vegetables and cook 10 minutes. Remove from oven and set aside. In a saucepan, combine stewed tomatoes, tomato sauce, oregano, and basil. Simmer 15 to 20 minutes. In a separate dish, blend ricotta cheese, mozzarella cheese, and parsley. Set aside. Bring 2 quarts of water to a boil in a large kettle. Add lasagna noodles and boil gently, uncovered, 10 to 15 minutes. Drain and rinse.

Preheat oven to 350°. Spray a 9-by-13-inch baking dish with nonstick cooking spray. Layer ¹/₄ of the sauce, 4 noodles, ¹/₃ of the cheese mixture, ¹/₃ of the vegetables, 4 noodles, etc., ending with sauce. Bake, uncovered, 35 minutes or until bubbling hot (cover if needed). Remove from the oven and let stand 20 minutes before serving.

⌐ Per Serving ⌐	
Calories:	278
Sodium:	567 mg
Fiber:	4 gm
Total fat:	5 gm
Saturated fat:	2 gm
Cholesterol:	16 mg
Cholesterol–saturated fat index:	3

Savory Eggplant Sauce
with Pasta

·– Makes 6 servings (2 cups each).

If you like eggplant, this dish may well become one of your favorites.

2 eggplants, $1/2$ pound each
5 shallots, peeled and thinly sliced
1 teaspoon fennel seeds
1 tablespoon dried rosemary leaves
1 teaspoon red pepper flakes
$1/2$ cup red wine
1 can ($14^{1/2}$ ounces) vegetable broth,
   divided
4 red *or* yellow bell peppers, cut into
   thin strips

1 can (16 ounces) unsalted tomatoes
1 to 2 tablespoons minced garlic
1 tablespoon unsalted tomato paste
Pepper, to taste (we like
   fresh-ground)

6 cups cooked pasta
$1/2$ cup grated Parmesan cheese

Peel eggplants and cut each in half. Remove seeds, chop into $1/2$-inch cubes, place in a mixing bowl, and set aside. In a large skillet, combine shallots, fennel seeds, rosemary, pepper flakes, wine, and $1/2$ cup vegetable broth. Boil, stirring frequently, until almost dry. Add to eggplant.

Heat $1/4$ cup vegetable broth in the same skillet. When hot, add bell peppers and stir-fry until liquid is almost cooked away. Add eggplant mixture, the remaining broth, tomatoes, garlic, tomato paste, and pepper. Simmer 10 minutes or until thickened. Toss with cooked spaghetti or other pasta and top with Parmesan cheese.

·– Per Serving *(Includes Parmesan Cheese) –·*	
Calories:	314
Sodium:	517 mg
Fiber:	5 gm
Total fat:	4 gm
Saturated fat:	2 gm
Cholesterol:	7 mg
Cholesterol–saturated fat index:	2

Spicy Si-Cuan Noodles

⌐ Makes 6 cups.

Chuka soba noodles are available in the Asian section of most grocery stores. Be sure to read the label to avoid buying fried noodles, which have a similar label.

Hot Oil
2 teaspoons vegetable oil
1/2 to 1 teaspoon red pepper flakes

Noodles
2 packages (5 ounces each) chuka
    soba noodles (not fried)
1 tablespoon sesame oil
1 cup chopped green onions

Si-Cuan Sauce
1/4 cup lower-sodium soy sauce*
3 tablespoons vinegar
3/4 teaspoon sugar
2 teaspoons grated fresh gingerroot
2 cloves garlic, minced

Prepare Hot Oil by heating oil in a small pan. Stir in red pepper flakes and heat for a few minutes to bring out the flavor. Set aside.

Boil noodles in unsalted water according to package directions until just done, about 2 minutes. Drain well and immediately mix with Hot Oil, sesame oil, and green onions. Prepare Si-Cuan Sauce by combining soy sauce, vinegar, sugar, ginger, and garlic; toss with noodles. Serve chilled.

* Kikkoman Lite Soy Sauce is available.

⌐ Per Cup ⌐	
Calories:	239
Sodium:	404 mg
Fiber:	2 gm
Total fat:	5 gm
Saturated fat:	1 gm
Cholesterol:	0 mg
Cholesterol–saturated fat index:	1

Thai Fusilli

~ Makes 11 cups.

The key to this dish is to toss the sauce with the hot noodles, and to serve it immediately so the noodles do not become sticky. It is great with barbecued teriyaki chicken or fish.

16 ounces uncooked fusilli
   (corkscrew-shaped pasta)

1 cup picante sauce

3 tablespoons reduced-fat peanut
   butter

1 tablespoon honey

1/3 cup orange juice

1 teaspoon lower-sodium soy sauce*

1/2 teaspoon ground ginger

1/4 cup chopped fresh cilantro

2 tablespoons chopped unsalted
   peanuts

1/4 cup thinly sliced red bell pepper

Cook fusilli in unsalted water according to package directions. Meanwhile, combine picante sauce, peanut butter, honey, orange juice, soy sauce, and ginger in a small saucepan. Cook and stir over low heat until blended and smooth. Toss mixture with hot cooked fusilli. Sprinkle with cilantro, peanuts, and bell pepper. Serve immediately.

* Kikkoman Lite Soy Sauce is available.

~ Per Cup ~	
Calories:	210
Sodium:	196 mg
Fiber:	2 gm
Total fat:	3 gm
Saturated fat:	Trace gm
Cholesterol:	0 mg
Cholesterol–saturated fat index:	Trace

Yakisoba Stir-Fry

An eye-pleasing recipe that can be used as either a main dish or side dish. Any combination of vegetables can be used.

2 packages (5 ounces each)
  uncooked chuka soba noodles*
1 cup hot water
2 tablespoons reduced-fat peanut
  butter
2 tablespoons lower-sodium soy
  sauce†
1 to 3 teaspoons vinegar
1 teaspoon sesame oil
1/4 teaspoon crushed red pepper
  flakes

1 cup thinly sliced green onions
2 cloves garlic, minced
1 package (6 ounces) frozen snow
  peas, thinly sliced
1 1/2 cups chopped red bell pepper
1 cup thinly sliced carrot
1/2 cup diagonally sliced celery
1 cup sliced mushrooms
1/4 cup chopped fresh cilantro

In a large cooking pot, bring unsalted water to boil. Cook chuka soba noodles 2 1/2 to 3 minutes. Drain and rinse; set aside. Combine 1 cup hot water with peanut butter, soy sauce, vinegar, sesame oil, and pepper flakes in small bowl. Set aside.

Spray wok or large skillet with nonstick cooking spray. Add green onions and garlic; sauté 2 minutes. Add snow peas, bell pepper, carrots, celery, and mushrooms and stir-fry until crisp-tender. Add peanut butter mixture and cooked noodles; cook 2 minutes, stirring constantly. Garnish with cilantro and serve immediately.

* Look for soba noodles in the Asian-food section of your supermarket.
† Kikkoman Lite Soy Sauce is available.

⁓ Per Serving ⁓	
Calories:	241
Sodium:	322 mg
Fiber:	5 gm
Total fat:	4 gm
Saturated fat:	1 gm
Cholesterol:	0 mg
Cholesterol–saturated fat index:	1

Cranberry Rice Pilaf

Makes 5 servings (a generous 1 cup each).

1 teaspoon vegetable oil
¹/₂ large onion, finely chopped
1¹/₂ teaspoons minced garlic
¹/₈ teaspoon cardamom
¹/₄ teaspoon cinnamon
1 teaspoon (or less) Lite Salt
¹/₄ teaspoon pepper

2 cups water
1 cup uncooked basmati rice *or* other
    long-grain white rice
¹/₂ cup dried cranberries
2 tablespoons chopped fresh cilantro
    or parsley

Heat oil in a saucepan. Add onion, garlic, cardamom, cinnamon, Lite Salt, and pepper and cook until onion is soft. Add water and bring to a boil. Add rice, stir, cover, and reduce heat to low. Cook for 20 minutes; remove pan from heat and let rest 5 minutes. Add cranberries and cilantro; fluff with a fork and serve.

Per Serving	
Calories:	210
Sodium:	199 mg
Fiber:	1 gm
Total fat:	1 gm
Saturated fat:	Trace mg
Cholesterol:	0 mg
Cholesterol–saturated fat index:	Trace

Gobi Pilaf

Gobi *is the Hindi word for* cabbage. *Anu, our friend from India, says adding a pinch of cardamom and a pinch of cinnamon to the oil is essential. To fully develop the flavors, cook the ingredients for the length of time specified in the recipe.*

1 teaspoon vegetable oil
Pinch of cardamom
Pinch of cinnamon
3/4 cup chopped onion
4 cups finely cut cabbage, well
  packed
1 cup uncooked white rice (we like
  basmati)
2 large cloves garlic, minced
1 teaspoon cumin
1/4 teaspoon turmeric
1 teaspoon garam marsala *

1 can (14 1/2 ounces) vegetable broth
1/4 cup water
1 teaspoon (or less) Lite Salt
1/4 teaspoon pepper
1/2 cup cooked diced red potato
3/4 cup frozen peas and carrots,
  thawed
1 1/2 teaspoons freshly squeezed
  lemon juice
1 cup chopped plum tomatoes

Lemon wedges, for garnish

Heat oil, cardamom, and cinnamon in a large cooking pot. Add onion and sauté over medium heat 10 minutes, or until onion is well cooked and golden in color. Add cabbage, cover, and cook 5 minutes over low heat, stirring often, until cabbage is wilted. Add rice, garlic, cumin, turmeric, and garam marsala and sauté 2 minutes, stirring constantly. Stir in broth, water, Lite Salt, and pepper. Bring to a boil, reduce heat, cover and cook 20 minutes. Mix in potatoes. *If making ahead, refrigerate at this point.* When ready to serve, add peas and carrots and lemon juice. Sprinkle tomatoes on top. Cover and cook 5 minutes on the stovetop or place pilaf in a serving bowl, cover, and heat in the microwave oven on high for 5 minutes or until steaming. Remove from heat and let stand 5 minutes. Serve with lemon wedges.

* A blend of spices that is available in Indian specialty stores.

~ Per Cup ~	
Calories:	143
Sodium:	377 mg
Fiber:	3 gm
Total fat:	1 gm
Saturated fat:	Trace gm
Cholesterol:	0 mg
Cholesterol–saturated fat index:	Trace

Golden Risotto Cakes
(Grilled Rice Cakes)

⤳ Makes 12 cakes and ½ cup sauce.

It is usually a "no-no" to stir rice while it is cooking, but there are different rules for risotto. To make the desired creamy texture, a lot of stirring is necessary. After the rice is cooked, small pattylike cakes are formed and cooked on a grill. The sauce makes a delicious accompaniment, but the cakes are tasty served alone.

Red Pepper Sauce
1 clove garlic
Scant ½ cup roasted and peeled red
    peppers*
1 teaspoon freshly squeezed lemon juice
2 tablespoons nonfat mayonnaise

Risotto Cakes
1 teaspoon olive oil
1¼ cups uncooked medium-grain white rice
    such as pearl *or* Calrose

1 can (14½ ounces) lower-salt
    chicken broth*
¼ teaspoon (or less) Lite Salt
1½ cups water
¾ cup grated light part-skim
    mozzarella cheese
¼ cup grated Parmesan cheese
4 green onions, minced

Fresh basil sprigs, for garnish

To prepare Red Pepper Sauce: Purée garlic, red peppers, lemon juice, and mayonnaise in a food processor or blender until smooth. Place in covered container and chill in refrigerator.

To prepare Risotto Cakes: Combine olive oil and uncooked rice in a 3-quart pan over medium-high heat. Stir until rice is opaque, about 3 minutes. Add broth, Lite Salt, and water; bring to boiling, stirring occasionally. Reduce heat to low and cook with liquid bubbling lightly, uncovered, 25 minutes or until rice is tender and liquid has been absorbed. Stir frequently as the mixture thickens. Remove from heat and stir in cheeses and green onions. Let cool uncovered.

Divide rice mixture into 12 equal portions and shape each portion into a ¾-inch cake. Spray a skillet or grill with nonstick cooking spray and heat to medium-high. Add cakes, but do not let them touch. Cook cakes 10 minutes or until golden brown, turn and cook 10 minutes or until golden brown. (If you cannot cook cakes all at once, place grilled cakes in a single layer in a shallow pan or platter. Cover loosely with foil and place in a 300° oven to keep warm. Spray skillet again with nonstick spray, and cook remaining cakes.) To serve, place cakes onto plates and top each cake with 2 teaspoons of Red Pepper Sauce and garnish with a basil sprig.

* Can be purchased in most supermarkets.

⤳ Per Serving (2 Cakes and 4 Teaspoons Sauce) ⤳	
Calories:	232
Sodium:	553 mg
Fiber:	1 gm
Total fat:	4 gm
Saturated fat:	2 gm
Cholesterol:	11 mg
Cholesterol–saturated fat index:	3

Jollof Rice

— Makes 10 cups.

This is a meatless version of a dish from Ghana in West Africa. It can be hot and spicy or mild, depending on your taste. The name jollof *means a mixture of spices.*

1 tablespoon vegetable oil

2 cloves garlic, minced

2 tablespoons grated fresh
    gingerroot

1 cup chopped onion

1/2 green bell pepper, cut into thin
    strips

1/2 red bell pepper, cut into thin strips

1/2 teaspoon cayenne pepper (double
    if you like fire)

3/4 teaspoon nutmeg

3/4 teaspoon hot curry powder

1 1/2 teaspoons (or less) Lite Salt

1/4 cup unsalted tomato paste

1 can (8 ounces) unsalted tomato
    sauce

2 cups uncooked long-grain white
    rice

4 cups water

Garnish

1 cup frozen peas, cooked

Heat oil in skillet on medium heat. Add garlic, ginger, and onions and cook 10 minutes, stirring frequently, until onion is golden in color. Add bell pepper strips and cook 5 minutes. Add cayenne pepper, nutmeg, curry powder, Lite Salt, and tomato paste. Stir and cook 5 minutes. Add tomato sauce, reduce heat, cover, and cook 15 minutes. Add rice and water. Bring to a boil, stir, reduce heat to low, cover and cook 15 minutes. Remove from heat and let stand 10 minutes. Put Jollof Rice in a serving bowl and sprinkle peas over the top.

~ Per Cup ~	
Calories:	195
Sodium:	172 mg
Fiber:	2 gm
Total fat:	2 gm
Saturated fat:	Trace gm
Cholesterol:	Trace mg
Cholesterol—saturated fat index:	Trace

Rice and Currant Pilaf

*Makes 4 cups.

1 teaspoon cumin seed
1 can (14¹/₂ ounces) lower-salt
   chicken broth*
1 cup uncooked rice
2 tablespoons dried currants

1 tablespoon chopped fresh parsley
1 tablespoon chopped fresh cilantro
1 tablespoon chopped fresh basil
   or 1 teaspoon dried basil

Place cumin seeds in medium saucepan and heat over low heat for about 1 minute. Add chicken broth, rice, and currants. Bring to a boil, reduce heat to low; cover and cook 20 minutes. Remove from heat and let rice stand 5 minutes. Add parsley, cilantro, and basil and stir.

* Swanson Natural Goodness with ¹/₃ less sodium is available.

Per Cup	
Calories:	210
Sodium:	294 mg
Fiber:	1 gm
Total fat:	1 gm
Saturated fat:	Trace gm
Cholesterol:	0 mg
Cholesterol–saturated fat index:	Trace

Rice with Sweet Onions, Red Pepper, and Broccoli

·‑ Makes 5 cups.

We like sweet onions so much that we use them in as many recipes as we can find.

1 tablespoon olive oil
2$^1/_2$ cups chopped Walla Walla *or*
  Vidalia sweet onion
$^1/_2$ teaspoon (or less) Lite Salt
1 teaspoon curry powder

1 can lower-salt chicken broth*
1 cup uncooked rice
1 cup chopped red bell pepper
1$^1/_2$ cups chopped broccoli
$^1/_4$ cup grated Parmesan cheese

Heat oil in a medium saucepan. Sauté onion for 1 to 2 minutes. Add Lite Salt, curry powder, chicken broth, and rice. Bring to a boil, cover, reduce heat, and cook 20 minutes. Remove from heat, add chopped bell pepper and broccoli (do not stir), cover, and set aside for 10 minutes. When ready to serve, stir and then sprinkle with Parmesan cheese.

* Swanson Natural Goodness with $^1/_3$ less sodium is available.

·‑ Per Cup ·‑	
Calories:	247
Sodium:	434 mg
Fiber:	3 gm
Total fat:	5 gm
Saturated fat:	2 gm
Cholesterol:	4 mg
Cholesterol–saturated fat index:	2

Spiced Fruit Pilaf

1 teaspoon vegetable oil

1 1/2 cups uncooked basmati rice

2 cloves garlic, minced

1 tablespoon mustard seeds

2 teaspoons grated fresh gingerroot

1/4 teaspoon hulled cardamom seeds

1 cup orange juice

2 cups lower-salt chicken broth*

1/4 teaspoon (or less) Lite Salt

1/2 cup dried cranberries

1/4 cup golden raisins

1 cinnamon stick

1 tablespoon grated orange peel

1 bay leaf

1 medium-sized carrot, cut into
   matchstick-sized strips

1/8 cup slivered almonds

Heat oil in a 3-quart pan. Add rice, garlic, mustard seeds, ginger, and cardamom seeds; stir until rice is golden brown, about 10 minutes. Add orange juice, broth, Lite Salt, cranberries, raisins, the cinnamon stick, orange peel, bay leaf, and carrot. Bring to a boil, reduce heat to low, cover, and simmer 20 minutes. Remove from heat and let stand 10 minutes. Remove bay leaf and cinnamon stick. Place in serving bowl and garnish with slivered almonds.

* Swanson Natural Goodness with 1/3 less sodium is available.

·– Per Cup ·–	
Calories:	227
Sodium:	250 mg
Fiber:	2 gm
Total fat:	2 gm
Saturated fat:	Trace gm
Cholesterol:	0 mg
Cholesterol–saturated fat index:	Trace

Thai Sandwiches

•~ Makes 12 sandwiches.

Looking for a new lunch idea? Try this flavorful rice-peanut filling in flour tortillas or in pocket bread. Some of us prefer to warm the sandwiches in a microwave oven, but they are good either warm or cold.

1 tablespoon sesame oil
1 clove garlic, minced
2 tablespoons honey
2 tablespoons lower-sodium soy sauce*
1/2 teaspoon (or less) Lite Salt
4 cups cooked brown rice
2 tablespoons chopped fresh cilantro
1/4 cup finely cut napa *or* Chinese cabbage

1/4 cup grated carrot
1/2 cup chopped green onions
2 tablespoons coarsely chopped unsalted peanuts
2 tablespoons freshly squeezed lemon juice

12 whole wheat tortillas (8-inch diameter)
or 12 small pocket breads

Heat sesame oil in a saucepan. Stir in garlic and cook slightly. Add honey, soy sauce, and Lite Salt. Stir to combine and set aside. When cool, add brown rice and mix well. Cover and refrigerate. When ready to make the sandwiches, add cilantro, cabbage, carrots, green onions, peanuts, and lemon juice.

To Prepare Thai Sandwiches: Cover tortillas and warm in the microwave oven or conventional oven to make them pliable. Spoon about 1/2 cup filling into center of each tortilla and fold all sides inward to make a pocket. The filling can also be spooned into pocket bread. Add more chopped cilantro, if desired.

* Kikkoman Lite Soy Sauce is available.

•~ Per Sandwich (1 Tortilla and 1/2 Cup Filling) ~•	
Calories:	178
Sodium:	298 mg
Fiber:	4 gm
Total fat:	3 gm
Saturated fat:	1 gm
Cholesterol:	0 mg
Cholesterol—saturated fat index:	1

Tropical Rice

We are always looking for new ways to prepare rice. This dish goes with fish, chicken, and curries of any kind.

1 teaspoon vegetable oil
1 tablespoon grated fresh gingerroot
1 teaspoon minced garlic
½ teaspoon cardamom
½ teaspoon (or less) Lite Salt
1 can (11½ ounces) papaya *or* mango
   nectar
   or 1 can (11½ ounces) papaya *or*
   mango juice

1½ cups water
1½ cups uncooked long-grain white
   rice such as basmati *or* jasmine
1 cup diced ripe papaya *or* ripe
   mango

In a heavy 2- or 3-quart saucepan, heat oil over medium heat. Add ginger and garlic; cook, stirring, for 1 minute (lift pan from heat if garlic and ginger start to brown). Stir in cardamom and Lite Salt. Add juice and water. Bring to a boil and add rice. Return to a boil, stir, reduce heat to low, cover, and cook 20 minutes. Remove from heat and let stand 10 minutes. Add diced papaya or mango, fluff the rice, and serve warm.

⤳ Per Cup ⤳	
Calories:	216
Sodium:	78 mg
Fiber:	2 gm
Total fat:	1 gm
Saturated fat:	Trace gm
Cholesterol:	0 mg
Cholesterol–saturated fat index:	Trace

Wild Mushroom Risotto

1 tablespoon olive oil
1/2 cup finely chopped onion
1 can (14 1/2 ounces) lower-salt
   chicken broth*
3 cups water
3 cups assorted mushrooms (crimini,
   shitake, hedgehog, porcini, oyster,
   button, etc.)

1 1/2 cups uncooked Arborio, Calrose,
   pearl, *or* other medium-grain rice
1/2 cup dry white wine
1/2 teaspoon (or less) Lite Salt
1/4 cup grated Parmesan cheese
1/8 teaspoon freshly ground pepper
2 tablespoons chopped fresh parsley
   (we like Italian flat-leaf parsley)

Heat oil in a skillet, add onion, and sauté until golden brown in color. In a saucepan, combine broth and water, heat to boiling, reduce heat to low and save for later use. Add mushrooms to the skillet and sauté until tender, about 5 minutes. Add rice and stir to coat grains. Add wine, 1/2 cup of the hot broth mixture and Lite Salt. Cook, stirring constantly, until all liquid has been absorbed. Continue to add broth mixture in 1/2-cup amounts and cook, stirring constantly, until liquid is absorbed and rice mixture is creamy and al denté (still firm), about 20 to 25 minutes. Remove from heat, add Parmesan cheese, pepper, and parsley and mix well. Serve immediately.

* Swanson Natural Goodness with 1/3 less sodium is available.

— Per Serving —	
Calories:	305
Sodium:	412 mg
Fiber:	2 gm
Total fat:	5 gm
Saturated fat:	1 gm
Cholesterol:	3 mg
Cholesterol–saturated fat index:	2

Apple and Dried Fruit Bread Dressing

↝ Makes 11 cups.

This is the dressing served in the Connors' home every Thanksgiving. Bill loves it and would like to have it made more often. It makes a great stuffing for squash.

1 tablespoon vegetable oil
1¹/₂ cups finely chopped celery
³/₄ cup finely chopped onion
9 cups bread cubes (¹/₂ whole wheat
    bread and ¹/₂ cubed herbed
    stuffing mix works well)
2 teaspoons dried sage
1 teaspoon chopped fresh lemon
    thyme leaves
    or ¹/₂ teaspoon dried thyme leaves
1 teaspoon chopped fresh marjoram
    leaves
    or ¹/₂ teaspoon dried marjoram
    leaves

1 apple, chopped
2 tablespoons chopped pecans
    or filberts
2 dried figs, chopped
2 tablespoons currants *or*
    golden raisins
2 tablespoons dried cranberries
3 tablespoons chopped fresh parsley
1 can (14¹/₂ ounces) lower-salt
    chicken broth* *or* vegetable broth

If not cooking in the microwave oven, preheat conventional oven to 350°. Heat oil in a skillet. Add celery and onion; cook until transparent. Set aside. In a large bowl, combine bread cubes, sage, thyme, marjoram, apple, nuts, figs, currants or raisins, cranberries, and parsley. Add celery and onion and stir to combine. Add broth and mix well. Spray a shallow 3-quart baking dish with nonstick cooking spray. Put dressing in the baking dish. Cover and refrigerate until ready to cook. Cover with foil and bake in the oven 30 to 45 minutes, or cover with plastic wrap or wax paper and heat in the microwave oven 5 to 10 minutes. Garnish with sprigs of fresh herbs, if desired.

* Swanson Natural Goodness with ¹/₃ less sodium is available.

↝ Per Cup ↝	
Calories:	195
Sodium:	484 mg
Fiber:	4 gm
Total fat:	4 gm
Saturated fat:	1 gm
Cholesterol:	Trace mg
Cholesterol–saturated fat index:	1

Baked Barley Pilaf

1 tablespoon oil
2 cloves garlic, minced
1 cup chopped onion
$^1/_2$ cup chopped green bell pepper
$^1/_2$ cup chopped red bell pepper
$^1/_2$ cup chopped celery
$^1/_2$ cup chopped carrots
$^3/_4$ teaspoon dried thyme leaves
$^3/_4$ teaspoon dried oregano leaves

$1^1/_2$ teaspoons (or less) Lite Salt
$^1/_2$ teaspoon pepper
$1^1/_2$ cups uncooked barley
1 can (14$^1/_2$ ounces) lower-salt
   chicken broth*
$2^1/_2$ cups water

$^1/_4$ cup chopped fresh parsley

Preheat oven to 350°. In a nonstick skillet, heat oil and sauté garlic for a few seconds. Add onion, bell peppers, celery, carrots, thyme, oregano, Lite Salt, and pepper. Continue cooking for about 5 minutes or until liquid has evaporated. Combine with uncooked barley, chicken broth, and water and mix well. Put in 9-by-13-inch baking dish that has been sprayed with nonstick cooking spray and cover tightly. Bake 1$^1/_4$ hours or until barley is tender and liquid is absorbed. Garnish with parsley and serve warm.

* Swanson Natural Goodness with $^1/_3$ less sodium is available.

Per Cup	
Calories:	170
Sodium:	343 mg
Fiber:	7 gm
Total fat:	2 gm
Saturated fat:	Trace gm
Cholesterol:	Trace mg
Cholesterol—saturated fat index:	Trace

Baked Corn Casserole

Corn bread mix makes this dish very easy to make, but be sure to choose a mix that contains no beef fat or lard.

3/4 cup chopped green bell pepper

1/3 cup chopped onion

1 can (17 ounces) unsalted
   whole-kernel corn, including liquid

1 can (8 ounces)
   or 1/2 can (17 ounces) cream-style
   corn

1 1/2 cups Krusteaz Honey Corn
   Bread Mix (1/2 of 15-ounce box)

3/4 cup egg substitute

2 tablespoons grated Parmesan
   cheese

Heat oven to 350°. Cook peppers and onion in nonstick skillet until crisp-tender, stirring constantly. In a separate bowl, combine all corn, including liquid, corn bread mix, and egg substitute. Add sautéed vegetables and mix lightly. Spray an 8- or 10-inch square baking dish with nonstick cooking spray. Pour mixture in dish and sprinkle top with cheese. Bake 45 to 60 minutes or until a wooden pick or knife inserted in the center comes out clean.

~ Per Serving ~	
Calories:	272
Sodium:	500 mg
Fiber:	6 gm
Total fat:	4 gm
Saturated fat:	2 gm
Cholesterol:	2 mg
Cholesterol–saturated fat index:	2

Holiday Corn Bread Dressing

⸗ Makes 12 cups.

A festive side dish for roasted turkey or chicken.

Corn Bread
1½ cups cornmeal
1½ cups white flour
1½ tablespoons baking powder
¾ teaspoon (or less) Lite Salt
1½ cups skim milk
⅓ cup egg substitute
3 tablespoons vegetable oil

Dressing
Corn Bread (see above)
1½ teaspoons dried sage
½ teaspoon pepper

1 teaspoon (or less) Lite Salt
1 can (14½ ounces) lower-salt
  chicken broth*
3 cups water
1 cup chopped celery
1 cup chopped onion
¾ cup chopped green bell pepper
¾ cup chopped red bell pepper
1 cup frozen corn, thawed
½ cup egg substitute

Garnish
¼ cup chopped green onions

To prepare Corn Bread: Preheat oven to 400°. In large bowl, combine cornmeal, flour, baking powder, and Lite Salt and stir well. In small bowl, combine milk, egg substitute, and oil; add to flour mixture, stirring just until dry ingredients are moistened. Pour batter into a 9-by-13-inch baking pan coated with nonstick cooking spray. Bake 15 to 20 minutes, or until wooden pick inserted in the center comes out clean. Let cool completely on wire rack.

To prepare Dressing: Preheat oven to 400°. In a large bowl, crumble corn bread into small pieces; add sage, pepper, and Lite Salt. Set aside. In a saucepan, bring broth and water to a boil. Add celery, onion, and bell peppers. Reduce heat and simmer, uncovered, 5 minutes. Add broth mixture to corn bread mixture and stir just until moistened. Add corn and egg substitute; stir well. Spoon dressing mixture into a 9-by-13-inch baking dish that has been coated with nonstick cooking spray.

Bake, uncovered, 50 to 60 minutes. Remove from oven. Cover loosely with a towel and let stand 10 to 15 minutes. Garnish with green onions and serve.

* Swanson Natural Goodness with ⅓ less sodium is available.

⸗ Per Cup ⸗	
Calories:	194
Sodium:	472 mg
Fiber:	3 gm
Total fat:	4 gm
Saturated fat:	Trace gm
Cholesterol:	1 mg
Cholesterol–saturated fat index:	Trace

Polenta with Late Summer Garden Vegetables

This tasty dish is hard to describe, so we'll let you find out for yourselves. . . .

Polenta
3 cups water
1/2 teaspoon (or less) Lite Salt
1 cup polenta (coarse cornmeal)

Vegetable Mixture
2 teaspoons olive oil, divided
1 1/2 cups fresh *or* frozen corn
1/2 teaspoon (or less) Lite Salt
1 1/2 cups chopped tomatoes

1/8 teaspoon pepper
3/4 cup chopped fresh basil leaves
1 jalapeño pepper, seeded and thinly
   sliced

1 cup Italian Marinara Sauce
   (page 172)

1/4 cup grated Parmesan cheese

To prepare Polenta: Bring water to a boil; add Lite Salt. Slowly stir in polenta. Reduce heat and simmer about 10 minutes, stirring with long-handled spoon (mixture can bubble up and cause a burn). Coat a 7-by-11-inch baking dish with nonstick cooking spray. Pour polenta into dish and cool. Cut mixture in half lengthwise and then cut into triangles.

To prepare Vegetable Mixture: Heat 1 teaspoon olive oil in large skillet; add corn and cook until tender, 5 to 10 minutes. Add Lite Salt. In a separate bowl, combine tomatoes, 1 teaspoon olive oil, and pepper. Cool the corn and mix with tomatoes, 1/2 cup basil, and jalapeño peppers.

To assemble: Preheat oven to 375°. Pour the Italian Marinara Sauce into a 9-by-13-inch baking dish. Arrange polenta triangles upright and overlapping in rows across the width of the dish. Spoon vegetable mixture among the polenta triangles. Sprinkle with Parmesan cheese. Cover and bake 25 minutes. Uncover and bake 10 minutes or until bubbly. Sprinkle remaining 1/4 cup basil over the top and serve.

~ Per Serving ~	
Calories:	193
Sodium:	322 mg
Fiber:	4 gm
Total fat:	4 gm
Saturated fat:	1 gm
Cholesterol:	3 mg
Cholesterol–saturated fat index:	1

Polenta with Tomato Sauce and GardenSausage

⁀ Makes 6 servings.

This recipe can be simplified by purchasing already prepared polenta.

Polenta
3 cups water
1/2 teaspoon (or less) Lite Salt
1 cup polenta (coarse cornmeal)

Tomato Sauce
1 cup onion, chopped
1 teaspoon olive oil
2 medium cloves garlic, minced
1 tablespoon dried basil leaves
2 teaspoons dried oregano leaves

1/4 teaspoon red pepper flakes
8 ounces GardenSausage, thawed
   and crumbled*
2 cans (14 1/2 ounces each) unsalted
   diced tomatoes
1/2 teaspoon sugar
1/2 teaspoon (or less) Lite Salt
1/4 teaspoon pepper

1/4 cup grated Parmesan cheese

To prepare Polenta: Bring water to a boil; add Lite Salt. Slowly stir in polenta. Reduce heat and simmer about 10 minutes, stirring with long-handled spoon (mixture can bubble up and cause a burn). Coat a 7-by-11-inch baking dish with nonstick cooking spray. Pour polenta into dish and cool. Cut mixture in 24 pieces.

To prepare Tomato Sauce: In a large saucepan, sauté onion in olive oil until tender, about 5 minutes. Add garlic, basil, oregano, and red pepper flakes. Sauté 2 minutes. Add crumbled GardenSausage, tomatoes, sugar, Lite Salt, and pepper. Bring to a boil, lower heat, and simmer, uncovered, for 30 minutes, stirring occasionally.

⁀ Per Serving ⁀	
Calories:	284
Sodium:	487 mg
Fiber:	9 gm
Total fat:	4 gm
Saturated fat:	2 gm
Cholesterol:	3 mg
Cholesterol–saturated fat index:	2

To assemble: Preheat oven to 375°. Put polenta pieces in a 9-by-13-inch baking dish that has been sprayed with nonstick cooking spray. Cover with Tomato Sauce. Sprinkle top with Parmesan cheese. Bake in oven 20 to 30 minutes or until bubbly.

* A frozen vegetable sausage by Wholesome and Hearty Foods.

Peppers Stuffed with Red Lentils and Drizzled with "Tire"

◦ Makes 4 servings.

This dish looks spectacular. We always double the lentil mixture and freeze half of it to use for a quick meal on another day.

1 teaspoon olive oil

³/₄ cup chopped onion

1 large clove garlic, minced

¹/₂ teaspoon cumin

1 cup vegetable broth

³/₄ cup uncooked red lentils, rinsed

¹/₄ cup uncooked bulgur

1¹/₂ teaspoons unsalted tomato paste

¹/₂ teaspoon (or less) Lite Salt

¹/₈ teaspoon cayenne pepper

¹/₂ teaspoon paprika

1 bay leaf

1¹/₂ teaspoons freshly squeezed
    lemon juice

¹/₂ cup finely chopped tomato

¹/₂ cup chopped fresh spinach

2 tablespoons chopped fresh cilantro

Spicy Pepper Oil

1 teaspoon olive oil

¹/₂ teaspoon paprika

¹/₂ teaspoon cayenne pepper

4 medium bell peppers (green, red,
    or yellow *or* a mixture of colors)

Fresh parsley, for garnish

Heat oil in a 3-quart pan. Add onions and cook several minutes, stirring, until softened. Add garlic and cumin and cook 1 minute. Add vegetable broth, lentils, bulgur, tomato paste, Lite Salt, ¹/₈ teaspoon cayenne pepper, ¹/₂ teaspoon paprika, and bay leaf. Bring to a boil, reduce heat, cover, and cook, stirring occasionally, 25 minutes. *Red lentils turn yellow when cooked and have the mushy texture needed for this recipe.* Discard bay leaf. Stir in lemon juice, tomato, spinach, and cilantro. Set aside. In a small skillet, heat 1 teaspoon olive oil and add ¹/₂ teaspoon paprika and ¹/₂ teaspoon cayenne pepper. Set aside. *This is the* Spicy Pepper Oil *to use later.*

Cut bell peppers in half lengthwise. Remove stems, seeds, and white membrane. Place pepper halves in a shallow baking dish, cover, and cook in the microwave oven on high for 4 minutes. Drain well. Return peppers to shallow baking dish and divide lentil mixture among the pepper halves.

Cover and cook in the microwave oven until heated through, 5 to 10 minutes, depending on whether peppers have been refrigerated or not. When serving, drizzle a few drops of the Spicy Pepper Oil over each pepper half. Garnish with parsley.

◦ Per Serving ◦	
Calories:	239
Sodium:	408 mg
Fiber:	11 gm
Total fat:	3 gm
Saturated fat:	Trace gm
Cholesterol:	0 mg
Cholesterol–saturated fat index:	Trace

Syrian Lentils with Tomatoes

⌐ Makes 5 cups.

Serve as a main entrée or as a side dish.

2 quarts water	2 cups chopped tomatoes
1 cup uncooked lentils	1 teaspoon cumin
1 tablespoon vegetable oil	$3/4$ teaspoon turmeric
2 cups finely chopped onion	1 teaspoon (or less) Lite Salt
1 cup finely chopped green bell	$1/8$ teaspoon cayenne pepper
pepper	$1/4$ cup chopped fresh cilantro
$1/2$ cup chopped pimiento, drained	

Bring water to a boil. Add lentils and simmer 20 minutes, or until lentils are tender. Drain and set aside. Heat oil in skillet and sauté onion and bell pepper until onions are wilted. Stir in pimiento, tomatoes, and cooked lentils. Cook, uncovered, over low heat for 30 minutes, stirring occasionally. Add cumin, turmeric, Lite Salt, and cayenne pepper. Garnish with cilantro.

⌐ Per Cup ⌐	
Calories:	205
Sodium:	210 mg
Fiber:	8 gm
Total fat:	4 gm
Saturated fat:	Trace gm
Cholesterol:	0 mg
Cholesterol–saturated fat index:	Trace

Beans and Tomatoes Provençale

·— Makes 4 servings (1¹/₄ cups each).

This is the meatless version of Prawns and Beans Tuscan Style *(page 259).*

1 teaspoon olive oil

2 cloves garlic, minced

3 cans (15¹/₂ ounces each) large
white beans, drained and rinsed

1 can (16 ounces) unsalted chopped
tomatoes, undrained

¹/₄ cup chopped fresh basil
or 1 tablespoon dried basil leaves

2 tablespoons chopped fresh parsley
or 1¹/₂ teaspoons dried parsley

¹/₄ teaspoon pepper

Heat olive oil in large skillet, add garlic, and sauté until golden. Add beans, undrained tomatoes, basil, parsley, and pepper. Cook for several minutes until heated through. Serve warm.

·— Per Serving ·—	
Calories:	357
Sodium:	573 mg
Fiber:	14 gm
Total fat:	2 gm
Saturated fat:	Trace gm
Cholesterol:	0 mg
Cholesterol–saturated fat index:	Trace

Best Ever Black Beans

Beans are wonderfully versatile, as they can be cooked in advance, covered, and refrigerated to be reheated when ready to eat. We like to serve these black beans as a side dish with Halibut Olé *(page 249) and* Pineapple Salsa *(page 42) or use to fill flour tortillas for a great burrito. Canned beans can be used easily, but dried beans make this dish very economical.*

6 cups canned black beans, drained
   and rinsed*
   or 1 pound (2¹/₄ cups) dried black
   beans
1 tablespoon olive oil
1 cup finely chopped onion
1¹/₂ cups chopped green bell pepper
1¹/₂ cups chopped red bell pepper
4 cloves garlic, minced
1 tablespoon cumin

1 teaspoon dried basil leaves
1 can (8 ounces) unsalted
   tomato sauce
¹/₄ cup red wine vinegar
1 teaspoon (or less) Lite Salt
¹/₂ teaspoon pepper
¹/₄ to ¹/₂ teaspoon Tabasco sauce

¹/₃ cup chopped green onions *or*
   chopped fresh cilantro, for garnish

If using canned beans: Drain and rinse beans and continue with recipe.

If using dried beans: Soak beans in a heavy saucepan in cold water for 8 to 24 hours. Drain and cover with cold water. Bring to a boil, reduce heat to low, cover, and simmer for 1 to 2 hours. Add water to keep level above beans. When beans are soft, drain.

   Heat oil in a heavy skillet. Add onions, bell peppers, garlic, and cumin. Cook and stir over medium heat until vegetables are soft. Add basil and tomato sauce and cook for 2 minutes. Add drained beans, vinegar, Lite Salt, pepper, and Tabasco sauce and simmer for 15 minutes or until thickened. Ladle beans into serving bowl and top with green onions or cilantro.

* S&W has a 50% Less Salt product available.

·⁓ Per Serving ⁓·	
Calories:	176
Sodium:	335 mg
Fiber:	8 gm
Total fat:	2 gm
Saturated fat:	Trace gm
Cholesterol:	0 mg
Cholesterol–saturated fat index:	Trace

Black Bean Enchiladas

Molly has given us several recipes that many of us like very much. Try this no-fuss dish that calls for canned beans, tomatoes, and salsa as well as instant rice. Joyce first ate it when Molly preassembled the enchiladas at home to feed hungry hikers on a weekend outing. After a strenuous day, all she had to do was heat them in the microwave oven and serve them with toppings, warm tortillas, and fruit.

1 teaspoon vegetable oil

2 cloves garlic, minced

1 1/2 cups cooked black beans
  or 1 can (15 ounces) black beans,
  drained and rinsed*

1 can (16 ounces) unsalted tomatoes,
  chopped

1 cup uncooked instant rice

1 cup S&W Salsa with Cilantro *or*
  picante sauce (mild, medium *or*
  hot—it's your choice)

1/3 cup water

1 teaspoon cumin

1/2 teaspoon dried oregano leaves

16 flour tortillas (8-inch diameter)

3/4 cup finely chopped red *or* green
  bell pepper

1/2 cup chopped green onions

3/4 cup grated light part-skim
  mozzarella cheese

2 tablespoons chopped fresh cilantro

Optional toppings: Shredded lettuce,
  diced tomatoes, nonfat yogurt,
  additional salsa

Heat oil in skillet and cook garlic until golden. Stir in beans, tomatoes, uncooked rice, 1/2 cup salsa, water, cumin, and oregano. Cover and simmer 1 minute. Remove from heat and let stand 5 minutes. Warm tortillas in microwave oven or wrap in foil and place in warm oven. Add bell pepper, green onions, and 1/4 cup of cheese to the bean mixture.

Spoon about 1/4 cup bean mixture down the center of each tortilla and roll up. Place seam-side-down in a 9-by-13-inch baking dish. Spoon remaining salsa over tortillas. *Enchiladas can be covered and refrigerated for up to 24 hours at this point, if desired.*

Thirty minutes before serving, preheat oven to 350° and bring enchiladas to room temperature. Bake, covered, 20 minutes or until bubbling hot, or cover with plastic wrap and heat 5 to 10 minutes in the microwave oven on high. After baking, sprinkle with remaining cheese and cilantro. Optional toppings can be placed in small dishes and served with the enchiladas.

* S&W has a 50% Less Salt product available.

Per Serving	
Calories:	436
Sodium:	609 mg
Fiber:	7 gm
Total fat:	8 gm
Saturated fat:	2 gm
Cholesterol:	3 mg
Cholesterol–saturated fat index:	2

Black Bean Pizza

Bean Sauce

1 can (15 ounces) black beans,
  drained and rinsed*
1 teaspoon olive oil
2 tablespoons chopped fresh cilantro
1 teaspoon cumin
1 teaspoon Tabasco sauce
2 cloves garlic, minced

1 round loaf (15 to 16 ounces)
  unbaked, whole wheat focaccia
  bread, sliced in half horizontally

Topping

1 cup grated light part-skim
  mozzarella cheese
1/2 cup sliced mushrooms
1/2 cup finely sliced red or green
  bell pepper
1/4 cup chopped green onions

Condiments

Taco sauce or fresh salsa, as desired
Nonfat sour cream or nonfat plain
  yogurt, as desired

Preheat oven to 425°. Combine black beans, oil, cilantro, cumin, Tabasco sauce, and garlic and blend in a food processor or mash with a fork until smooth. Place bread on baking sheet with cut side-up and spread bean sauce on each piece. Top with grated cheese, mushrooms, bell peppers, and onions. Bake 7 to 12 minutes. Serve warm with condiments, as desired.

* S&W has a 50% Less Salt product available.

⁓ Per Serving ⁓	
Calories:	351
Sodium:	694 mg
Fiber:	6 gm
Total fat:	10 gm
Saturated fat:	2 gm
Cholesterol:	6 mg
Cholesterol–saturated fat index:	3

Blackeye Peas and Plantains (Red Red)

The name Red Red *comes from the red palm oil used for cooking in western Africa. This meal consists of three parts—couscous, spicy blackeye peas, and plantains. In Africa, the plantains are used as scoops to eat the beans and couscous.*

Blackeye Peas

1 cup dried blackeye peas
   or 2 cans (16 ounces each)
   blackeye peas, drained and rinsed
$^1/_2$ onion, chopped
1 teaspoon (or less) Lite Salt (omit if
   using canned beans)

1 teaspoon vegetable oil
$^1/_2$ onion, chopped
$^1/_2$ teaspoon black pepper
$^1/_4$ teaspoon cayenne pepper
1 teaspoon grated fresh gingerroot
$^1/_4$ teaspoon nutmeg
$^1/_4$ teaspoon paprika

$^1/_2$ teaspoon curry powder
1 cup chopped fresh tomatoes

Couscous

$2^1/_4$ cups water
$^1/_2$ teaspoon (or less) Lite Salt
$1^1/_2$ cups couscous

Fried Plantains

$^1/_2$ teaspoon grated fresh gingerroot
$^1/_4$ teaspoon pepper
$^1/_4$ teaspoon (or less) Lite Salt
2 large ripe plantains*
2 teaspoons vegetable oil

To prepare Blackeye Peas: To use dried blackeye peas, sort and wash dried blackeye peas and cover with a generous amount of hot water. Soak peas at least 4 hours. Drain, put in large cooking pot, and cover peas with water plus 1 inch more. Add $^1/_2$ chopped onion and 1 teaspoon Lite Salt. Bring to a boil, reduce heat, cover, and simmer 30 minutes. Remove cover and cook until peas are very soft and all the water is absorbed, about 30 minutes.

To use canned blackeye peas, drain blackeye peas and rinse with cold water. Place in large cooking pot and add 1 cup water and $^1/_2$ chopped onion. Bring to a boil, reduce heat, and simmer until peas are very soft, about 15 minutes.

Begin here after dried or canned blackeye peas have been cooked: When peas are close to being done, heat 1 teaspoon oil in skillet on medium heat and sauté ½ chopped onion until golden brown, 10 to 15 minutes. Add black pepper, cayenne pepper, ginger, nutmeg, paprika, curry powder, and tomatoes. Stir until heated through. Add tomato mixture to the blackeye peas, cover, and simmer on low heat 30 minutes or until peas are thick and mushy with a few peas left whole. They are now ready to serve with the Fried Plantains.

To prepare Couscous: In a saucepan, bring 2¼ cups water to a boil. Stir in Lite Salt and couscous; cover. Remove from heat and let stand, covered, until plantains are ready. Fluff lightly with a fork before serving.

To prepare Fried Plantains: Start preparing at the same time you add the tomatoes to the peas. Mix ginger, pepper, and Lite Salt in shallow dish. Peel plantains and slice each into diagonal pieces ½ inch thick. Coat each piece with the ginger-pepper-salt mixture. Heat oil in nonstick skillet. Sauté plantain slices until deep brown. Drain on paper towels. Serve immediately.

* Let plantains ripen for 3 days or until they resemble a firm banana.

·~ Per Serving (Including Couscous, Peas, and Plantains) ~·	
Calories:	502
Sodium:	362 mg
Fiber:	14 gm
Total fat:	4 gm
Saturated fat:	Trace gm
Cholesterol:	0 mg
Cholesterol–saturated fat index:	Trace

Chickpea Masala

This east Indian dish works well as either a side or a main dish. You can adjust the spices to suit your taste. Chickpeas are also called garbanzo beans.

1 teaspoon vegetable oil
1$\frac{1}{2}$ cups chopped onion
3 cloves garlic, minced
2 teaspoons grated fresh gingerroot
2 teaspoons water
1$\frac{1}{2}$ cups chopped tomato
$\frac{1}{4}$ to $\frac{1}{2}$ teaspoon crushed red
    pepper flakes

$\frac{3}{4}$ teaspoon (or less) Lite Salt
$\frac{1}{4}$ to $\frac{1}{2}$ teaspoon pepper
1 tablespoon coriander
$\frac{1}{2}$ to 1$\frac{1}{2}$ teaspoons garam masala*
2 cans (15 ounces each) garbanzo
    beans, drained and rinsed†

2 tablespoons chopped fresh cilantro

Heat oil in a large nonstick skillet; sauté onion, garlic, and ginger until onion is lightly browned (about 5 minutes). Add water, tomato, pepper flakes, Lite Salt, pepper, coriander, and garam masala. Cover and cook, stirring often, about 3 minutes. Add beans to sauce. Heat, adding water if mixture becomes too dry. Serve with basmati rice, if desired, and garnish with cilantro.

* A blend of spices that is available in Indian specialty stores.
† S&W has a 50% Less Salt product available.

~ Per Cup ~	
Calories:	296
Sodium:	545 mg
Fiber:	10 gm
Total fat:	6 gm
Saturated fat:	1 gm
Cholesterol:	0 mg
Cholesterol–saturated fat index:	1

Kung Pao Vegetarian Style

Makes 4 servings.

Kung Pao Chicken has been a favorite Chinese dish for years. This version has a new twist—it's vegetarian and low-fat.

Kung Pao Vegetarian
Cooking Sauce

2 tablespoons cornstarch

2 tablespoons lower-sodium
soy sauce *

1 tablespoon white wine vinegar

1 tablespoon dry sherry

1½ cups water

2 tablespoons sugar

1½ tablespoons dry sherry

1 tablespoon cornstarch

½ teaspoon (or less) Lite Salt

⅛ teaspoon white pepper

1½ cups (approximately 6 ounces)
tempeh, cubed†
or extra-firm low-fat tofu
(10½ ounces), cubed

2 teaspoons sesame oil

4 to 6 small dried hot red chiles,
sliced in half lengthwise

3 tablespoons unsalted peanuts,
dry roasted

1 teaspoon minced garlic

1 teaspoon grated fresh gingerroot

6 green onions (including tops), cut
into 1½-inch lengths

To prepare Cooking Sauce: Dissolve cornstarch in soy sauce and add vinegar, sherry, water, and sugar. Set aside.

In a separate bowl, stir together sherry, cornstarch, Lite Salt, and white pepper. Add cubed tempeh or tofu and stir to coat. When ready to cook, place a wok over medium heat and, when hot, add 1 teaspoon sesame oil. When oil is hot, add chiles and peanuts. Stir until chiles just begin to char; remove chiles and peanuts from the wok and set aside. Pour remaining 1 teaspoon sesame oil into wok and increase heat to high. When oil is hot, add garlic and ginger and stir. Add tempeh or tofu and stir-fry until heated through, about 2 minutes. Add peanuts, chiles, and green onions. Add Cooking Sauce and continue stirring until sauce boils and thickens. Serve with steamed rice.

* Kikkoman Lite Soy Sauce is available.
† Tempeh is fermented whole soybeans and is available in specialty food stores.

Per Serving with Tempeh	
Calories:	264
Sodium:	435 mg
Fiber:	8 gm
Total fat:	10 gm
Saturated fat:	1 gm
Cholesterol:	0 mg
Cholesterol–saturated fat index:	1

Per Serving with Low-Fat Tofu	
Calories:	171
Sodium:	502 mg
Fiber:	4 gm
Total fat:	6 gm
Saturated fat:	1 gm
Cholesterol:	0 mg
Cholesterol–saturated fat index:	1

"Pile-Ons"
(Our Favorite Tostada)

This recipe can be expanded to accommodate any size group. Let everyone create masterpieces and "pile on" low-fat favorites. Here is one way to do it.

2 small corn tortillas (6¹/₂-inch diameter)

²/₃ cup vegetarian refried beans

¹/₄ cup chopped tomatoes

2 tablespoons chopped green onions

¹/₂ cup chopped lettuce

¹/₄ cup (1 ounce) grated fat-free cheese

¹/₄ cup nonfat plain yogurt

Taco sauce, as desired

Preheat oven to 350°. Bake tortillas 10 to 15 minutes or until crisp but not overbrowned. (Turn tortillas over after 5 minutes.) Warm refried beans.

To assemble, spread ¹/₃ cup refried beans onto each tortilla. Sprinkle with tomatoes, onions, and lettuce. Top with cheese and yogurt. Add taco sauce, if desired. This tostada may be a bit messy to eat, but it makes for a great, casual meal.

·— Per Tostada ·—	
Calories:	192
Sodium:	644 mg
Fiber:	6 gm
Total fat:	2 gm
Saturated fat:	1 gm
Cholesterol:	1 mg
Cholesterol–saturated fat index:	1

Black Beans with Shrimp and Noodles
Breaded Honey Dijon Salmon
Chilean Sea Bass with Ginger Sesame Sauce
Curried Snapper
Dungeness Crab Cakes with Red Pepper Sauce
Fish and Vegetable Kabobs Asian Style
Fish in Saffron Broth with Garlic Mayonnaise
Fish Nuggets with Tartar Sauce
Fish Poached in Court Bouillon
Fran's Stir-Fry
Fresh Fish with Mediterranean Herbs
Halibut in Garlic Tomato Sauce
Halibut Olé
Lemon Garlic Halibut
Mrs. Plancich's Barbecued Salmon
Northwestern Salmon Cakes
Oven-Poached Cod with Red Peppers, Onion, and Ginger
Paella
Pan-Seared Fish Steaks
Party Shrimp Casserole
Polynesian "Fried Rice" with Shrimp
Prawns and Beans Tuscan Style (The Longer Version)
Prawns and Beans Tuscan Style (The Quick and Easy Way)
Red Snapper Primavera
Scallops à la Mistral
Seafood Pasta with Spinach and Lemon
Sesame Shrimp with Couscous
Shrimp Creole
Stir-Fried Shrimp and Scallops

Dishes with seafood

Black Beans with Shrimp and Noodles

·– Makes 4 servings (2¼ cups each).

This seems like a soup when it is being prepared, but it is really a juicy noodle dish.

1 tablespoon freshly squeezed
   lemon juice
½ teaspoon chili powder
¼ teaspoon cumin
⅛ teaspoon pepper
½ pound shelled fresh *or* frozen
   shrimp (rock shrimp make it easy,
   as they come shelled)
4 cups water
2 packages (3 ounces each) low-fat
   ramen noodle soup (do not use
   the seasoning packets)

1 can (14½ ounces) S&W Salsa with
   Cilantro
1 can (15 ounces) black beans, rinsed
   and drained*
1 package (10 ounces) frozen
   whole-kernel corn
¼ cup chopped fresh cilantro
½ cup thinly sliced green onions

In a medium mixing bowl, combine lemon juice, chili powder, cumin, and pepper; add shrimp. Toss to coat. Let shrimp sit for 20 minutes at room temperature to pick up some of the spicy flavors; stir occasionally. Meanwhile, in a large soup pot, bring water to a boil. Break up ramen noodles and stir into boiling water. Return to a boil and cook 1 minute. Add shrimp and cook 2 minutes or until shrimp turn pink. Stir in salsa, beans, corn, cilantro, and green onions. Heat through. Serve in bowls.

* S&W has a 50% Less Salt product available.

·– Per Serving ·–	
Calories:	404
Sodium:	604 mg
Fiber:	14 gm
Total fat:	2 gm
Saturated fat:	1 gm
Cholesterol:	81 mg
Cholesterol–saturated fat index:	5

Breaded Honey Dijon Salmon ·~ *Makes 4 servings.*

Fish truly has become our quick meal. The topping adds a subtle flavor that does not overwhelm the delicate salmon flavor.

4 teaspoons honey

2 tablespoons Dijon-style mustard

$^1/_2$ cup bread crumbs, toasted
   if desired

1 tablespoon chopped pecans,
   hazelnuts, *or* walnuts

2 teaspoons chopped fresh parsley

$^1/_2$ teaspoon (or less) Lite Salt

$^1/_8$ teaspoon pepper

4 salmon fillets (6 ounces each)

4 lemon wedges

Preheat oven to 450°. In a small bowl, combine honey and mustard. In a separate bowl, mix bread crumbs, nuts, parsley, Lite Salt, and pepper. Place salmon fillets in a baking dish that has been sprayed with nonstick cooking spray. Pat salmon with a paper towel to dry the top. Spread honey mustard sauce evenly over fish. Sprinkle with the crumb mixture. Bake, uncovered, 10 to 15 minutes or until salmon is almost opaque in the center. Serve with lemon wedges.

·~ Per Serving ~·	
Calories:	337
Sodium:	438 mg
Fiber:	1 gm
Total fat:	12 gm
Saturated fat:	3 gm
Cholesterol:	112 mg
Cholesterol–saturated fat index:	9

Chilean Sea Bass with Ginger Sesame Sauce

⁃ Makes 4 servings.

It is nice to serve this fish with steamed rice so every drop of the delicious sauce can be enjoyed. To shorten the cooking time, simply sprinkle the marinade ingredients on the fish and bake, microwave, or grill it.

1 pound Chilean sea bass, red
    snapper, *or* halibut, cut into
    4 pieces

Marinade
1 teaspoon lower-sodium soy sauce*
1/2 teaspoon grated fresh gingerroot
1/4 teaspoon sesame oil

Ginger Sesame Sauce
1 teaspoon sesame seeds
1 teaspoon vegetable oil

1/2 teaspoon grated fresh gingerroot
1 teaspoon minced garlic
2 teaspoons lower-sodium
    soy sauce*
2 teaspoons freshly squeezed
    lemon juice
1/2 teaspoon cornstarch
1/4 cup water

2 tablespoons finely chopped
    green onions

Rinse fish under cold water and pat dry. Place fish in shallow baking dish.

To prepare Marinade: Combine soy sauce, ginger, and sesame oil; drizzle over fish and let stand, uncovered, for 30 to 60 minutes.

Preheat oven to 400°. Bake fish, uncovered, 8 to 15 minutes (time depends on thickness of the fish). While fish is baking, prepare Ginger Sesame Sauce. Toast sesame seeds in nonstick skillet over medium heat, stirring constantly, until golden brown. Set aside. Heat oil in nonstick skillet; add ginger and garlic and cook 1 minute. Combine soy sauce, lemon juice, cornstarch, and water; stir into ginger-garlic mixture and cook until slightly thickened and mixture is clear.

Remove fish from oven and place on warm serving platter. Stir sesame seeds and juices from baking dish into sauce and bring to a boil. Spoon sauce over fish and sprinkle with green onions. Serve immediately.

* Kikkoman Lite Soy Sauce is available.

⁃ Per Serving ⁃	
Calories:	128
Sodium:	245 mg
Fiber:	Trace gm
Total fat:	3 gm
Saturated fat:	1 gm
Cholesterol:	60 mg
Cholesterol–saturated fat index:	4

Curried Snapper

Serve with steamed rice or Best Ever Black Beans *(page 227) for a marvelous meal.*

Curry Sauce
1 tablespoon vegetable oil
2 cloves garlic, minced
1 medium onion, finely chopped
1/2 green bell pepper, finely chopped
1/2 red bell pepper, finely chopped
1/2-inch piece fresh gingerroot,
   finely chopped
1 1/2 tablespoons curry powder
2 tablespoons flour
1 can (14 1/2 ounces) lower-salt
   chicken broth*

3 medium tomatoes, finely chopped,
   or 1 can (16 ounces) unsalted
   tomatoes, drained and chopped
1/2 teaspoon (or less) Lite Salt
1 tablespoon freshly squeezed
   lime juice
1/8 teaspoon pepper

4 red snapper fillets (6 ounces each)

2 tablespoons chopped fresh cilantro,
   for garnish

To prepare Curry Sauce (can be made ahead and stored in refrigerator or freezer until ready to use): Heat oil in a large skillet and add garlic. When it starts to sizzle, add onions and bell peppers. When vegetables are soft, add ginger and continue cooking for a minute or so. Add curry powder and flour and stir with a whisk for 3 to 4 minutes. Continue to whisk and slowly add chicken broth; bring to a boil. Reduce heat, stir in chopped tomatoes, and continue to cook slowly for 3 to 4 minutes. Add Lite Salt, lime juice, and black pepper.

To prepare fish: Preheat oven to 350°. Reheat sauce if cooled. Place snapper in baking dish and cover with Curry Sauce. Cover tightly and bake 10 minutes or until fish is done. Sprinkle with chopped cilantro, if desired.

* Swanson Natural Goodness with 1/3 less sodium is available.

·⁓ Per Serving ·⁓	
Calories:	255
Sodium:	564 mg
Fiber:	3 gm
Total fat:	7 gm
Saturated fat:	1 gm
Cholesterol:	90 mg
Cholesterol–saturated fat index:	5

Dungeness Crab Cakes with Red Pepper Sauce

⁓ Makes 8 crab cakes and 1 cup sauce.

We like these crab cakes with Red Pepper Sauce, *although they taste great by themselves.*

Red Pepper Sauce
2 cloves garlic
³/₄ cup roasted and peeled red peppers
2 teaspoons freshly squeezed lemon juice
¹/₄ cup nonfat mayonnaise

Crab Cakes
1 teaspoon olive oil
¹/₄ cup minced green onions
3 tablespoons minced red bell pepper
1 tablespoon rice vinegar *or* other vinegar
³/₄ pound (2 cups) fresh crabmeat
  or 2 cups canned salmon (14³/₄ ounce
  can) *or* tuna (12-ounce can)

3 tablespoons freshly squeezed
  lemon juice
¹/₄ cup dried bread crumbs
2 egg whites, lightly beaten,
  or ¹/₄ cup egg substitute,
  lightly beaten
1 teaspoon Dijon-style mustard
¹/₄ cup chopped fresh parsley
¹/₈ teaspoon Tabasco sauce
¹/₄ teaspoon paprika
¹/₈ teaspoon pepper

¹/₄ cup dried bread crumbs (omit for
  salmon and tuna cakes)
2 teaspoons olive oil

To prepare Red Pepper Sauce: Purée garlic, red peppers, lemon juice, and mayonnaise in food processor or blender until smooth. Place in covered container and chill in refrigerator.

To prepare Crab Cakes: Heat 1 teaspoon oil in a small nonstick skillet. Add green onions and bell pepper and sauté, stirring often, until green onions are wilted. Add vinegar and boil rapidly until it has evaporated. Set aside to cool.

Place crabmeat in a bowl and sprinkle with lemon juice. *If using canned salmon, discard skin; mash bones well. If using tuna, mash well.* Blend in cooled green onion–pepper mixture. Stir in ¹/₄ cup bread crumbs, egg whites or egg substitute, mustard, parsley, Tabasco sauce, paprika, and pepper. Cover and chill at least 2 hours.

When ready to cook, mold mixture into 8 cakes. Coat lightly on both sides with remaining ¹/₄ cup bread crumbs. *Do not coat salmon or tuna cakes.* Heat remaining 2 teaspoons oil in a nonstick skillet. Add cakes, cover, and cook over medium heat 4 minutes or until nicely browned. Turn carefully and cook, uncovered, 4 minutes or until browned.

⁓ Per Cake (and 2 Tablespoons Sauce) ⁓	
Calories:	109
Sodium:	411 mg
Fiber:	1 gm
Total fat:	3 gm
Saturated fat:	Trace gm
Cholesterol:	43 mg
Cholesterol–saturated fat index:	3

Fish and Vegetable Kabobs
Asian Style

Vegetables and fish are marinated in a ginger-garlic sauce and then grilled on the barbecue. The kabobs are loaded with vegetables, so a simple rice dish, great bread, and some fresh fruit are all that is required for a very satisfying meal.

Kabob Marinade

3 tablespoons lower-sodium
    soy sauce*

1 teaspoon sesame oil

2 tablespoons rice vinegar

2 teaspoons minced garlic

1 tablespoon grated fresh
    gingerroot†

1 green onion, thinly sliced

¼ teaspoon pepper

Kabobs

1 pound shark *or* other firm fish

1 large onion, cut into 1-inch pieces

1 red *or* green bell pepper, cut into
    1-inch pieces

24 large mushrooms

1 zucchini, sliced into ¼-inch rounds

8 small skewers *or* 4 large skewers

Start early in the day or the day before you plan to serve the kabobs. In a shallow dish, prepare marinade by whisking together soy sauce, sesame oil, vinegar, garlic, ginger, green onion, and pepper. Cut shark into 1½-inch pieces (about 16) and add to marinade, stirring to coat. Cover and refrigerate 3 hours or overnight.

When nearly ready to cook, soak wooden skewers, if using, in water 30 minutes. Place onions, bell peppers, mushrooms, and zucchini in a large bowl, add fish and marinade, and stir to coat the vegetables. If time allows, let vegetables marinate 15 minutes. Make the kabobs by alternating vegetables and shark on the skewers. When ready to barbecue, preheat grill. Cook kabobs over medium-hot coals until shark is done and vegetables are crisp-tender. Baste with marinade while kabobs are cooking.

* Kikkoman Lite Soy Sauce is available.
† To make grating easier, freeze ginger first—no need to peel it.

·– Per Serving –·	
Calories:	221
Sodium:	519 mg
Fiber:	3 gm
Total fat:	8 gm
Saturated fat:	2 gm
Cholesterol:	67 mg
Cholesterol–saturated fat index:	5

Fish in Saffron Broth with Garlic Mayonnaise

⌐ Makes 4 servings.

Garlic Mayonnaise
2 tablespoons nonfat mayonnaise
$^1/_2$ teaspoon minced garlic

1 tablespoon olive oil
$1^1/_2$ cups finely chopped onion
3 cloves garlic, minced
Pinch of saffron *or* turmeric
$^1/_8$ to $^1/_4$ teaspoon red pepper flakes
$^1/_2$ teaspoon (or less) Lite Salt
1 can (16 ounces) unsalted tomatoes,
   chopped (reserve liquid)

$^3/_4$ cup clam juice
2 cups water
$^1/_2$ cup white wine
4 halibut fillets, 6 ounces each (some
   other options include sea bass, red
   snapper, salmon)

2 tablespoons minced parsley,
   for garnish

Prepare Garlic Mayonnaise by combining mayonnaise with minced garlic.

Heat oil in a large cooking pot. Add onion and garlic and sauté 5 minutes or until onion is golden brown. Add saffron or turmeric, pepper flakes, Lite Salt, and tomatoes (including reserved liquid) and cook 3 minutes. Add clam juice, water, and white wine. Bring to a boil, reduce heat to simmer, and cook 10 minutes. Place fish fillets in the broth, cover, and simmer 5 minutes or until fish is done. Ladle fish and broth into bowls. Top with parsley and a heaping teaspoon of Garlic Mayonnaise.

⌐ Per Serving ⌐	
Calories:	264
Sodium:	475 mg
Fiber:	3 gm
Total fat:	6 gm
Saturated fat:	1 gm
Cholesterol:	92 mg
Cholesterol—saturated fat index:	6

Fish Nuggets with Tartar Sauce

Tartar Sauce

2 tablespoons nonfat mayonnaise
2 tablespoons nonfat plain yogurt
4 teaspoons sweet pickle relish
1 teaspoon freshly squeezed
   lemon juice
1/4 teaspoon onion powder
1/4 teaspoon dillweed

Fish Nuggets

1/2 cup crushed corn flakes
2 tablespoons grated Parmesan
   cheese
1 teaspoon paprika
2 egg whites, lightly beaten (1/2 cup
   skim milk can be used in place of
   the egg whites)
1 pound white fish fillets, cut into
   1 1/2-inch nuggets (snapper, cod, *or*
   perch work well)

To prepare Tartar Sauce: Combine mayonnaise, yogurt, pickle relish, lemon juice, onion powder, and dillweed in a bowl and mix well. Cover and refrigerate.

To prepare Fish Nuggets: Preheat oven to 500°. Combine crushed corn flakes, Parmesan cheese, and paprika. Put beaten egg whites in a separate bowl. Dip fish nuggets in egg whites or skim milk; roll in crushed corn flake mixture. Place on a baking sheet that has been sprayed with nonstick cooking spray. Bake 7 to 8 minutes or until crisp and brown. Serve hot with Tartar Sauce.

·~ Per Serving (Including Tartar Sauce) ~·	
Calories:	158
Sodium:	354 mg
Fiber:	Trace gm
Total fat:	2 gm
Saturated fat:	1 gm
Cholesterol:	63 mg
Cholesterol–saturated fat index:	4

Fish Poached in Court Bouillon

Makes 2 servings of poached fish (uses 4 cups bouillon).

One of the secrets of successful poaching is to use the correct pan. The fish needs to be covered with the liquid, so choose one that is deep enough (a wok or wok-type skillet works well). This recipe makes enough Court Bouillon to poach 4 pounds of fish—so freeze the unused "bouillon" in 4-cup portions for future use. Also, you can save the bouillon after poaching and use it in soup.

Court Bouillon
9 whole cloves
3 onions, unpeeled
3 quarts water
1 quart white wine
1 cup wine vinegar
4 carrots, finely chopped
2 stalks celery, chopped
1 bay leaf
1 teaspoon dried thyme leaves

4 to 5 sprigs parsley
1 tablespoon (or less) Lite Salt

Fish
1 pound salmon *or* halibut fillets
  or steaks

Fresh parsley, chopped
Pepper
Paprika

The Court Bouillon can be made ahead of time: Insert 3 cloves into each onion. Combine all Court Bouillon ingredients in a deep pan. Bring liquid to a boil, reduce heat, cover, and simmer for 1 hour. Strain and save the liquid. Makes 16 cups bouillon.

When ready to poach fish: Cut fish into serving-size pieces. Place 4 cups bouillon* in skillet or wok and increase heat until it is barely moving (soft boil). Add fish carefully and simmer (liquid is softly boiling) until done; if fish is not entirely covered with liquid, spoon it over the fish as it cooks. When fish is done, remove it from liquid and sprinkle with chopped parsley, black pepper, and paprika. Serve immediately.

* Fish can also be poached in chicken or vegetable broth or a dry white wine.

~ Per Serving ~	
Calories:	173
Sodium:	249 mg
Fiber:	0 gm
Total fat:	10 gm
Saturated fat:	2 gm
Cholesterol:	65 mg
Cholesterol–saturated fat index:	6

Fran's Stir-Fry

Want to learn to stir-fry? This is the dish for you. Take a few minutes to get all the ingredients ready and then have fun preparing it and smelling the wonderful aroma.

1 pound raw, shelled shrimp

4 ounces uncooked spaghetti

1 teaspoon vegetable oil

2 teaspoons grated fresh gingerroot

2 teaspoons minced garlic

1/3 cup sliced green onions

1 medium red bell pepper, cut into thin strips

3 tablespoons rice wine vinegar

1/8 teaspoon cayenne pepper

1 teaspoon lower-sodium soy sauce *

1 cup snow peas, sliced diagonally

1 1/2 cups bean sprouts, blanched (dipped in boiling water for a few seconds)

1/4 cup grated carrots

1/2 teaspoon sesame oil

4 teaspoons chopped fresh cilantro

2 tablespoons chopped unsalted peanuts

Rinse shrimp under cold water and drain; pat dry and set aside. Cook spaghetti in unsalted water until it is al dente (still firm); drain well and set aside.

Heat oil in a nonstick skillet. Sauté ginger and garlic. Add green onions, bell pepper, vinegar, cayenne pepper, and soy sauce. Stir and cook until onions are soft. Add snow peas, bean sprouts, carrots, sesame oil, and shrimp. Mix carefully. Add cooked spaghetti; toss. Sprinkle top with chopped cilantro and peanuts and serve immediately.

* Kikkoman Lite Soy Sauce is available.

⤳ Per Serving ⤳	
Calories:	264
Sodium:	245 mg
Fiber:	3 gm
Total fat:	5 gm
Saturated fat:	1 gm
Cholesterol:	161 mg
Cholesterol–saturated fat index:	9

Fresh Fish with Mediterranean Herbs

·⁓ Makes 4 servings (6 ounces each).

If you have the time (and can remember), marinate the fish overnight or for a few hours in this wonderful combination of flavors. The final cooking is done quickly in the microwave oven. Roasted Potatoes and Mushrooms with Fennel *(page 196) is a good dish to serve with it.*

2 teaspoons olive oil	$^1/_8$ to $^1/_2$ teaspoon pepper
6 cloves garlic, minced	$^1/_2$ teaspoon dried oregano leaves
1 large tomato, chopped	$^1/_2$ teaspoon dried basil leaves
2 stalks celery, thinly sliced	$^1/_8$ teaspoon nutmeg
$^1/_3$ cup chopped fresh parsley	
or 2 tablespoons dried parsley	2 pounds red snapper, perch, halibut,
flakes	or Chilean sea bass (the fresher,
1 teaspoon (or less) Lite Salt	the better)

Early in the day: Combine oil, garlic, tomato, celery, parsley, Lite Salt, pepper, oregano, basil, and nutmeg to make marinade. Place mixture in a glass bowl, cover well, and cook in the microwave oven on high for 3 minutes. *This combines the flavors and gets it ready to meet the next addition.* Stir well and let cool. Add fish fillets and turn fish so each piece is coated with marinade mixture. Cover dish and refrigerate for a few hours or overnight. It takes at least 3 hours to develop the flavor, but you can charge ahead and get it cooked and on the table if you need to.

When ready to cook: Cover baking dish with plastic wrap or waxed paper and cook in microwave oven on high for 5 minutes or until fish is done.

·⁓ Per Serving ⁓·	
Calories:	250
Sodium:	455 mg
Fiber:	1 gm
Total fat:	5 gm
Saturated fat:	1 gm
Cholesterol:	120 mg
Cholesterol—saturated fat index:	7

Halibut in Garlic Tomato Sauce

Makes 4 servings.

One of Sonja and Bill's favorites.

1 tablespoon vegetable oil

2 tablespoons minced garlic

2 tablespoons grated fresh
gingerroot

2 teaspoons jalapeño pepper, seeded
and minced, *or* use bottled
jalapeño slices (add more if you
like fire)

1/2 teaspoon cumin

1/2 teaspoon turmeric

1 teaspoon (or less) Lite Salt

2 cups coarsely chopped Roma
tomatoes

1 cup water

1 1/2 pounds halibut, red snapper,
perch, etc., cut into 2-inch pieces

2 to 4 tablespoons chopped fresh
cilantro, for garnish

Hot steamed rice

Heat oil in a large nonstick skillet over medium heat. Add garlic and ginger and cook until golden, stirring often to prevent sticking. Add jalapeño pepper, cumin, turmeric, Lite Salt, tomatoes, and water. Stir and bring the mixture to a boil, cover, reduce heat to simmer, and cook 15 minutes or until sauce thickens somewhat. Stir several times and mash tomatoes with a fork.

Bring sauce to a boil, add fish, cover and cook 4 to 5 minutes or until fish is done. Sprinkle with cilantro and serve over hot steamed rice.

Per Serving (Rice Not Included)	
Calories:	205
Sodium:	370 mg
Fiber:	2 gm
Total fat:	6 gm
Saturated fat:	1 gm
Cholesterol:	74 mg
Cholesterol–saturated fat index:	4

Halibut Olé

The lightly flavored fish is marinated in fresh lime juice, cooked, and served over stir-fried corn, peppers, and black beans. One serving is very filling and contains lots of fiber.

Marinated Fish

4 halibut steaks (about 6 ounces each) *or* other similar fish
1/4 teaspoon (or less) Lite Salt
1/4 teaspoon pepper
1/2 teaspoon cumin
2 teaspoons olive oil
1/4 cup freshly squeezed lime juice
1 large clove garlic, minced

Stir-Fried Vegetables

1 bag (16 ounces) frozen corn
1/2 cup chopped green bell pepper
1/2 cup chopped red bell pepper
1/4 to 1/2 teaspoon red pepper flakes
1 can (15 ounces) black beans, drained and rinsed*
1/2 cup sliced avocado
3 tablespoons chopped fresh cilantro

Lemon slices
Fresh salsa, if desired
Hot steamed rice

Forty-five minutes before meal time: Sprinkle halibut with Lite Salt, pepper, and cumin and rub into fish. Combine olive oil, lime juice, and garlic and pour over halibut. Cover and refrigerate for about 30 minutes.

When ready to cook, remove halibut from marinade (reserve marinade) and cook. Fish can be broiled, grilled over charcoal, sautéed lightly with some of the reserved marinade, or cooked in the microwave oven. Don't overcook. Keep warm until vegetables and beans are ready.

In large nonstick skillet, heat reserved marinade and add corn, bell peppers, and pepper flakes. Stir and cook 3 to 4 minutes. Add black beans and simmer, on low heat, for a few minutes, just until beans are hot and vegetables cooked to crisp-tender.

To serve, place corn-pepper mixture on platter; put avocado and cilantro over top. Place cooked fish around vegetables. Serve with lemon slices and fresh salsa, if desired, and hot steamed rice.

* S&W has a 50% Less Salt product available.

⌐ Per Serving (Rice Not Included) *⌐*	
Calories:	419
Sodium:	401 mg
Fiber:	11 gm
Total fat:	8 gm
Saturated fat:	1 gm
Cholesterol:	90 mg
Cholesterol–saturated fat index:	6

Lemon Garlic Halibut

The most critical taste tester on our staff describes this recipe as "concentrated deliciousness."

3 cloves garlic, minced

2 teaspoons olive oil

3 tablespoons chopped fresh basil

1/2 teaspoon (or less) Lite Salt

1 teaspoon pepper

3 tablespoons freshly squeezed lemon juice

2 teaspoons chopped fresh parsley, divided

4 halibut fillets (5 to 6 ounces each)

Combine garlic, oil, basil, Lite Salt, pepper, lemon juice, and 1 teaspoon parsley. Add fish and marinate at least 2 hours. Place on broiler pan or grill, reserving liquid. Broil about 5 minutes on each side. Brush with remaining marinade and heat 1 minute. Sprinkle with remaining parsley.

⁓ Per Serving ⁓	
Calories:	144
Sodium:	230 mg
Fiber:	Trace gm
Total fat:	4 gm
Saturated fat:	1 gm
Cholesterol:	68 mg
Cholesterol–saturated fat index:	4

Mrs. Plancich's
Barbecued Salmon

This is a great way to prepare salmon for a crowd. It requires a barbecue grill with a cover. Mrs. Plancich, of the Plancich Wholesale Fish Company, told us how to cook salmon for 100 people using three large grills (coals had to be added to the barbecue to keep the cooking going for 1 hour).

4 pounds salmon fillets, boned but
  not skinned (1 or 2 large pieces
  work best)
1 tablespoon vegetable oil

¼ teaspoon seasoned pepper
4 three-inch sprigs fresh rosemary
½ cup fresh parsley sprigs
3 lemons, cut into wedges

Place coals in barbecue grill. Make sure there is a solid layer of coals. Pile coals and light. After 25 minutes (coals will be very hot), spread coals. Brush skin side of salmon with oil. Place directly on grill skin-side-down. Sprinkle with seasoned pepper. Place rosemary on salmon. Cover. Leave vents open on both top and bottom of grill. *The length of time it will take to cook depends on the amount and thickness of the salmon.* Check after 15 minutes. Remove cover, insert knife at thickest part and separate to determine doneness. If it is still translucent, cover and check again in 5 minutes. Cook until the center of the thickest part of the salmon is almost opaque. Insert two spatulas either under the skin or between the skin and the meat and lift salmon onto a platter (a baking sheet covered with foil can serve as a platter). Garnish with parsley sprigs and serve with lemon wedges.

·– Per Serving –·	
Calories:	264
Sodium:	143 mg
Fiber:	Trace gm
Total fat:	15 gm
Saturated fat:	3 gm
Cholesterol:	94 mg
Cholesterol–saturated fat index:	8

Northwestern Salmon Cakes

Cook an extra potato and have it on hand to make these delicious and attractive grilled patties.

1 pound cooked salmon
   or 1 can (16 ounces) red *or*
   pink salmon
1 cold cooked potato, peeled
⅓ cup finely diced red bell pepper
⅓ cup diced red onion
1 tablespoon finely minced fresh basil
2 soda crackers, crushed (with
   unsalted tops)

1 teaspoon Worcestershire sauce
¾ cup egg substitute
   or 6 egg whites
1 teaspoon (or less) Lite Salt (omit if
   using canned salmon)
½ teaspoon pepper

Skin and bone salmon and flake into a large bowl. Grate cold potato (should measure 1 cup) and add to salmon with bell pepper, onion, basil, cracker crumbs, and Worcestershire sauce. Toss to combine. Add egg substitute, Lite Salt and pepper and mix well.

Form salmon mixture into 6 cakes, using about ½ cup per cake. Spray a large skillet with nonstick cooking spray and heat to medium. Cook the salmon cakes until golden brown, about 3 minutes per side. Serve on a toasted bun with Tartar Sauce (page 244) or alone with other side dishes.

·~ Per Cake ~	
Calories:	194
Sodium:	305 mg
Fiber:	1 gm
Total fat:	9 gm
Saturated fat:	2 gm
Cholesterol:	58 mg
Cholesterol–saturated fat index:	5

Oven-Poached Cod with Red Peppers, Onion, and Ginger

⁓ Makes 6 servings.

Keep Icelandic cod in your freezer to make this easily prepared fish entrée.

1 cup white wine

2 pounds frozen Icelandic cod, thawed and cut in 2-inch pieces

2 cups thinly sliced red bell pepper

4 cups chopped tomato

1 onion, cut in half and thinly sliced

1/4 cup chopped fresh basil

1/4 cup chopped fresh parsley

1 tablespoon olive oil

1 teaspoon (or less) Lite Salt

1/8 teaspoon pepper

3 cloves garlic, minced

2 teaspoons grated fresh gingerroot

Preheat oven to 350°. Spray a 9-by-13-inch baking dish with nonstick cooking spray. Pour wine into dish and arrange cod pieces on top of wine. In a bowl, combine bell pepper, tomatoes, onion, basil, parsley, olive oil, Lite Salt, pepper, garlic, and ginger. Mix together and spread over cod. Bake 35 minutes or until fish flakes easily when tested with a fork. Serve immediately.

⁓ Per Serving ⁓	
Calories:	231
Sodium:	303 mg
Fiber:	2 gm
Total fat:	5 gm
Saturated fat:	1 gm
Cholesterol:	80 mg
Cholesterol–saturated fat index:	5

Paella

•‒ Makes 6 servings (2 cups each).

Paella is the national dish of Spain. This dish is a real "show-off" with its colorful blend of seafood, saffron rice, and stir-fried peppers and onions.

12 prawns

1 pound small steamer clams

1½ pounds seafood (Chilean sea bass, halibut, salmon, scallops, etc.)*

2 teaspoons olive oil

1 teaspoon minced garlic

½ cup finely chopped onion

1 medium red, yellow, *or* green bell pepper, cut into thin strips

3 plum tomatoes, finely chopped *or* 1 large tomato, finely chopped

2 cups basmati rice

1 teaspoon (or less) Lite Salt

⅛ teaspoon ground saffron

4 cups boiling water

1 cup fresh or frozen and defrosted peas *or* water-packed *or* frozen artichoke hearts

2 lemons, each cut into 6 wedges, for garnish

12 tomato wedges, for garnish

Clean and rinse prawns. Rinse clams and scallops under cold water, if using, and drain in a colander. Rinse other seafood and cut into 2-inch pieces. Refrigerate until ready to use.

Preheat oven to 400°. Heat oil in a large skillet and add garlic. When it begins to bubble, add onions, bell pepper, and tomato. Cook on medium-high heat and stir frequently until mixture is thick and most of the liquid evaporated, about 15 minutes. Add rice, Lite Salt, saffron, and boiling water. Stirring constantly, bring to a full boil; remove from heat and put in a warm 9-by-13-inch baking dish. Arrange seafood that takes longer to cook (Chilean sea bass, halibut, or salmon) on top of the rice mixture. Push seafood into rice mixture so it is covered with liquid. Scatter peas or artichoke hearts over the top. Place pan on the lowest rack or on the bottom of the oven and bake, uncovered, 15 minutes. Add prawns, steamer clams, and scallops, if using, and cook 10 minutes. *Do not stir after paella has been placed in the oven.*

Remove from oven, cover loosely with a towel, and let stand 5 minutes. Garnish with lemon wedges and tomato wedges. Serve directly from the pan. It is important to squeeze some lemon juice on each serving of Paella.

Options: 1. If you use a 14-inch paella pan, increase all the ingredients by 1½ times (for example, use 3 cups rice, 6 cups boiling water, etc.). 2. To make a more elaborate paella, remove and dis-card the tips from 6 chicken wings, remove the skin, and brown remaining pieces in 1 teaspoon olive oil. Brown 1 ounce hot Italian chicken sausage and cut into small pieces or use 1 ounce smoked turkey or chicken sausage cut into small pieces. Add chicken wings and sausage along with the seafood.

•‒ Per Serving (with Seafood Only) ‒•	
Calories:	465
Sodium:	283 mg
Fiber:	4 gm
Total fat:	8 gm
Saturated fat:	2 gm
Cholesterol:	92 mg
Cholesterol–saturated fat index:	7

* You can use just one type of fish, or as many as you like.

Pan-Seared Fish Steaks

Our version of fresh tuna teriyaki, but any fish can be used. Serve with steamed rice and drizzle remaining marinade on top.

Teriyaki Marinade

3 tablespoons lower-sodium
   soy sauce*

1 tablespoon water

1/4 cup dry sherry

1/4 cup freshly squeezed lemon juice

4 teaspoons grated fresh gingerroot

2 teaspoons sugar

4 cloves garlic, minced

4 tuna *or* halibut steaks *or* red
   snapper fillets (5 to 6 ounces
   each), cut 1/2 to 3/4 inch thick

2 teaspoons peanut *or* other
   vegetable oil

2 tablespoons chopped green onions

Hot steamed rice

Two hours before cooking, mix soy sauce, water, sherry, lemon juice, ginger, sugar, and garlic together and stir until sugar dissolves. Place fish in shallow container and cover with marinade. Turn fish to coat well. Refrigerate for 2 hours, turning several times.

To cook, remove fish and save marinade. Blot fish with paper towels to remove moisture and brush both sides with oil. Heat a heavy 8-inch nonstick skillet on medium heat; add fish and cook 5 to 8 minutes, stirring often. Do not overcook; the fish is done when it is opaque throughout.

Transfer fish to a warm platter, pour marinade into the skillet and heat until marinade boils, about 30 seconds. Pour over fish. Top with green onions and serve with hot steamed rice.

* Kikkoman Lite Soy Sauce is available.

・~ Per Serving (Rice Not Included) ~・	
Calories:	235
Sodium:	535 mg
Fiber:	Trace gm
Total fat:	8 gm
Saturated fat:	2 gm
Cholesterol:	70 mg
Cholesterol–saturated fat index:	5

Party Shrimp Casserole *–Makes about 6 servings (1⅓ cups each).*

For shrimp lovers—a beautiful shrimp and rice dish that can be prepared ahead of time.
It is great for company occasions.

1½ pounds raw, shelled shrimp
   or 1½ pounds ready-to-serve,
   cooked and shelled shrimp
1 tablespoon freshly squeezed
   lemon juice
1 tablespoon olive oil
1 cup minced green bell pepper
1 cup minced green onion

3 cups cooked white rice
⅛ teaspoon mace
Dash cayenne pepper
1 can (10¾ ounces) Campbell's
   Healthy Request Tomato Soup
1 cup skim milk
½ cup sherry *or* water
¼ cup slivered almonds

If shrimp is raw, cook in boiling water 5 minutes. Drain well. Place cooked shrimp in 9-by-13-inch baking dish. Sprinkle with lemon juice. Cover and refrigerate while you prepare the other ingredients.

Preheat oven to 350°. Heat olive oil in skillet. Sauté bell pepper and onion until tender. Add cooked rice, mace, and cayenne. In a separate bowl, mix tomato soup, milk, and sherry or water until smooth. Add to rice mixture. Remove shrimp from refrigerator and set aside 8 shrimp to decorate top of casserole. Leave shrimp and lemon juice in the baking dish and pour rice mixture over shrimp. Add slivered almonds and remaining shrimp to the top and bake, uncovered, 35 minutes or until heated through.

– Per Serving –	
Calories:	318
Sodium:	405 mg
Fiber:	2 gm
Total fat:	7 gm
Saturated fat:	1 gm
Cholesterol:	162 mg
Cholesterol–saturated fat index:	9

Polynesian "Fried Rice" with Shrimp

·— Makes 4 servings (2 cups each).

For a fancy meal or buffet, start with a big, sweet fresh pineapple, remove the fruit for use in this stir-fried main dish, and then serve the cooked "fried rice" in two pineapple shells. This also makes a delicious rice side dish when the seafood is omitted.

1½ cups pineapple chunks, fresh
   or canned
½ cup red bell pepper, cut into
   thin strips
3 small green onions, thinly sliced
1½ tablespoons lower-sodium
   soy sauce*
1 teaspoon sugar
½ teaspoon turmeric
1 tablespoon water
1 tablespoon vegetable oil

2 cloves garlic, minced
½ to 2 teaspoons chopped fresh
   jalapeño pepper *or* to taste
   (these can be hot!)
1 pound raw shrimp, shelled and
   deveined, *or* 1 pound scallops
6 cups cooked rice (we like basmati
   for this dish)†
½ teaspoon (or less) Lite Salt
¼ cup chopped fresh cilantro

If using fresh pineapple, cut lengthwise and remove the fruit, leaving about a ½-inch-thick shell. Reserve the shells to use as serving dishes for the finished rice. Cut the pineapple fruit into ½-inch chunks until you have 1½ cups and use the remaining fruit for something else. Combine pineapple chunks with bell pepper and green onions. In another small dish, combine soy sauce, sugar, turmeric, and water.

When ready to prepare the finished dish, heat oil in a wok or heavy skillet. Add garlic and jalapeño pepper and stir for about 30 seconds. Add shrimp or scallops and stir-fry until seafood is just cooked (about 1½ minutes). Remove shrimp or scallops from the skillet. Stir in cooked rice and continue stirring and cooking until rice is hot (about 2 minutes). Add soy sauce mixture and stir-fry until golden color is uniform. Add pineapple/peppers, Lite Salt, and seafood and heat through. Remove from heat and add chopped cilantro. Serve the "fried rice" in pineapple shells, if desired.

·— Per Serving —·	
Calories:	465
Sodium:	537 mg
Fiber:	2 gm
Total fat:	5 gm
Saturated fat:	1 gm
Cholesterol:	161 mg
Cholesterol–saturated fat index:	9

*Kikkoman Lite Soy Sauce is available.
† It is essential to cook the rice a day before and refrigerate until needed or rice will be sticky.

Prawns and Beans Tuscan Style (The Longer Version)

✦ *Makes 4 servings.*

An Italian friend brought this popular recipe to a potluck—a great place to get ideas for new recipes.

1½ cups dried small white beans
1 bay leaf
2 cloves garlic
½ teaspoon (or less) Lite Salt
1 pound prawns in shells
    or ¾ pound raw, shelled shrimp
1 teaspoon olive oil
1 clove garlic, minced
3 cups chopped plum tomatoes
2 teaspoons olive oil

2 cloves garlic, minced
½ cup chopped fresh basil
    or 2 tablespoons dried basil leaves
2 tablespoons chopped fresh
    Italian parsley
1¼ teaspoons (or less) Lite Salt
½ teaspoon pepper
1 tablespoon freshly squeezed lemon
    juice or to taste

In a 3-quart pan, cover beans with water several inches above top of beans. Add bay leaf, 2 cloves garlic, and ½ teaspoon Lite Salt. Bring to a boil, reduce heat, cover, and cook 2 hours or until beans are tender. Drain beans, reserving ½ cup liquid, and remove bay leaf. Set beans and reserved liquid aside.

Remove shells from prawns, if using, and rinse and drain. Prawns can be left whole or cut into pieces. In a large skillet, heat 1 teaspoon olive oil. Add garlic and sauté until golden. Add chopped tomatoes and sauté 1 minute. Remove tomatoes from skillet and set aside. Heat 2 teaspoons olive oil in the skillet. Add prawns or shrimp and sauté until almost cooked. Add garlic, basil, parsley, Lite Salt, pepper, beans, and the ½ cup reserved bean liquid. Heat until beans are warm. Add tomatoes and lemon juice, heat through, and serve.

✦ Per Serving ✦	
Calories:	355
Sodium:	574 mg
Fiber:	11 gm
Total fat:	5 gm
Saturated fat:	1 gm
Cholesterol:	107 mg
Cholesterol–saturated fat index:	6

Prawns and Beans Tuscan Style (The Quick and Easy Way)

⌐ Makes 4 servings (1½ cups each).

Add a green vegetable, salad, fresh bread, and a dessert for a terrific dinner.

³/₄ pound raw, shelled shrimp
   or 1 pound prawns in shells
1 teaspoon olive oil
2 cloves garlic, minced
2 cans (15½ ounces each) small
   white beans, drained and rinsed
1 can (15½ ounces) unsalted
   chopped tomatoes, not drained

2 tablespoons dried basil leaves
   or ½ cup chopped fresh basil
1½ teaspoons dried parsley
   or 2 tablespoons chopped fresh
   parsley
¼ teaspoon pepper
2 teaspoons freshly squeezed
   lemon juice

Remove shells, if needed, from prawns and rinse in cold water. Heat olive oil in large skillet, add garlic, and sauté until golden. Add shrimp or prawns and sauté until almost cooked (not quite pink and opaque); add beans, undrained tomatoes, basil, parsley, and pepper. Cook for several minutes until heated and prawns are cooked. Stir in lemon juice. Serve hot.

⌐ Per Serving ⌐	
Calories:	304
Sodium:	509 mg
Fiber:	10 gm
Total fat:	3 gm
Saturated fat:	Trace gm
Cholesterol:	107 mg
Cholesterol–saturated fat index:	6

Red Snapper Primavera

·~ Makes 6 servings.

Fish baked over shrimp and vegetables makes a wonderful sauce to thicken and serve over rice or pasta.

1 cup chopped tomato
1/2 cup chopped onion
1/2 cup chopped green bell pepper
1 cup chopped mushrooms
3 tablespoons chili sauce
2 tablespoons lower-sodium
    chicken broth*
2 tablespoons freshly squeezed
    lemon juice
2 tablespoons chopped fresh parsley
2 cloves garlic, minced

1/2 teaspoon dried thyme leaves
1/4 teaspoon (or less) Lite Salt
1/8 teaspoon pepper
1/4 pound shrimpmeat *or* chopped
    cooked shrimp
1/4 cup white wine
1 1/2 pounds red snapper fillets

2 teaspoons cornstarch
1/4 cup water

Preheat oven to 350°. Spray a 9-by-13-inch baking dish with nonstick cooking spray. Place tomato, onion, bell pepper, mushrooms, chili sauce, chicken broth, lemon juice, parsley, garlic, thyme, Lite Salt, and pepper in the prepared baking dish. Bake until vegetables are tender, about 10 to 15 minutes. Stir in shrimp and wine. Place snapper fillets on top. Bake 15 to 20 minutes or until fish flakes easily with a fork.

Place snapper on warm platter. Pour remaining sauce into a small pan. In a small dish, dissolve cornstarch in water and add to the sauce. Cook over medium heat, stirring constantly, until thickened; spread sauce over the fish. Serve with steamed rice or fresh-cooked pasta.

* Swanson Natural Goodness with 1/3 less sodium is available.

·~ Per Serving ~·	
Calories:	144
Sodium:	263 mg
Fiber:	1 gm
Total fat:	2 gm
Saturated fat:	Trace gm
Cholesterol:	80 mg
Cholesterol–saturated fat index:	4

Scallops à la Mistral

These scallops are always moist and tender. We like this dish so much we make it for ourselves and serve it to company. Serve over hot steamed rice to take advantage of the delicious sauce.

1 pound fresh scallops	1 teaspoon dried oregano leaves
1 tablespoon olive oil	$^1/_4$ to $^1/_2$ teaspoon fennel seed
2 teaspoons garlic, minced	$^3/_4$ cup dry white wine
3 cups green, red, and/or yellow bell peppers, cut into 1$^1/_2$-inch thin strips	$^1/_8$ to $^1/_4$ teaspoon red pepper flakes
	$^1/_8$ teaspoon seasoned pepper
1$^1/_2$ cups sliced onion	2 tablespoons grated Parmesan cheese
1$^1/_2$ cups sliced fresh mushrooms	

Preheat oven to 375°. Place scallops in colander and rinse thoroughly with cold water until froth disappears. Drain well and place scallops in a 7-by-11-inch or 10-inch square baking dish.

Heat oil and garlic in a heavy skillet. Add peppers, onion, and mushrooms. Stir-fry over high heat until crisp-tender. Add oregano, fennel, wine, pepper flakes, and pepper. Bring to a boil and cook 1 to 2 minutes. Spoon mixture evenly over the scallops. Sprinkle Parmesan cheese over the top. Bake 15 to 20 minutes or until lightly browned. Serve immediately.

·⁓ Per Serving ⁓·	
Calories:	252
Sodium:	366 mg
Fiber:	3 gm
Total fat:	6 gm
Saturated fat:	1 gm
Cholesterol:	39 mg
Cholesterol–saturated fat index:	3

Seafood Pasta with Spinach and Lemon

·~ Makes 4 servings (1½ cups each).

8 ounces uncooked angel hair pasta
2 teaspoons olive oil, divided
2 cloves garlic, minced
¼ teaspoon red pepper flakes
¼ cup freshly squeezed lemon juice
1 teaspoon freshly grated lemon peel
2 tablespoons chopped fresh basil
½ teaspoon (or less) Lite Salt
¼ teaspoon pepper
6 ounces shrimpmeat *or* chopped
   cooked shrimp
6 ounces scallops

2 cups chopped tomatoes
½ cup lower-salt chicken broth*
1 package (10 ounces) frozen
   chopped spinach, thawed and
   drained
¼ cup grated Parmesan cheese

Cook pasta in unsalted water according to package directions until just tender. Drain. Meanwhile, in a medium bowl, combine 1 teaspoon oil, garlic, pepper flakes, lemon juice, lemon peel, basil, Lite Salt, and pepper. Add shrimpmeat and scallops; stir to coat. In a large skillet, heat remaining teaspoon of oil. Add tomatoes and cook 3 minutes. Add broth, shrimp-and-scallop mixture, and spinach. Cook, stirring frequently, until shrimp and scallops are done.

Place pasta in a large serving bowl and pour the seafood mixture on top. Sprinkle with Parmesan cheese. Serve immediately.

* Swanson Natural Goodness with ⅓ less sodium is available.

·~ Per Serving ~·	
Calories:	387
Sodium:	532 mg
Fiber:	4 gm
Total fat:	7 gm
Saturated fat:	2 gm
Cholesterol:	58 mg
Cholesterol–saturated fat index:	5

Sesame Shrimp with Couscous ·~ *Makes 4 servings.*

An easy stir-fried dish with marinated shrimp, garlic, and ginger served over couscous.

3/4 pound shrimp, shelled and
   deveined
1/2 cup sliced green onions
2 teaspoons grated fresh gingerroot
2 tablespoons lower-sodium
   soy sauce*
1 tablespoon sesame oil
3 cloves garlic, minced
1/8 teaspoon red pepper flakes

4 cups unsalted chicken broth,
   divided, *or* 4 cups water, divided
1 1/2 cups uncooked couscous

1 cup broccoli flowerets
1 cup sliced red bell pepper
1 cup fresh *or* frozen pea pods
1 tablespoon cornstarch

1 teaspoon toasted sesame seeds
2 tablespoons chopped fresh cilantro

Combine shrimp, green onions, ginger, soy sauce, sesame oil, garlic, and pepper flakes in a bowl. Cover and marinate in refrigerator for 30 minutes.

Bring 3 1/2 cups chicken broth or water to a boil. Stir in couscous. Remove from heat, cover, and let stand 5 minutes. Fluff with a fork and set aside.

Meanwhile, place a nonstick skillet or wok over medium-high heat until hot. Add marinated shrimp, and cook 4 minutes. Remove from skillet and set aside. Add broccoli, bell pepper, and pea pods and stir-fry until tender, about 5 minutes. Dissolve cornstarch in remaining 1/2 cup chicken broth or water and add to vegetable mixture. Cook 1 minute or until sauce is slightly thickened and clear. Stir in shrimp mixture, and cook only until heated through, about 1 minute. Serve over couscous. Sprinkle with toasted sesame seeds and cilantro.

* Kikkoman Lite Soy Sauce is available.

·~ Per Serving ~·	
Calories:	428
Sodium:	457 mg
Fiber:	6 gm
Total fat:	6 gm
Saturated fat:	1 gm
Cholesterol:	121 mg
Cholesterol–saturated fat index:	7

Shrimp Creole

⁓ Makes 4 servings (1¹/₄ cups each)

Simple to prepare, this colorful dish should be served over a large plate of hot steamed rice.

1¹/₄ pounds unshelled medium-sized shrimp
   or 1 pound raw, shelled shrimp
1 tablespoon oil
¹/₂ cup chopped green onions
¹/₂ cup chopped green bell pepper
¹/₂ cup chopped celery
2 cups chopped tomatoes
1 can (8 ounces) unsalted
   tomato sauce

¹/₂ teaspoon (or less) Lite Salt
¹/₄ teaspoon cayenne pepper
   (this can be hot!)
2 bay leaves
3 tablespoons chopped fresh parsley

Hot steamed rice

Shell and devein shrimp, if necessary, and rinse in cold water. Set aside.

Heat oil in a large skillet. Sauté green onions, bell pepper, and celery until slightly cooked. Add remaining ingredients, including shrimp, and continue cooking just until shrimp turns pinkish-white. Remove bay leaves and serve immediately over hot steamed rice.

⁓ Per Serving (Rice Not Included) ⁓	
Calories:	181
Sodium:	397 mg
Fiber:	2 gm
Total fat:	5 gm
Saturated fat:	1 gm
Cholesterol:	202 mg
Cholesterol–saturated fat index:	11

Stir-Fried Shrimp and Scallops ⸱⁓ Makes 6 cups.

Master the art of stir-frying and you will open the door to many tasty dishes—this being one of them. Choose your favorite pasta or hot steamed rice to serve under it.

3 tablespoons lower-sodium
   soy sauce*
1/4 cup brown sugar
1 teaspoon curry powder (we like
   Sharwood's Mild)
1 teaspoon dry mustard

1 tablespoon vegetable oil, divided
1 cup thinly sliced carrots
1 1/2 cups broccoli flowerets
3/4 cup sliced red bell pepper

1/2 cup sliced water chestnuts
1 teaspoon grated fresh gingerroot
1 clove garlic, minced

3/4 pound shrimp, shelled and
   deveined
3/4 pound medium-sized scallops
1/4 cup chopped walnuts
1/4 cup chopped green onions

Hot steamed rice or hot pasta

Combine soy sauce, brown sugar, curry powder, and mustard. Set aside. Heat 1 teaspoon oil in wok or skillet. Add carrots and stir-fry 2 minutes. Add broccoli and stir-fry 2 minutes. Add bell pepper, water chestnuts, ginger, and garlic and stir-fry 3 minutes. Stir constantly and add a little water if necessary to prevent sticking. Remove vegetables from wok. Add remaining 2 teaspoons oil to wok, add shrimp and scallops and stir-fry 3 minutes or until seafood is cooked. Add vegetables and soy sauce mixture, tossing gently. Heat 1 to 2 minutes. Sprinkle with nuts and green onions and serve immediately over hot steamed rice or hot pasta.

* Kikkoman Lite Soy Sauce is available.

⸱⁓ Per Cup (Rice or Pasta Not Included) ⸝	
Calories:	229
Sodium:	564 mg
Fiber:	2 gm
Total fat:	7 gm
Saturated fat:	1 gm
Cholesterol:	99 mg
Cholesterol–saturated fat index:	6

Dishes with Chicken and Turkey

Baked Chicken with Caramelized Onions
Chicken and Spinach with Creamy Ginger Sauce
Chicken with Cranberries
East Indian Chicken with Apricot Rice
East Indian Curry
Kung Pao Chicken
La Paz Chicken and Corn Stir-Fry
Sausage and Mushroom Spaghetti Torta
Savory Lemon Chicken
South-of-the-Border Casserole
Spicy Sesame Linguine with Chicken

Baked Chicken with Caramelized Onions

Caramelized Onions

2 large onions, thinly sliced

3 tablespoons brown sugar

3/4 cup dry red wine

3 tablespoons balsamic vinegar

3 tablespoons Dijon-style mustard

1 1/2 teaspoons freshly squeezed
   lemon juice

1/2 teaspoon pepper

1 teaspoon Worcestershire sauce

1 teaspoon minced garlic

4 chicken breasts, boned and skinned
   (about 4 ounces each)

To prepare Caramelized Onions: Combine onions and brown sugar in a nonstick skillet. Cook over moderate heat, stirring often, until onions begin to caramelize and turn golden, 15 to 20 minutes. Stir in wine and vinegar; increase heat to medium-high and bring to a boil. Reduce heat and cook, stirring often, until most of liquid has evaporated, at least 30 minutes—the longer, the better. Set aside.

Preheat oven to 350°. While onions are cooking, combine mustard, lemon juice, pepper, Worcestershire sauce, and garlic. Place chicken breasts in a baking dish that has been sprayed with nonstick cooking spray and cover with the mustard-lemon mixture. Bake, uncovered, 30 minutes or until chicken is no longer pink inside. Place on a warm platter and cover with warm Caramelized Onions.

·⁓ Per Serving (Including Onions) ⁓·	
Calories:	250
Sodium:	226 mg
Fiber:	2 gm
Total fat:	4 gm
Saturated fat:	1 gm
Cholesterol:	65 mg
Cholesterol–saturated fat index:	4

Chicken and Spinach with Creamy Ginger Sauce

~ Makes 4 servings

This dish has a sauce that is tasty over fresh pasta. If you use prewashed spinach, this stir-fry takes about 6 minutes to prepare.

4 chicken breasts, skinned and boned

2 teaspoons olive oil

1 cup chopped onion

3 tablespoons grated fresh gingerroot*

1 can (14½ ounces) lower-salt chicken broth†

1 cup nonfat plain yogurt

2 tablespoons flour

4 teaspoons Dijon country-style mustard

6 cups fresh spinach, torn into large pieces

or 1 package (10 ounces) frozen spinach, thawed and well drained

Cut chicken into ¾-inch pieces. Heat olive oil in wok or nonstick skillet. Stir-fry chicken, onion, and ginger until chicken is browned, stirring often. Combine chicken broth, yogurt, flour, and mustard. Stir until the sauce is thoroughly mixed (a whisk works well for this). Add sauce to chicken mixture. Stir while cooking for 2 minutes. Add spinach and continue cooking until sauce thickens. Continue to stir. Add water if sauce is too thick. Serve over cooked rice or pasta.

* To make grating easier, freeze ginger first, no need to peel it.
† Swanson Natural Goodness with ⅓ less sodium is available.

~ Per Serving ~	
Calories:	259
Sodium:	531 mg
Fiber:	3 gm
Total fat:	7 gm
Saturated fat:	2 gm
Cholesterol:	67 mg
Cholesterol–saturated fat index:	5

Chicken with Cranberries

⤳ Makes 8 servings.

This is the kind of dish families request over and over again. Keep cranberries in the freezer so you can make it on the spur of the moment and please them. If fresh or frozen cranberries are unavailable, canned jellied cranberries work well, also. Serve over hot steamed rice.

8 chicken breasts, skinned and boned
1 teaspoon vegetable oil
3/4 cup thinly sliced onion
1 cup ketchup
1 to 3 teaspoons Thai chili sauce, optional*
1/2 cup brown sugar
1 1/2 tablespoons vinegar

1 1/2 teaspoons dry mustard
2 cups cranberries, fresh or frozen and thawed
or 1 can (16 ounces) whole jellied cranberries
1/4 cup chopped green onions, for garnish

Preheat oven to 400°. Place chicken in a 9-by-13-inch baking dish that has been sprayed with nonstick cooking spray. Bake 25 minutes, uncovered. While chicken is cooking, heat oil in a nonstick skillet. Brown onion slices until softened. Remove from heat and add ketchup, Thai chili sauce, if using, brown sugar, vinegar, mustard, and cranberries. Remove chicken from the oven after 25 minutes and spoon the sauce over it. Return to the oven and bake 10 to 15 minutes, or until chicken is done. Serve warm.

* Thai chili sauce can be found in the Asian-food section of supermarkets or in Asian grocery stores.

⤳ Per Serving (Not Including Rice) ⤳	
Calories:	249
Sodium:	422 mg
Fiber:	1 gm
Total fat:	4 gm
Saturated fat:	1 gm
Cholesterol:	65 mg
Cholesterol–saturated fat index:	4

East Indian Chicken with Apricot Rice

An irresistible one-pot meal.

1 can (14½ ounces) lower-salt
   chicken broth*
1 cup water
2 cloves garlic, minced
2 cinnamon sticks (3 inches each),
   broken in pieces
1 tablespoon coriander
1 teaspoon cumin
2 teaspoons onion powder
1 teaspoon ground ginger
½ teaspoon turmeric

½ teaspoon (or less) Lite Salt
⅛ teaspoon cayenne pepper

1¼ cups uncooked long grain white
   rice
1 pound chicken breasts, skinned,
   boned, and cut into ½-inch cubes
   (3 breasts)
1 cup frozen peas
½ cup light apricot preserves

In a medium saucepan, combine chicken broth, water, garlic, cinnamon sticks, coriander, cumin, onion powder, ginger, turmeric, Lite Salt, and cayenne; bring to a boil. Stir in rice and return to a boil; reduce heat, cover, and simmer 12 minutes.

Add chicken cubes and simmer, covered, until chicken is almost cooked, about 7 minutes. Stir in peas and apricot preserves; simmer, covered, 2 to 3 minutes, just until chicken loses its pink color. Remove cinnamon sticks and serve warm.

* Swanson Natural Goodness with ⅓ less sodium is available.

·- Per Serving -·	
Calories:	432
Sodium:	517 mg
Fiber:	4 gm
Total fat:	4 gm
Saturated fat:	1 gm
Cholesterol:	62 mg
Cholesterol–saturated fat index:	4

East Indian Curry

The aroma while this curry dish is cooking is hard to beat. We like to serve this one over a heaping pile of steamed rice and offer a variety of condiments to sprinkle on top. It's a great party dish.

6 chicken breasts, skinned and boned
1 to 2 tablespoons water
1 tablespoon vegetable oil
1½ cups chopped onion
2 large cloves garlic, minced
1 cup chopped celery
1 large cucumber, peeled, seeded, and chopped
3½ cups peeled and chopped Granny Smith apples (about 3 apples)
1 can (14½ ounces) lower-salt chicken broth*
¼ cup flour
1 teaspoon nutmeg
1 teaspoon dry mustard
3 tablespoons curry powder (we like Sharwood's Mild)

1½ teaspoons (or less) Lite Salt
1 can (12 ounces) evaporated skim milk
¼ teaspoon coconut extract
2 tablespoons freshly squeezed lemon juice
   or ½ teaspoon tamarind paste dissolved in a small amount of water
1 cup finely chopped tomato
¼ cup chopped fresh parsley

Choice of condiments: Chopped green onions, raisins, and fruit chutney

Place chicken breasts in a single layer in a glass dish; add 1 to 2 tablespoons water and cover tightly with plastic wrap. Cook in microwave oven on high about 8 minutes or until chicken is no longer pink. Drain, cool, and cut into ³/₄-inch cubes. Set aside.

Heat oil in a large nonstick skillet. Add onions, garlic, celery, cucumber, and apples and sauté, while stirring constantly, until tender, about 5 minutes. Add 2 tablespoons of the chicken broth and all of the flour, nutmeg, mustard, and curry powder; stir constantly (a wire whisk works well) until mixture begins to thicken. Slowly add remaining chicken broth and Lite Salt. Bring the mixture to a boil, reduce heat to low, and cook for 1 hour, partially covered. Add evaporated milk, coconut extract, lemon juice, tomato, and cooked chicken cubes; simmer on low heat, stirring often, until heated through, about 15 minutes. Garnish with fresh parsley. Serve over hot steamed rice and pass the condiments.

— Per Cup —	
Calories:	210
Sodium:	435 mg
Fiber:	3 gm
Total fat:	5 gm
Saturated fat:	1 gm
Cholesterol:	37 mg
Cholesterol–saturated fat index:	3

* Swanson Natural Goodness with ⅓ less sodium is available.

Kung Pao Chicken

People love Kung Pao Chicken. This version has a new twist—it's low-fat!

Kung Pao Chicken Cooking Sauce
2 tablespoons lower-sodium soy
 sauce*
1 tablespoon white wine vinegar
1 tablespoon dry sherry
3/4 cup water
2 tablespoons sugar
2 tablespoons cornstarch

Marinade and Chicken
1 1/2 tablespoons dry sherry
1 tablespoon cornstarch
1/2 teaspoon (or less) Lite Salt
1/8 teaspoon white pepper
4 chicken breasts, skinned, boned,
 and cubed

1 tablespoon sesame oil, divided
4 to 6 small dried hot red chiles,
 sliced in half lengthwise
 (watch the amount, these can be
 spicy)
3 tablespoons unsalted peanuts, dry
 roasted
1 teaspoon minced garlic
1 teaspoon grated fresh gingerroot
6 green onions (including tops), cut
 into 1 1/2-inch lengths

Hot steamed rice

Combine soy sauce, vinegar, sherry, water, sugar, and cornstarch to make Cooking Sauce; set aside. In a separate bowl, prepare marinade by stirring together sherry, cornstarch, Lite Salt, and white pepper. Add cubed chicken and stir to coat. When ready to cook, place a wok over medium heat; when hot, add 1 1/2 teaspoons sesame oil. When oil is hot, add chiles and peanuts and stir until chiles just begin to char. *Be very careful not to let chiles turn black.* Remove peanuts and chiles from wok; set aside. Pour 1 1/2 teaspoons sesame oil into wok and increase heat to high. When oil begins to sizzle, add garlic and ginger, stir; add chicken and stir-fry 5 to 7 minutes. Add peanuts, chiles, and green onions. Add Cooking Sauce and continue stirring until sauce boils and thickens. Serve with hot steamed rice.

* Kikkoman Lite Soy Sauce is available.

⌐ Per Serving (Rice Not Included) ⌐	
Calories:	287
Sodium:	490 mg
Fiber:	1 gm
Total fat:	10 gm
Saturated fat:	2 gm
Cholesterol:	65 mg
Cholesterol–saturated fat index:	5

La Paz Chicken and Corn Stir-Fry

A colorful marinated chicken dish that goes together fairly quickly. The lightly flavored chicken is sautéed and served over stir-fried corn, peppers, and black beans. Try Fresh Tomato Salsa (page 36) as a side dish.

Marinated Chicken

4 chicken breast halves, skinned and boned
$^1/_4$ teaspoon (or less) Lite Salt
$^1/_4$ teaspoon pepper
$^1/_2$ teaspoon cumin
2 teaspoons olive oil
$^1/_4$ cup freshly squeezed lime juice
1 large clove garlic, minced

Stir-Fried Vegetables

1 bag (16 ounces) frozen corn
$^1/_2$ cup chopped green bell pepper
$^1/_2$ cup chopped red bell pepper
$^1/_4$ to $^1/_2$ teaspoon red pepper flakes
1 can (15 ounces) black beans, drained and rinsed*

$^1/_4$ cup sliced avocado
3 tablespoons chopped fresh cilantro

Forty-five minutes before mealtime, sprinkle chicken with Lite Salt, pepper, and cumin and rub into chicken. Combine olive oil, lime juice, and garlic; pour over chicken. Cover and refrigerate 30 minutes.

When ready to cook, remove chicken from marinade (save marinade). Place chicken in a nonstick skillet and sauté over medium heat, stirring often, 15 minutes or until lightly browned and chicken is done. Remove chicken and keep warm until serving time.

In the same skillet, heat marinade saved from the chicken. Add corn, bell peppers, and pepper flakes, stir and cook 3 to 4 minutes; add black beans. Simmer on low until beans are heated and vegetables cooked but crunchy. To serve, place corn-pepper mixture on a warm platter; top with avocado and cilantro. Slice chicken crosswise into thick slices and place around vegetables.

* S&W has a 50% Less Salt product available.

•~ Per Serving ~•	
Calories:	389
Sodium:	321 mg
Fiber:	11 gm
Total fat:	8 gm
Saturated fat:	2 gm
Cholesterol:	65 mg
Cholesterol–saturated fat index:	5

Sausage and Mushroom Spaghetti Torta

This dish can be served with any marinara sauce, but we prefer the Spicy Tomato Sauce.

3 cups Spicy Tomato Sauce
  (page 178)
  or 3 cups of your favorite marinara
  sauce
8 ounces uncooked spaghetti
4 ounces turkey or chicken Italian
  sausage
  or 8 ounces GardenSausage*
1 cup chopped onion
1¹/₂ cups sliced fresh mushrooms

¹/₄ cup sliced black olives
¹/₂ cup egg substitute
¹/₄ cup chopped fresh parsley
¹/₂ teaspoon (or less) Lite Salt
¹/₄ teaspoon pepper
1 cup grated Jarlsberg Lite Reduced
  Fat Swiss Cheese
¹/₄ cup grated Parmesan cheese

Prepare Spicy Tomato Sauce, if using, and set aside. Cook spaghetti in unsalted water according to package directions; drain well. Transfer cooked spaghetti to a large bowl and set aside.

Remove sausage from casing and discard casing. Crumble sausage into a nonstick skillet. *If using GardenSausage, crumble while cooking.* Sauté over medium heat until cooked, about 10 minutes. Transfer sausage to bowl with spaghetti. Add onion to skillet and sauté until tender, about 5 minutes (add water if necessary). Stir in mushrooms and sauté 5 minutes. Mix onions, mushrooms, and olives into spaghetti-sausage mixture along with egg substitute, parsley, Lite Salt, pepper, and cheeses. Toss to combine thoroughly.

Coat a 7-by-11-inch or 10-inch square baking dish with nonstick cooking spray. Turn the spaghetti mixture into baking dish. *The torta can be prepared a day ahead up to this point. Cover and refrigerate. Increase cooking time by 10 minutes if torta is chilled when placed in oven.* Preheat oven to 350°. Before baking torta, top with 3 cups Spicy Tomato Sauce or marinara sauce. Cover with foil (leave some room at the top so the sauce will not be crushed) and bake 35 to 40 minutes or until heated through. Remove from the oven and let stand 10 minutes. Cut into squares and serve.

* A frozen vegetable sausage by Wholesome and Hearty Foods.

·– Per Serving (with Turkey or Chicken Sausage and Sauce) –·	
Calories:	331
Sodium:	612 mg
Fiber:	4 gm
Total fat:	8 gm
Saturated fat:	3 gm
Cholesterol:	23 mg
Cholesterol–saturated fat index:	7

·– Per Serving (with GardenSausage and Sauce) –·	
Calories:	421
Sodium:	514 mg
Fiber:	10 gm
Total fat:	9 gm
Saturated fat:	4 gm
Cholesterol:	9 mg
Cholesterol–saturated fat index:	6

Savory Lemon Chicken

This chicken has a generous amount of tart lemon sauce that is delicious served over hot steamed rice.

Lemon Marinade
5 tablespoons freshly squeezed
  lemon juice
1 to 2 tablespoons Dijon-style
  mustard
2 cloves garlic, minced
1/4 teaspoon white pepper
1 tablespoon olive oil
1/4 cup water

6 chicken breasts, skinned and boned

Savory Lemon Sauce
Lemon Marinade (see above)
1 cup lower-salt chicken broth*

4 teaspoons cornstarch
2 tablespoons cold water
2 tablespoons lemon marmalade
  or 2 tablespoons orange
  marmalade and 1 tablespoon
  freshly squeezed lemon juice
1/8 to 1/4 teaspoon cayenne pepper

1/4 cup sliced almonds

Garnish
Lemon slices, cut in half
1/4 cup chopped fresh parsley

Hot steamed rice

Combine lemon juice, mustard, garlic, white pepper, oil, and water to make the Lemon Marinade. Place chicken breasts in a shallow dish; pour marinade over the chicken. Cover and refrigerate 1 to 2 hours. When ready to cook, preheat oven to 350°. Remove chicken from marinade (reserving marinade) and place in a baking dish that has been sprayed with nonstick cooking spray. Bake 20 to 30 minutes or until chicken is no longer pink inside.

Meanwhile, prepare the Savory Lemon Sauce by combining reserved marinade and chicken broth in saucepan and bringing to a boil. In small bowl, dissolve cornstarch in water, add to broth mixture, and cook over medium heat until slightly thickened, stirring constantly. Add marmalade and cayenne pepper and stir until well combined.

Remove chicken from the oven and cover with the sauce. Sprinkle with sliced almonds and bake an additional 10 minutes. Garnish with lemon slices and parsley. Serve with hot steamed rice.

Per Serving (Rice Not Included)	
Calories:	219
Sodium:	222 mg
Fiber:	1 gm
Total fat:	8 gm
Saturated fat:	2 gm
Cholesterol:	66 mg
Cholesterol–saturated fat index:	5

* Swanson Natural Goodness with 1/3 less sodium is available.

South-of-the-Border Casserole ·~ *Makes 4 servings.*

An easily prepared casserole that looks and tastes great. It's a good one to make when you have leftover chicken or turkey.

3 (6-inch) corn tortillas, each cut into 6 wedges
1 cup cubed cooked chicken breast
1 cup frozen whole-kernel corn
1 cup black beans, drained and rinsed*
1 cup canned S&W Salsa with Cilantro
$1/4$ teaspoon (or less) Lite Salt
$1^1/2$ cups finely diced tomato
3 tablespoons nonfat sour cream
3 tablespoons chopped fresh cilantro
$1/2$ cup grated low-fat Jack cheese

1 jalapeño pepper, thinly sliced
2 tablespoons chopped fresh cilantro
$1/4$ cup chopped tomato
2 tablespoons sliced black olives

Optional
Nonfat sour cream
Salsa (you can use the rest of the canned salsa)

Preheat oven to 350°. Spray an $8^1/2$-by-11-inch baking dish with nonstick cooking spray. Place tortilla wedges in the bottom of the dish. In a separate bowl, combine chicken, corn, black beans, salsa, Lite Salt, tomatoes, sour cream, cilantro, and cheese. Place mixture in baking dish on top of tortilla wedges. Bake, uncovered, 20 to 30 minutes. Sprinkle jalapeño pepper, cilantro, tomato, and olives on top of casserole. Serve with sour cream and salsa, if desired.

* S&W has a 50% Less Salt product available.

·~ Per Serving ~·	
Calories:	281
Sodium:	523 mg
Fiber:	7 gm
Total fat:	5 gm
Saturated fat:	2 gm
Cholesterol:	34 mg
Cholesterol–saturated fat index:	4

Spicy Sesame Linguine with Chicken

•⁓ Makes 8 servings.

Select a colorful platter or bowl to set off this dish. Sliced tomatoes make a nice accompaniment.

1 can (14½ ounces) lower-salt
   chicken broth *
1 cup water
4 chicken breasts, skinned and boned

1 teaspoon sesame oil
1¼ cups chopped green onions
8 cloves garlic, minced
2 tablespoons grated fresh gingerroot
¼ to ½ teaspoon red pepper flakes
3½ tablespoons sugar

3 tablespoons rice vinegar
3 tablespoons lower-sodium soy
   sauce †
2 tablespoons tahini ‡
16 ounces uncooked linguine, broken
   in half
1 small English cucumber, thinly sliced
   and cut in half

2 teaspoons toasted sesame seeds
¼ cup chopped green onions

In a large skillet, bring chicken broth and water to a boil. Add chicken breasts, reduce heat to low, cover and simmer for 7 to 8 minutes, or until the chicken is cooked. Remove from broth and cut into ½-by-3-inch slices. Reserve 1½ cups of the chicken broth.

In a nonstick skillet, heat sesame oil over medium heat. Add green onions, garlic, ginger, and pepper flakes; sauté 2 to 3 minutes. Add the reserved chicken broth, sugar, vinegar, soy sauce, and tahini. Bring to a boil and cook for 5 minutes, stirring constantly, until well combined. Meanwhile, cook linguine in unsalted water according to package directions. Drain and return to pan. Pour the tahini mixture over the linguine and toss to coat. Place on a shallow serving platter. Top with chicken and cucumber slices. Sprinkle with sesame seeds and remaining green onions. Serve warm or at room temperature.

* Swanson Natural Goodness with ⅓ less sodium is available.
† Kikkoman Lite Soy Sauce is available.
‡ Tahini (sesame seed butter) is available in most supermarkets.

•⁓ Per Serving ⁓	
Calories:	372
Sodium:	411 mg
Fiber:	3 gm
Total fat:	6 gm
Saturated fat:	1 gm
Cholesterol:	33 mg
Cholesterol–saturated fat index:	3

Desserts

Bars

Apricot Bars
Frosted Hazelnut Coffee Bars
Lazy Daisy Bars
Mocha Squares
Paula's Date Nut Bars
Raisin Spice Bars with Lemon Glaze

Cakes

Apple Cheesecake Torte
Apricot and Pineapple Downside-Up Cake
Chocolate Cherry Cheesecake
Devil's Food Cake
Devil's Frosting
Dorothy's Lemon Sponge Cake with Glazed Berry Topping
Fresh Ginger Cake
Million Dollar Torte
Peach Streusel Cake
Pumpkin Cheesecake with Chocolate Crumb Crust
Roxy Road Cheesecake
Tiramisù
Whiskey Cake

Candy

Best Ever Divinity
Espresso Almond Brittle
Peanut Brittle Thin as Glass

Cookies

Cardamom Holiday Cookies
Chocolate Lovers' Cookies
Chocolate Mint Cookies
Italian Biscotti
Oat Chip Cookies
Ranger Cookies
Soft Ginger Cookies
Soft Lemon Cookies

Frozen Desserts

Chocolate Chip Mint Ice Milk
Chocolate Sorbet
Creamy Chocolate Ice Milk
Frozen Maple Yogurt
Frozen Yogurt Sandwiches
Fruit Cassis Sorbet
Grapefruit Tequila Sorbet
Lemon Gelati
Mandarin Orange and Pineapple Sherbet
Quick Fruit Sherbets
Vanilla Frozen Yogurt

Fruit

Baked Pears with Sherry Sauce
Berry Rhubarb Crisp
Cranberry Orange Crisp
Fabulous Fruit Tart
Fruit Trifle
Summer Fruit on Lemonade Squares
Summer Pudding
Three Berry Cobbler

Apricot Bars

¹/₂ cup margarine, softened
¹/₂ cup sugar
¹/₄ cup brown sugar
2 cups flour

¹/₄ teaspoon baking soda
1 cup apricot preserves
1 tablespoon freshly squeezed lemon
   juice

Preheat oven to 350°. Spray a 9-inch square baking pan with nonstick cooking spray. In a mixing bowl, cream margarine and sugars. Stir in flour and baking soda and mix until crumbly. Set aside 1 cup of the crumb mixture.

Press remaining crumb mixture into prepared pan. In a separate bowl, combine apricot preserves and lemon juice and spread over crumbs in pan. Sprinkle 1 cup crumbs evenly on top. Bake 35 to 40 minutes or until lightly browned. Cool completely before cutting into bars.

· Per Bar ·	
Calories:	172
Sodium:	94 mg
Fiber:	1 gm
Total fat:	5 gm
Saturated fat:	1 gm
Cholesterol:	0 mg
Cholesterol–saturated fat index:	1

Frosted Hazelnut Coffee Bars   *- Makes 24 bars.*

*These dessert bars are a great way to show off the official nut of Oregon—hazelnuts
(also known as filberts).*

Bars
1/4 cup margarine, softened
1/2 cup brown sugar
1/2 cup strong hot brewed coffee
1 1/2 cups flour
1 teaspoon baking powder
1/4 teaspoon baking soda
1/4 teaspoon (or less) Lite Salt
1 teaspoon cinnamon

1/2 cup golden raisins
   (optional)
1/4 cup chopped hazelnuts

Coffee Frosting
2/3 cup powdered sugar
1/2 teaspoon vanilla
1 tablespoon brewed coffee (does
   not need to be hot)

Preheat oven to 350°. Spray a 9-by-13-inch baking pan with nonstick cooking spray. In a large bowl, cream margarine and brown sugar. Add 1/2 cup hot coffee, flour, baking powder, baking soda, Lite Salt, and cinnamon; blend. Stir in raisins, if using, and nuts. Spread batter into prepared pan. Bake 20 minutes. Cool.

When bars are cool, prepare frosting. Mix together powdered sugar, vanilla, and 1 tablespoon coffee until smooth. Spread over cooled dessert and cut into bars.

- Per Frosted Bar -	
Calories:	84
Sodium:	71 mg
Fiber:	Trace gm
Total fat:	3 gm
Saturated fat:	Trace gm
Cholesterol:	0 mg
Cholesterol–saturated fat index:	Trace

Lazy Daisy Bars

A sweet, light bar with a delicious topping that is toasted under the broiler.

Cake
1¼ cups boiling water
1 cup uncooked oatmeal
½ cup margarine
½ cup sugar
½ cup brown sugar
½ cup egg substitute
   or 3 egg whites
1 teaspoon vanilla
1½ cups flour
½ teaspoon (or less) Lite Salt

½ teaspoon baking soda
1 teaspoon cinnamon

Lazy Daisy Topping
3 tablespoons margarine, melted
½ cup brown sugar
¼ cup evaporated skim milk
1 teaspoon vanilla
½ cup uncooked oatmeal

To prepare Cake: Pour boiling water over oatmeal. Let sit 10 minutes. Preheat oven to 350°. Spray an 11-by-15-inch baking pan with nonstick cooking spray. In a mixing bowl, cream margarine and sugars. Add egg substitute or whites and vanilla; blend well. Add soaked oatmeal. Blend in flour, Lite Salt, baking soda, and cinnamon. Pour into prepared pan. Bake 20 to 25 minutes or until a wooden pick inserted in the center comes out clean.

   Near the end of the baking time, prepare Lazy Daisy Topping: Combine melted margarine and brown sugar. Add milk, vanilla, and oatmeal. Spread evenly on top of warm cake. Place under broiler until nicely browned, about 2 to 3 minutes (watch carefully). Cut into bars.

⁓ Per Bar ⁓	
Calories:	120
Sodium:	105 mg
Fiber:	1 gm
Total fat:	5 gm
Saturated fat:	1 gm
Cholesterol:	Trace mg
Cholesterol–saturated fat index:	1

Mocha Squares

²/₃ cup brown sugar

3 tablespoons margarine

1 tablespoon instant coffee granules

2 teaspoons vanilla

¹/₂ cup egg substitute

1 cup flour

1 teaspoon baking powder

¹/₄ cup mini semisweet chocolate
chips

Preheat oven to 350°. Combine sugar, margarine, and coffee granules in a small saucepan. Place over low heat; cook and stir until margarine melts. In a separate bowl, combine sugar-coffee mixture, vanilla, and egg substitute. Beat until smooth.

Add flour and baking powder to creamed mixture; beat well. Stir in chocolate chips. Spread in an 8-inch square baking pan that has been coated with nonstick cooking spray. Bake 10 to 15 minutes or just until wooden pick inserted in the center comes out clean (be careful not to overbake). Let cool in pan and cut into bars.

~ Per Bar ~	
Calories:	99
Sodium:	74 mg
Fiber:	1 gm
Total fat:	3 gm
Saturated fat:	1 gm
Cholesterol:	0 mg
Cholesterol–saturated fat index:	1

Paula's Date Nut Bars

How lucky we were to get this tasty recipe from Paula, who is a marvelous cook. She was a little dubious about our ability to alter it for lower fat and still have a delicious bar, but she was pleasantly surprised with our results.

1 pound pitted dates, chopped	1/4 teaspoon ground cloves
1/4 cup margarine	1 1/2 cups white flour
1/2 cup brown sugar	1/2 cup whole wheat flour
1 cup water	2 teaspoons baking powder
1 teaspoon vanilla	1/4 cup chopped walnuts
1 teaspoon cinnamon	
1/2 teaspoon nutmeg	2 teaspoons powdered sugar

Combine dates, margarine, brown sugar, and water in saucepan and simmer on low heat for about 5 minutes. Cool.

Preheat oven to 325°. To the cooled date mixture, add vanilla, cinnamon, nutmeg, cloves, flours, and baking powder. When well mixed, stir in chopped nuts. Spread in an 8-inch square baking pan that has been sprayed with nonstick cooking spray. Bake for 30 minutes or until a wooden pick inserted in the center comes out clean. Cool. Sprinkle powdered sugar over top and cut into squares to serve.

~ Per Square ~	
Calories:	133
Sodium:	69 mg
Fiber:	1 gm
Total fat:	3 gm
Saturated fat:	Trace gm
Cholesterol:	0 mg
Cholesterol–saturated fat index:	Trace

Raisin Spice Bars with Lemon Glaze

1 cup raisins
2 cups water
1/4 cup margarine
3/4 cup sugar
1 cup whole wheat flour
3/4 cup white flour
1 teaspoon baking soda
1 teaspoon cinnamon
1 teaspoon nutmeg
1/4 cup chopped walnuts

Lemon Glaze
1/2 cup powdered sugar
3 tablespoons freshly squeezed
  lemon juice
1/2 teaspoon freshly grated
  lemon peel

Preheat oven to 350°. Boil raisins in 2 cups water for 10 minutes. Remove from heat (do not drain liquid). Add margarine and stir to melt. Cool. In a separate bowl, mix together sugar, flours, baking soda, cinnamon, and nutmeg. Add raisin mixture to dry ingredients. Stir in nuts. Spread batter into a 9-by-13-inch baking pan that has been sprayed with nonstick cooking spray. Bake for 20 to 25 minutes, just until a wooden pick inserted in the center comes out clean. Do not overbake.

To prepare Lemon Glaze: Combine powdered sugar, lemon juice, and lemon peel. Pour over raisin spice bars while they are still warm. Let cool, cut into bars, and serve.

⏤ Per Bar ⏤	
Calories:	83
Sodium:	60 mg
Fiber:	1 gm
Total fat:	2 gm
Saturated fat:	Trace gm
Cholesterol:	0 mg
Cholesterol–saturated fat index:	Trace

Apple Cheesecake Torte

$^1/_4$ cup margarine

$^3/_4$ cup sugar, divided

1 teaspoon vanilla

1 cup flour

8 ounces fat-free cream cheese

$^1/_4$ cup egg substitute

$^1/_2$ cup raisins

1 teaspoon cinnamon

$^1/_2$ teaspoon grated lemon peel

2 cups sliced Granny Smith apples

($^1/_4$ inch thick)

Preheat oven to 350°. In a medium mixing bowl, beat margarine, $^1/_4$ cup sugar, and vanilla until light and fluffy. Add flour; stir until well combined. Spread over bottom and 1$^1/_2$ inches up the sides of a 9-inch springform pan. Bake 20 minutes.

In another bowl, beat cream cheese, $^1/_4$ cup sugar, and egg substitute until smooth. Spread over crust; top with raisins. Mix remaining $^1/_4$ cup sugar, cinnamon, lemon peel, and apples. Arrange apples in a circular pattern, overlapping them slightly, on top of raisins. Bake 40 minutes or until filling is set in the center (does not jiggle when pan is shaken). Cool at least 30 minutes before serving. Remove rim of pan and cut into wedges.

Per Serving	
Calories:	170
Sodium:	173 mg
Fiber:	1 gm
Total fat:	4 gm
Saturated fat:	1 gm
Cholesterol:	Trace mg
Cholesterol–saturated fat index:	1

Apricot and Pineapple Downside-Up Cake

When made in a round pan, this pretty cake looks like a pinwheel.

1 tablespoon margarine

1/3 cup brown sugar

5 slices fresh pineapple, 1/4 inch thick,
    or 5 slices juice-packed pineapple

14 dried apricot halves

3 tablespoons margarine

1/2 cup sugar

3 egg whites

1 teaspoon vanilla

1/2 cup white flour

1/2 cup whole wheat flour

1 1/4 teaspoons baking powder

1/3 cup water

Preheat oven to 350°. Spray a 9-inch round or square baking pan with nonstick cooking spray. Combine 1 tablespoon margarine and brown sugar and press onto the bottom of the pan. Cut 4 pineapple rings in half and arrange on top of the sugar mixture. Add 12 dried apricot halves, smooth side down. Finely chop the remaining pineapple and apricots and set aside.

Cream together 3 tablespoons margarine and sugar until light and fluffy. Beat in egg whites and vanilla. Add flours and baking powder alternately with the water. Fold in the chopped pineapple and apricots and stir just until mixed. Pour batter over the fruit and bake 30 minutes or until a wooden pick inserted in the center comes out clean.

Let the cake cool only 5 minutes (or you won't be able to get it out of the pan in one piece). Invert it onto a cake plate. Cut into wedges or squares and serve warm.

~ Per Serving ~	
Calories:	209
Sodium:	159 mg
Fiber:	2 gm
Total fat:	5 gm
Saturated fat:	1 gm
Cholesterol:	0 mg
Cholesterol–saturated fat index:	1

Chocolate Cherry Cheesecake ·- Makes 12 servings.

A cheesecake with a chocolate crust and cherries on the top. A new version of the popular cherry cheesecake from the 1960s.

Chocolate Graham Cracker Crust
1¹/2 cups chocolate graham cracker
    crumbs (1 package of 11 crackers)
2 tablespoons honey
2 tablespoons vegetable oil

Cheesecake
2 packages (8 ounces each) fat-free
    cream cheese, softened
¹/2 cup sugar
2 egg whites
    or ¹/4 cup egg substitute
1 tablespoon amaretto
    or 1 teaspoon almond extract

Topping
1 can (20 ounces) cherry pie filling

To prepare Chocolate Graham Cracker Crust: It's important to use the designated size of pan for the cheesecake baking time to be correct. Preheat oven to 350°. Prepare graham cracker crumbs by crushing with a rolling pin or using a blender or food processor. Combine graham cracker crumbs, honey, and oil in bowl. Mix well. Press crumbs firmly into bottom of 9-inch springform pan. Bake 15 minutes. Remove from oven. Cool to room temperature before adding filling.

To prepare Cheesecake: When crust has cooled, heat oven to 325°. In large mixing bowl, beat cream cheese until fluffy. Beat in sugar gradually and add egg whites or egg substitute. Add amaretto or almond extract and beat until well blended. Pour over crust. Bake 40 minutes. Cool completely; top with cherry pie filling, cover with plastic wrap, and refrigerate 12 hours or overnight. Before serving, remove rim of springform pan and place cheesecake on a serving platter.

·- Per Serving ·-	
Calories:	188
Sodium:	303 mg
Fiber:	1 gm
Total fat:	4 gm
Saturated fat:	1 gm
Cholesterol:	1 mg
Cholesterol—saturated fat index:	1

Devil's Food Cake

This cake is good with or without frosting. Devil's Frosting (page 293) is wonderful to add for special occasions.

¹/₄ cup margarine	¹/₂ teaspoon (or less) Lite Salt
¹/₂ cup sugar	1 teaspoon baking soda
¹/₂ cup maple syrup	1 teaspoon baking powder
¹/₂ cup egg substitute	¹/₄ cup unsweetened cocoa powder
1¹/₂ cups flour	²/₃ cup buttermilk

Preheat oven to 350°. Cream margarine and sugar. Add syrup and egg substitute. Beat well. Combine flour, Lite Salt, baking soda, baking powder, and cocoa powder; add to batter alternately with buttermilk. *Mix well* and pour into a 9-by-13-inch baking dish that has been sprayed with nonstick cooking spray. Bake for 20 to 25 minutes or until a wooden pick inserted in the center comes out clean. If icing is to be added, cool cake thoroughly before frosting it.

~ Per Serving of Unfrosted Cake ~	
Calories:	137
Sodium:	214 mg
Fiber:	1 gm
Total fat:	3 gm
Saturated fat:	1 gm
Cholesterol:	Trace mg
Cholesterol–saturated fat index:	1

Devil's Frosting

A dark, rich cocoa frosting that tastes as good as it looks. We seldom frost cakes, but if you wish to make a special occasion treat, you will be happy with the results. This is especially good on Devil's Food Cake *(page 292).*

¹/₃ cup unsweetened cocoa powder	¹/₂ cup skim milk
¹/₂ cup sugar	¹/₄ teaspoon vanilla
2¹/₂ tablespoons cornstarch	

In a small saucepan, combine cocoa powder and sugar. In a small bowl, mix cornstarch and milk until well blended. Stir cornstarch mixture into cocoa mixture (a whisk works well). Cook over medium heat, stirring constantly until glossy and thick, about 5 minutes. Remove from heat; add vanilla and beat to remove any lumps. Stir occasionally while cooling completely. Frost cake when cool.

⁓ Per 2¹/₂ Teaspoons	
(the Amount on ¹/₁₅ th of a Cake) ⁓	
Calories:	38
Sodium:	5 mg
Fiber:	1 gm
Total fat:	Trace gm
Saturated fat:	Trace gm
Cholesterol:	Trace mg
Cholesterol–saturated fat index:	Trace

Dorothy's Lemon Sponge Cake with Glazed Berry Topping

This cake is the ultimate in quick cooking. Sonja got the cake part of this recipe from her mother when attending an all-school reunion in the town of her childhood in western Kansas—where Dorothy is from! The cake makes a great base to top with fruit.

Cake

1 package (1 pound) angel food
    cake mix
1 can (21 ounces) lemon pie filling
1 tablespoon freshly squeezed
    lemon juice
1 1/2 teaspoons grated lemon rind
    (optional)

Glazed Fruit

1/2 cup currant or raspberry jelly
1 tablespoon crème de cassis liqueur
    (optional)
6 cups fresh or frozen, thawed and
    drained berries (blueberries,
    blackberries, strawberries)
Mint sprigs for garnish

Preheat oven to 350°. Combine dry cake mix, pie filling, lemon juice, and lemon rind; mix until smooth. Spray a 9-by-13-inch pan or two 8-inch round cake pans with nonstick cooking spray. Put batter into pan and bake 18 to 20 minutes. Cool and cut into 16 pieces.

Heat jelly in a saucepan over medium heat until melted. Simmer 2 to 3 minutes. Do not boil. Remove from heat and stir in liqueur, if using. Let glaze cool 2 to 3 minutes and then add the berries. Stir to coat.

To serve: Place pieces of cake on a dessert plate. Spoon a generous 1/3 cup of fruit over the top. Garnish with a mint sprig, if desired.

~ Per Serving ~	
Calories:	190
Sodium:	195 mg
Fiber:	3 gm
Total fat:	Trace gm
Saturated fat:	Trace gm
Cholesterol:	0 mg
Cholesterol–saturated fat index:	Trace

Fresh Ginger Cake

How does warm gingerbread topped with lemon yogurt sound? Be sure to use fresh gingerroot for the grated ginger.

1/2 cup whole wheat flour
3/4 cup white flour
1 teaspoon baking soda
1/2 teaspoon cinnamon
1/4 teaspoon (or less) Lite Salt
1/8 teaspoon pepper (we do mean pepper)
1 tablespoon grated fresh lemon peel
1 heaping tablespoon finely grated fresh gingerroot*

2/3 cup brown sugar
1/4 cup margarine, softened
1/4 cup egg substitute
1/2 cup cold brewed coffee
1/4 cup dark molasses

2 teaspoons powdered sugar for topping
Nonfat lemon yogurt, if desired

Preheat oven to 350°. Spray an 8-inch square baking pan with nonstick cooking spray. Mix together flours, baking soda, cinnamon, Lite Salt, and pepper; set aside. In a mixing bowl, cream lemon peel, ginger, brown sugar, and margarine. Add egg substitute, coffee, and molasses and mix well. Add flour mixture and stir just until moistened. Pour batter into pan. Bake 30 minutes or until a wooden pick inserted in the center comes out clean. Cool slightly. Sift powdered sugar over the top. Serve warm or at room temperature. Lemon yogurt over the top is delicious.

* To make grating easier, freeze gingerroot first. There is no need to peel it.

Per Serving	
Calories:	198
Sodium:	255 mg
Fiber:	1 gm
Total fat:	5 gm
Saturated fat:	1 gm
Cholesterol:	0 mg
Cholesterol–saturated fat index:	1

Million Dollar Torte

A wonderful chocolate treat served with a colorful berry sauce.

Filling
1/4 cup cocoa powder

1/3 cup fat-free sweetened condensed milk (not evaporated)

Cake
1 package (18 1/4-ounce) light devil's food cake mix

1 1/2 teaspoons cinnamon

1/3 cup sweetened applesauce

1 can (16 ounces) juice-packed sliced pears, drained

1/2 cup egg substitute

2 teaspoons water

Sauce
1 cup raspberries or strawberries (fresh or frozen)

1 1/2 tablespoons (or less) sugar

1 1/2 tablespoons crème de cassis *or* 1 1/2 tablespoons freshly squeezed lemon juice

Nonfat vanilla frozen yogurt (optional)

Preheat oven to 350°.

To prepare Filling: In a small bowl, gradually add cocoa powder to condensed milk, stirring until dissolved; set aside.

To prepare Cake: In a large bowl, combine dry cake mix, cinnamon, and applesauce; mix at low speed for 20 to 30 seconds or until crumbly (mixture will be dry). Put 1 cup of this mixture in a small bowl and set aside.

Place pears in a blender or food processor and purée until smooth. Add puréed pears and egg substitute to the large bowl of cake mixture; beat at low speed until moistened, then at medium speed another 2 minutes. Spread batter evenly into 9-inch springform pan that has been coated with nonstick cooking spray. Drop filling by spoonfuls over batter. Stir the 2 teaspoons water into the 1 cup of reserved cake mix. Drop by spoonfuls over filling. Bake 45 to 50 minutes or until top springs back when touched lightly in center. Cool 10 minutes; remove side of pan. Put onto a cooling rack and let cool another 45 minutes. Cover with plastic wrap until serving.

To prepare Sauce: Stem, wash, and drain fresh berries (or thaw frozen berries). Put in a blender or food processor and purée until smooth (or push berries through a food mill). Add sugar and crème de cassis or lemon juice and stir.

To serve: Cut torte into 12 wedges. Spoon 1 tablespoon sauce onto each serving plate; top with wedge of torte. If desired, serve with nonfat vanilla frozen yogurt.

·~ Per Serving ~·	
Calories:	236
Sodium:	353 mg
Fiber:	3 gm
Total fat:	3 gm
Saturated fat:	1 gm
Cholesterol:	1 mg
Cholesterol–saturated fat index:	1

Peach Streusel Cake

This cake is well liked because it isn't too sweet, yet it's moist and has lots of flavor. The glaze is optional, but it is quickly prepared and makes the cake look quite fancy.

1/4 cup margarine	*Streusel Topping*
3/4 cup sugar	1/2 cup brown sugar
2 tablespoons egg substitute	2 teaspoons margarine, softened
1 1/2 cups flour	1 teaspoon cinnamon
1 teaspoon baking powder	
1/2 cup skim milk	*Glaze (optional)*
2 egg whites	1/4 cup powdered sugar
2 fresh peaches, sliced into wedges,	1 teaspoon skim milk
or 1 can (14 ounces) sliced	1/4 teaspoon vanilla
peaches, drained	

Spray a 9-inch square baking pan or springform pan with nonstick cooking spray. Preheat oven to 350°. In a large bowl, cream margarine, sugar, and egg substitute. Combine flour and baking powder and add to margarine mixture alternately with milk. In a separate bowl, beat egg whites until stiff and carefully fold into batter. Pour batter into prepared pan and arrange peach wedges over the top.

Combine Streusel Topping ingredients; mix with a fork until crumbly and sprinkle over peaches. Bake 35 to 45 minutes or until a wooden toothpick inserted in the center comes out clean. Cool.

Combine glaze ingredients, if using; mix until smooth and drizzle over cool cake.

⸾ Per Serving (Without Glaze) ⸾	
Calories:	199
Sodium:	122 mg
Fiber:	1 gm
Total fat:	5 gm
Saturated fat:	1 gm
Cholesterol:	Trace mg
Cholesterol—saturated fat index:	1

Pumpkin Cheesecake with Chocolate Crumb Crust

The chocolate crumb crust makes this a true winner. We've given you a choice of two toppings, both delicious.

Chocolate Graham Cracker Crust

1 1/2 cups chocolate graham cracker crumbs (1 package of 11 crackers)

2 tablespoons honey

2 tablespoons vegetable oil

Pumpkin Cheesecake

3 packages (8 ounces each) fat-free cream cheese, softened

1/2 cup sugar

1/4 cup brown sugar

1 can (16 ounces) pumpkin

3 egg whites

2/3 cup evaporated skim milk

2 tablespoons cornstarch

1 1/4 teaspoons cinnamon

1/2 teaspoon nutmeg

1/2 teaspoon ground ginger

1/8 teaspoon ground cloves

EITHER

Sour Cream Topping

2 cups nonfat sour cream (we prefer the Land O' Lakes brand)

1/4 cup sugar

1 teaspoon vanilla

OR

Walnut Topping

2 tablespoons brown sugar

2 tablespoons chopped walnuts

1 teaspoon vegetable oil

To prepare Chocolate Graham Cracker Crust: It's important to use the designated size of pan for the cheesecake baking time to be correct. Preheat oven to 350°. Prepare graham cracker crumbs by crushing with a rolling pin or using a blender or food processor. Combine graham cracker crumbs, honey, and oil in a bowl. Mix well. Press onto the bottom of a 9-inch springform pan. Bake 15 minutes. Remove from oven; cool.

To prepare Pumpkin Cheesecake: Preheat oven to 350°. Beat cream cheese and sugars in a large mixing bowl until fluffy. Beat in pumpkin, egg whites, and evaporated milk. Add cornstarch, cinnamon, nutmeg, ginger, and cloves; beat well. Pour over crust. Bake 1 hour and 15 minutes. *Choose either Sour Cream or Walnut Topping.*

To prepare Sour Cream Topping: While cheesecake is baking, combine sour cream, sugar, and vanilla in small bowl. Remove cheesecake from the oven and spread sour cream mixture over the surface of the warm cheesecake. Return to the oven and bake 5 minutes. Cool on wire rack. Chill several hours or overnight.

To prepare Walnut Topping: While cheesecake is baking, combine brown sugar, walnuts, and oil. Remove cheesecake from the oven and sprinkle with topping. Return to the oven and bake 10 minutes. Cool on wire rack. Chill several hours or overnight.

Per Serving (with Sour Cream Topping)	
Calories:	245
Sodium:	472 mg
Fiber:	1 gm
Total fat:	4 gm
Saturated fat:	1 gm
Cholesterol:	2 mg
Cholesterol–saturated fat index:	1

Roxy Road Cheesecake

This is a world-class chocolate mocha treat. By using a small amount of mini chocolate chips, this recipe remains low-fat. The name comes from a young woman in our office who has helped us with many low-fat recipes—this is one of her favorites.

Chocolate Graham Cracker Crust
1¹/₂ cups chocolate graham cracker
   crumbs (1 package of 11 crackers)
2 tablespoons honey
2 tablespoons vegetable oil

Roxy Road Cheesecake
3 packages (8 ounces each) fat-free
   cream cheese, softened

1 cup sugar
³/₄ cup egg substitute
¹/₃ cup skim milk
2 teaspoons instant coffee *or*
   espresso granules
1 teaspoon vanilla extract
¹/₄ cup mini chocolate chips

To prepare Chocolate Graham Cracker Crust: It's important to use the designated size of pan for the cheesecake baking time to be correct. Preheat oven to 350°. Prepare graham cracker crumbs by crushing with a rolling pin or using a blender or food processor. Combine graham cracker crumbs, honey, and oil in bowl. Mix well. *Save 2 tablespoons for later use* and press remaining crumbs firmly onto the bottom of a 9-inch springform pan. Bake 15 minutes. Remove from oven. Cool completely before adding the filling.

To prepare Cheesecake: When crust has cooled, preheat oven to 250°. In a large mixing bowl, beat cream cheese until fluffy. Beat in sugar gradually and add egg substitute. Add milk, coffee granules, and vanilla and beat until well blended. Swirl chocolate chips into cheesecake mixture with spatula. Pour over crust. Set pan on a baking sheet. Bake 1¹/₂ hours. Cool completely; cover with plastic wrap and refrigerate 12 hours or overnight. Before serving, remove rim of pan and press the remaining chocolate crumbs onto sides. Serve chilled.

⁓ Per Serving ⁓	
Calories:	212
Sodium:	431 mg
Fiber:	1 gm
Total fat:	5 gm
Saturated fat:	1 gm
Cholesterol:	1 mg
Cholesterol–saturated fat index:	1

Tiramisù

Tiramisù is an Italian "pick me up" dessert, but we think it means WONDERFUL. This dessert is not low-fat if you eat the other half of the candy bar! Prepare it beforehand so it has time to chill 8 hours.

1/2 cup extra-strong coffee, cooled	2 tablespoons cold water
4 tablespoons brandy, divided	1/8 teaspoon cream of tartar
6 ounces soft ladyfingers	1/4 cup nonfat sour cream
(24 ladyfingers)	4 ounces light cream cheese
2 large egg whites	1/2 Hershey chocolate bar
3/4 cup sugar	(1.55 ounces)

In a small bowl, combine the coffee and 3 tablespoons of brandy. Cut each ladyfinger in half. Lay the ladyfinger halves, flat-side-up, in a single layer on baking sheets. Brush the flat side with the coffee-brandy mixture. Set aside.

In the bottom pan of a double boiler, bring about 1 inch of water to a boil and reduce heat to simmer. In the top of the double boiler, combine egg whites, sugar, water, and cream of tartar. Beat at low speed until a candy thermometer reads 140° (about 4 to 5 minutes). Increase mixer speed to high and continue beating for 3 minutes, or until the mixture forms a ribbon trail. Remove the top of the double boiler from the heat and beat about 4 minutes, or until cool and fluffy. Set aside.

In a large bowl, beat sour cream and cream cheese until smooth. Add about 1/2 cup of the beaten egg white mixture and the remaining tablespoon of brandy and beat until smooth. *Gently* fold in the remaining egg white mixture.

Lay 12 split ladyfingers flat-side-down in a rectangle (6 ladyfingers long and 2 ladyfingers wide) on a serving plate. Spread 1/3 of the cream cheese mixture evenly over the top. Repeat to make 3 layers; top with ladyfingers. Sprinkle grated chocolate on the top and sides. Refrigerate 8 hours or overnight. Cut into squares and serve cold.

~ Per Serving ~	
Calories:	203
Sodium:	113 mg
Fiber:	Trace gm
Total fat:	4 gm
Saturated fat:	2 gm
Cholesterol:	40 mg
Cholesterol–saturated fat index:	4

Whiskey Cake

This is a very moist cake that requires no frosting and keeps very well for several days. It is a family favorite of one of our staff members; it has undergone some major revisions to make it low-fat. At holiday time, red and green cherries make it very festive.

1/2 cup fat-free margarine

7 egg whites

1 package (18 1/4 ounces) light yellow cake mix

1 package (3 ounces) vanilla pudding (not instant)

1/4 teaspoon baking soda

3/4 cup bourbon
  or 3/4 cup apple juice or 1/4 cup bourbon *and* 1/2 cup apple juice

1/2 cup maraschino cherries, cut in half

1/2 cup chocolate chips

1/2 cup chopped walnuts

Preheat oven to 350°. Cream margarine to soften. Add egg whites one at a time. Add dry cake mix, dry pudding mix, baking soda, and bourbon or juice and mix well. Fold in cherries, chocolate chips, and nuts. Spray a Bundt pan with nonstick cooking spray and pour batter into it. Bake 50 minutes or until a wooden pick inserted near the center comes out clean. Cool 10 minutes in pan and invert onto cooling rack. Cool before slicing.

~ Per Serving ~	
Calories:	166
Sodium:	233 mg
Fiber:	1 gm
Total fat:	4 gm
Saturated fat:	1 gm
Cholesterol:	0 mg
Cholesterol–saturated fat index:	1

Best Ever Divinity

Candymaking is more fun when done with friends. A group of us has made this a tradition at holiday time for 15 years. Here is one of our favorites and, as you can see, these delicious morsels are very low in fat. We have been known to blame it on the "weather" if it does not turn out perfect! Take the plunge and buy a candy thermometer. You really need one to make candy.

2²/₃ cups sugar	2 egg whites
²/₃ cup light corn syrup	1 teaspoon vanilla
¹/₂ cup water (use 1 tablespoon less on humid days)	²/₃ cup chopped walnuts

Combine sugar, corn syrup, and water in a thin-sided 2-quart pan. Stir, while heating to dissolve sugar, until mixture comes to a boil. Cook, without stirring, to 260°. Meanwhile, in a mixing bowl, beat egg whites until stiff peaks form. Continue beating while pouring hot syrup in a thin stream into egg whites. Add vanilla; beat until mixture holds its shape and becomes slightly dull. Mixture may become too stiff for mixer. If this happens, beat by hand. Fold in nuts. Drop mixture from tip of greased spoon onto waxed paper. *Have each person use 2 greased teaspoons to do this job.* Work fast at this point as it will set up quickly. Cool on waxed paper for a short time and store in airtight containers.

⤳ Per Candy ⤳	
Calories:	67
Sodium:	8 mg
Fiber:	Trace gm
Total fat:	1 gm
Saturated fat:	Trace gm
Cholesterol:	0 mg
Cholesterol–saturated fat index:	Trace

Espresso Almond Brittle

~ Makes 32 ounces (2 pounds).

A new twist to an old holiday favorite! It is definitely worth the effort to pull the brittle.
This works best if you have 3 people so you can work quickly to make this candy.

1 tablespoon margarine	1 cup light corn syrup
1/4 teaspoon baking soda	4 teaspoons instant espresso
1/2 cup water	coffee granules
2 cups sugar	2 cups slivered blanched almonds

Heat oven to 200°. Grease 3 baking sheets and warm them in the oven. Combine margarine and baking soda in a small dish and set aside. Combine water, sugar, and corn syrup in a heavy 3-quart pan. Heat and stir to dissolve sugar. Bring to a boil and cook to 250° (a candy thermometer is a must). Add espresso granules and stir to dissolve. While stirring, slowly add almonds. Stir occasionally to keep nuts from settling to the bottom and burning. Cook to 295°. Remove from heat and stir in margarine mixture. Pour the brittle down the center of each of the 3 warm baking sheets that have been removed from the oven just before the brittle reached 295°. Tilt the baking sheets to spread the brittle out a little. Grease your hands with margarine. Begin to pull the brittle from the edges. If the brittle is still too hot, it will not come loose from the pan. After you have pulled the brittle from the edges, pick up what you have pulled and stretch farther into the center. You can run the back side of a spatula under the brittle to help loosen it. Stop pulling the brittle when it begins to stretch out in threads. Let stand to cool completely. Carefully break into pieces and store in an airtight container.

~ Per Ounce ~	
Calories:	126
Sodium:	28 mg
Fiber:	1 gm
Total fat:	4 gm
Saturated fat:	Trace gm
Cholesterol:	0 mg
Cholesterol–saturated fat index:	Trace

Peanut Brittle
Thin as Glass

⤳ Makes 32 ounces (2 pounds).

It is definitely worth the effort to pull the peanut brittle as thin as glass! Sonja learned the technique from her Aunt Ola and Aunt Alta, who made it every Christmas. This works best if you have 3 people to do the job. Bill even lets his staff take off work during the holidays to make this for him.

1 tablespoon margarine	2 cups sugar
1/4 teaspoon baking soda	1 cup light corn syrup
1 teaspoon vanilla	2 cups raw Spanish peanuts
1 cup water	

Heat oven to 200°. Grease 3 baking sheets and warm them in the oven. Combine margarine, baking soda, and vanilla in a small dish and set aside. Combine water, sugar, and corn syrup in a heavy 3-quart pan. Heat and stir to dissolve sugar. Bring to a boil and cook to 250° (a candy thermometer is a must). While stirring, slowly add peanuts. Stir occasionally to keep nuts from settling to the bottom and burning. Cook to 295°. Remove from heat and stir in margarine mixture. Pour the brittle down the center of each of the 3 warm baking sheets that have been removed from the oven just before the brittle reached 295°. Tilt the baking sheets to spread the brittle out a little. Grease your hands with margarine. Begin to pull the brittle from the edges. If the brittle is still too hot, it will not come loose from the pan. After you have pulled the brittle from around the edges, pick up what you have pulled and stretch farther into the center. You can run the back side of a spatula under the brittle to help loosen it. Stop pulling the brittle when it begins to stretch out in threads. Let stand to cool completely. Carefully break into pieces and store in an airtight container.

⤳ Per Ounce ⤳	
Calories:	134
Sodium:	28 mg
Fiber:	1 gm
Total fat:	5 gm
Saturated fat:	1 gm
Cholesterol:	0 mg
Cholesterol–saturated fat index:	1

Cardamom Holiday Cookies

To make snickerdoodle cookies, use nutmeg in place of cardamom.

1¹/₂ cups flour	6 tablespoons margarine, melted
¹/₂ cup sugar	¹/₂ cup egg substitute
¹/₂ cup brown sugar	red and green sugar sprinkles to
¹/₄ teaspoon baking soda	decorate
1¹/₄ teaspoons cardamom	

Preheat oven to 350°. Combine flour, sugars, baking soda, and cardamom in a large mixing bowl. Stir well. Add melted margarine and egg substitute; mix well. Drop by rounded teaspoonfuls onto baking sheets coated with nonstick cooking spray. Top with sugar sprinkles. Bake 12 minutes. Cool on wire racks.

⁓ Per Cookie ⁓	
Calories:	67
Sodium:	45 mg
Fiber:	Trace gm
Total fat:	2 gm
Saturated fat:	Trace gm
Cholesterol:	0 mg
Cholesterol—saturated fat index:	Trace

Chocolate Lovers' Cookies

— Makes 32 cookies.

¹/₄ cup margarine, softened
2 ounces fat-free cream cheese
¹/₂ cup sugar
¹/₃ cup brown sugar
1 teaspoon vanilla

1 cup flour
¹/₄ teaspoon (or less) Lite Salt
¹/₂ cup cocoa powder
¹/₄ cup mini semisweet chocolate
  chips

Cream margarine, cream cheese, sugars, and vanilla. Combine flour, Lite Salt, and cocoa powder; add to margarine mixture. Blend in chocolate chips. Cover and chill dough in refrigerator for several hours or overnight.

When ready to bake, remove dough from refrigerator and let soften for a few minutes. Preheat oven to 350°. Roll dough into 1-inch balls and place on baking sheets that have been sprayed with nonstick cooking spray. Flatten cookies with back side of a fork that has been dipped in powdered sugar to keep from sticking. Bake 6 to 8 minutes until slightly puffed and soft to the touch. Let cool on pan for a minute before carefully removing to a cooling rack.

— Per Cookie —	
Calories:	59
Sodium:	39 mg
Fiber:	1 gm
Total fat:	2 gm
Saturated fat:	1 gm
Cholesterol:	0 mg
Cholesterol–saturated fat index:	1

Chocolate Mint Cookies

You may be surprised how moist these cookies are. The Chocolate Mocha and Chocolate Vanilla versions are wonderful also.

1/3 cup margarine, softened	2 1/4 cups flour
1/2 cup sugar	1 teaspoon baking powder
1/2 cup brown sugar	3/4 teaspoon baking soda
1/2 cup egg substitute	1/4 cup cocoa powder
1 teaspoon peppermint extract	1/4 cup chopped walnuts

Flavor Options

For Chocolate Mocha Cookies, substitute 5 teaspoons instant coffee dissolved in 2 teaspoons vanilla in place of peppermint extract.

For Chocolate Vanilla Cookies, substitute 1 teaspoon vanilla in place of peppermint extract.

Preheat oven to 350°. In a large bowl, cream margarine and sugars. Add egg substitute and peppermint extract. In a medium bowl, combine flour, baking powder, baking soda, and cocoa powder. Add flour mixture and nuts to creamed margarine, stirring just until blended. Drop by tablespoonfuls onto baking sheets coated with nonstick cooking spray. Bake 8 to 10 minutes (be careful not to overbake).

·~ Per Cookie ~·	
Calories:	63
Sodium:	59 mg
Fiber:	Trace gm
Total fat:	2 gm
Saturated fat:	Trace gm
Cholesterol:	0 mg
Cholesterol–saturated fat index:	Trace

Italian Biscotti

A great low-fat cookie. The word biscotti *means twice-baked. They are often referred to as "dunking cookies" because of their crisp texture.*

2¼ cups flour

⅓ cup chopped walnuts *or* toasted
   hazelnuts

1 teaspoon baking powder

¼ teaspoon (or less) Lite Salt

¾ cup sugar

2 tablespoons vegetable oil

½ cup egg substitute

1½ teaspoons anise seeds

2 teaspoons anise extract

1 egg white, lightly beaten

Preheat oven to 350°. Combine flour, nuts, baking powder, and Lite Salt. In a large mixing bowl, combine sugar, oil, and egg substitute. Beat at high speed until thick, about 5 minutes. Add anise seeds and anise extract and beat until blended. Stir in flour mixture until well blended. Turn dough onto a lightly floured surface, and divide into 2 equal parts. Shape each portion into an 11-inch-long roll. Place rolls about 2 inches apart on a baking sheet that has been sprayed with nonstick cooking spray. Flatten each roll to a thickness of 1 inch. Brush with egg white.

Bake 20 minutes. Let cool. Slice each roll diagonally into 15 slices, each slice ¾ inch thick. Place slices on baking sheet. Bake 5 to 10 minutes or until dry. Cool on wire racks.

·⤳ Per Cookie ⤳·	
Calories:	73
Sodium:	31 mg
Fiber:	Trace gm
Total fat:	2 gm
Saturated fat:	Trace gm
Cholesterol:	0 mg
Cholesterol—saturated fat index:	Trace

Oat Chip Cookies

A few chocolate chips can go a long way.

¼ cup margarine, softened	¾ cup plus 2 tablespoons white flour
½ cup brown sugar	½ teaspoon baking soda
⅓ cup sugar	1¼ cups uncooked old-fashioned
2 egg whites	oatmeal
1 tablespoon skim milk	½ cup mini semisweet chocolate
1 teaspoon vanilla	chips

Preheat oven to 375°. Beat margarine and sugars until creamy. Add egg whites, skim milk, and vanilla; beat well. Add flour, baking soda, and oatmeal. Mix well. Stir in chocolate chips. Drop by rounded tablespoonfuls onto a baking sheet that has been sprayed with nonstick cooking spray. Bake 9 to 10 minutes for a chewy cookie and 12 to 13 minutes for a crispy cookie.

~ Per Cookie ~	
Calories:	77
Sodium:	47 mg
Fiber:	1 gm
Total fat:	3 gm
Saturated fat:	1 gm
Cholesterol:	Trace mg
Cholesterol–saturated fat index:	1

Ranger Cookies

Low-fat cookies often become dry after a day or two. It's wise to freeze them and defrost as needed.

¹/₂ cup margarine	¹/₂ teaspoon nutmeg
¹/₂ cup sugar	1 teaspoon baking soda
¹/₂ cup brown sugar	¹/₂ teaspoon baking powder
¹/₂ cup egg substitute	2 cups uncooked oatmeal
2 teaspoons vanilla	2 cups Rice Krispies cereal
2 cups flour	1 cup corn flakes cereal
1 teaspoon cinnamon	1 cup raisins

Preheat oven to 350°. In a large mixing bowl, beat margarine, sugars, egg substitute, and vanilla until smooth. Add flour, cinnamon, nutmeg, baking soda, and baking powder. Stir in oatmeal, Rice Krispies, corn flakes, and raisins. Drop by tablespoonfuls on a baking sheet coated with nonstick cooking spray. Bake 8 to 10 minutes.

᠊ᵕ Per Cookie ᵕ᠊	
Calories:	49
Sodium:	67 mg
Fiber:	Trace gm
Total fat:	1 gm
Saturated fat:	Trace gm
Cholesterol:	0 mg
Cholesterol–saturated fat index:	Trace

Soft Ginger Cookies

¹/₄ cup margarine, softened

¹/₃ cup sugar

¹/₃ cup brown sugar

¹/₄ cup dark molasses

¹/₄ cup egg substitute

2 cups flour

2 teaspoons baking soda

1 teaspoon ground ginger

1 teaspoon cinnamon

¹/₄ teaspoon nutmeg

2 tablespoons granulated sugar

Preheat oven to 350°. Cream margarine and sugars until light and fluffy. Add molasses and egg substitute; beat well. In a separate bowl, combine flour, baking soda, ginger, cinnamon, and nutmeg; gradually add to creamed mixture. Mix well, shape dough into 1-inch balls and roll in remaining 2 tablespoons sugar. Place 2 inches apart on baking sheets that have been sprayed with nonstick cooking spray. Bake 12 to 14 minutes or until lightly browned.

•⤳ Per Cookie ⤳•	
Calories:	46
Sodium:	68 mg
Fiber:	Trace gm
Total fat:	1 gm
Saturated fat:	Trace gm
Cholesterol:	0 mg
Cholesterol—saturated fat index:	Trace

Soft Lemon Cookies

·‑ Makes 40 cookies.

Bill is very fond of cookies, so we like to develop new low-fat varieties—this is the fun part of our job.

1½ cups flour
½ cup cornmeal
1 teaspoon baking powder
½ teaspoon baking soda
¼ teaspoon (or less) Lite Salt
⅓ cup margarine
¾ cup brown sugar

¼ cup egg substitute
2 teaspoons finely grated lemon peel
5 tablespoons freshly squeezed
  lemon juice
½ cup buttermilk
⅓ cup finely chopped pecans

Preheat oven to 350°. In a mixing bowl, stir together flour, cornmeal, baking powder, baking soda, and Lite Salt. In a large mixing bowl, beat margarine and brown sugar until creamy. Add egg substitute, lemon peel, and lemon juice; beat well.

Add dry ingredients and buttermilk alternately to the margarine-sugar mixture. Beat well. Drop by tablespoonfuls 2 inches apart onto a baking sheet that has been sprayed with nonstick cooking spray. Sprinkle with chopped pecans. Bake 12 to 14 minutes. Remove from baking sheet and cool on a wire rack.

·‑ Per Cookie ·‑	
Calories:	61
Sodium:	69 mg
Fiber:	Trace gm
Total fat:	2 gm
Saturated fat:	Trace gm
Cholesterol:	Trace mg
Cholesterol–saturated fat index:	Trace

Chocolate Chip Mint Ice Milk *·– Makes 6 cups.*

1 cup sugar
2 tablespoons cornstarch
4½ cups skim milk
½ cup egg substitute

¼ cup crème de menthe liqueur *or*
    crème de menthe syrup
⅓ cup mini semisweet chocolate
    chips

In a medium saucepan, whisk together sugar, cornstarch, and skim milk. Bring to a boil, stirring constantly; boil 1 minute. Remove from heat. Add egg substitute. Cook over low heat, stirring constantly until slightly thickened *(do not boil)*. Remove from heat and add crème de menthe. Refrigerate mixture until chilled. Add chocolate chips just before freezing. Freeze in an ice cream freezer according to manufacturer's directions. A Donvier Frozen Dessert Maker greatly simplifies the freezing process.

·– Per Cup –·	
Calories:	283
Sodium:	124 mg
Fiber:	1 gm
Total fat:	3 gm
Saturated fat:	2 gm
Cholesterol:	3 mg
Cholesterol–saturated fat index:	2

Chocolate Sorbet

Makes 5 cups.

A very rich, dark chocolate treat. Top with fresh raspberries during the summer. For a special treat, add some peppermint or rum.

1½ cups sugar
¾ cup cocoa powder
⅛ teaspoon (or less) Lite Salt
⅛ teaspoon cinnamon
½ to 1 tablespoon instant coffee granules
3¾ cups water
1½ teaspoons vanilla

Optional
½ to 1½ teaspoons peppermint extract *or* 1 teaspoon rum *or* ¼ teaspoon rum flavoring

Early in the day, or the day before serving, mix sugar, cocoa powder, Lite Salt, cinnamon, coffee granules, and water in a saucepan. Boil 5 minutes, stirring frequently. Cool. Add vanilla and, if desired, peppermint extract or rum. Chill several hours or overnight. When ready to freeze, pour mixture into ice cream maker and process according to manufacturer's instructions. A Donvier Frozen Dessert Maker greatly simplifies the freezing process.

Per ½ Cup	
Calories:	133
Sodium:	14 mg
Fiber:	2 gm
Total fat:	1 gm
Saturated fat:	1 gm
Cholesterol:	0 mg
Cholesterol–saturated fat index:	1

Creamy Chocolate Ice Milk

1 cup sugar
1/3 cup cocoa powder
1 cup buttermilk

3 cups skim milk
1 1/4 teaspoons vanilla

In a mixing bowl, combine sugar and cocoa powder. Using a wire whisk, beat in buttermilk, skim milk, and vanilla until smooth. Chill mixture thoroughly. Freeze in an ice cream freezer according to manufacturer's directions. A Donvier Frozen Dessert Maker greatly simplifies the freezing process.

~ Per Cup ~	
Calories:	242
Sodium:	129 mg
Fiber:	2 gm
Total fat:	1 gm
Saturated fat:	1 gm
Cholesterol:	4 mg
Cholesterol—saturated fat index:	1

Frozen Maple Yogurt

↪ Makes 1 quart.

This recipe was originally developed to serve with Cranberry Orange Crisp *(page 326),*
but it tastes great with any crisp. It is best eaten when first made; otherwise, it becomes
rock hard. If this happens, take it out of the freezer and it will soften in about 10 minutes.

3 cups nonfat plain yogurt (Dannon
    yogurt is less tangy and many
    prefer it in frozen yogurt)
1 cup "real" maple syrup

¼ teaspoon nutmeg
¼ teaspoon cinnamon
1 teaspoon vanilla

Mix all ingredients and freeze in ice cream freezer according to manufacturer's directions.

↪ Per ¼ Cup ↩	
Calories:	78
Sodium:	37 mg
Fiber:	Trace gm
Total fat:	Trace gm
Saturated fat:	Trace gm
Cholesterol:	1 mg
Cholesterol—saturated fat index:	Trace

Frozen Yogurt Sandwiches

These frozen yogurt desserts can be ready at a moment's notice
(after some advance assembling).

2 cups of your favorite nonfat frozen dessert *or* nonfat frozen yogurt
   (we like Vanilla Raspberry Swirl from Häagen-Dazs; it's $1/2$ sorbet and $1/2$ yogurt)
17 chocolate graham cracker squares, each $2^1/2$ by $2^1/2$ inches
1 cup Grape-nuts cereal

Remove the frozen dessert or yogurt from the freezer and soften slightly; it takes about 10 minutes. Cut each graham cracker square in half (into rectangles) and set aside. Line a shallow pan with aluminum foil.

Assemble when frozen dessert or yogurt has softened: Place 2 tablespoons frozen dessert or yogurt on a graham cracker, cover with another graham cracker; compress the sandwich slightly. Set it on its edge and roll all sides in the Grape-nuts. Place the sandwich on the foil-covered pan and repeat. Freeze sandwiches until hard, then wrap individually in foil or plastic. Serve immediately after removing from the freezer, as they soften quickly.

·~ Per Serving ~·	
Calories:	85
Sodium:	70 mg
Fiber:	1 gm
Total fat:	2 gm
Saturated fat:	1 gm
Cholesterol:	1 mg
Cholesterol—saturated fat index:	1

Fruit Cassis Sorbet

Our plentiful Northwest blackberries and boysenberries give this dessert its elegant rich color (watch out, it stains!). With a Donvier Frozen Dessert Maker, it is a snap to prepare without the mess of ice and rock salt. Use the liqueur if you want to keep it for several weeks and still be able to serve it right from the freezer. If you use the syrup, it will turn into a popsicle when stored in the freezer.

6 cups unsweetened boysenberries
    or blackberries (thaw if you use
    frozen berries)
1 cup sugar

³/₄ cup water
¹/₄ cup crème de cassis liqueur *or*
    crème de cassis syrup
Fresh mint sprigs, for garnish

Purée thawed berries in a blender or food processor. Press fruit through a fine strainer by stirring fruit with the back of a spoon. You should have about 4 cups purée when finished. Stir sugar, water, and cassis liqueur or syrup into berry purée. Chill berry mixture. Transfer berry mixture into an ice cream maker and process according to manufacturer's instructions. It may be slushy at this point. Place in a covered container in the freezer for 2 or more hours. Serve in chilled bowls and garnish with fresh mint, if desired.

Per ¹/₂ Cup	
Calories:	138
Sodium:	0 mg
Fiber:	3 gm
Total fat:	Trace gm
Saturated fat:	0 gm
Cholesterol:	0 mg
Cholesterol–saturated fat index:	0

Grapefruit Tequila Sorbet

◦~ Makes 8 servings (½ cup each).

A friend, Elaine, brought this superb dessert to a staff party. It makes a wonderful finale for a Mexican meal. It is also a good palate refresher to serve between courses of a special meal. We like to make it in a Donvier Frozen Dessert Maker because it requires no ice or salt. If it does not freeze firm enough in the Donvier, place it in a covered container and put it in the freezer to firm up the texture. The tequila is optional, but if you use it, the sorbet will keep its nice texture in the freezer and not become an ice block.

1 cup sugar
½ cup water
2¼ cups freshly squeezed grapefruit juice
⅓–½ cup freshly squeezed lemon *or* lime juice

¼ cup tequila (optional)
NOTE: Do not add more tequila or sorbet won't freeze

Combine sugar and water in saucepan. Bring to a boil and cook 5 minutes. Cool. In a mixing bowl, combine grapefruit juice with cooled sugar-water mixture and add lemon or lime juice and tequila, if using. Freeze in an ice cream freezer according to the manufacturer's directions.

◦~ Per ½ Cup (Without Tequila) ~◦	
Calories:	126
Sodium:	4 mg
Fiber:	Trace gm
Total fat:	Trace gm
Saturated fat:	Trace gm
Cholesterol:	0 mg
Cholesterol–saturated fat index:	Trace

◦~ Per ½ Cup (With Tequila) ~◦	
Calories:	142
Sodium:	4 mg
Fiber:	Trace gm
Total fat:	Trace gm
Saturated fat:	Trace gm
Cholesterol:	0 mg
Cholesterol–saturated fat index:	Trace

Lemon Gelati

This light, frozen dessert is very easy to make and is especially attractive when served in lemon shells. Trim bottoms of 10 lemons so they stand up. Cut off the top third of each lemon, scoop out the fruit and place shells upside down on paper towels until well drained. Spoon frozen gelati into the lemon shells and serve immediately. Or if you want to prepare them earlier, place in freezer and remove 20 minutes before serving.

1⅓ cups sugar

2 tablespoons grated lemon peel

¾ to 1 cup freshly squeezed
    lemon juice

1 teaspoon vanilla

4 cups (1 quart) nonfat plain yogurt

Fresh mint sprigs (optional)

Combine sugar, lemon peel, lemon juice, and vanilla in a mixing bowl. Stir until sugar dissolves. Add yogurt; stir well. Chill thoroughly. Pour cold mixture into ice cream freezer and process according to manufacturer's directions. Garnish with mint sprigs, if desired.

✑ Per ½ Cup ✑	
Calories:	137
Sodium:	67 mg
Fiber:	Trace gm
Total fat:	Trace gm
Saturated fat:	Trace gm
Cholesterol:	1 mg
Cholesterol–saturated fat index:	Trace

Mandarin Orange and
Pineapple Sherbet

This dessert is easy to prepare and very refreshing. Any ice cream freezer will work. However, the Donvier Frozen Dessert Maker has become very popular among our staff because it is so easy to use.

1 can (12 ounces) Mandarin Orange
  Slice soda
1 can (20 ounces) juice-packed
  crushed pineapple

¼ cup sugar
1 cup buttermilk

Combine all ingredients and chill for several hours. Freeze in an ice cream freezer according to manufacturer's directions. Serve immediately for best texture.

Per Cup	
Calories:	162
Sodium:	62 mg
Fiber:	2 gm
Total fat:	1 gm
Saturated fat:	Trace gm
Cholesterol:	2 mg
Cholesterol–saturated fat index:	Trace

Quick Fruit Sherbets

With a Donvier Frozen Dessert Maker, you attain instant popularity with this delicious frozen dessert that can be ready in 30 minutes. Simply turn the handle every few minutes while you're cooking dinner. Or turn the job over to one of your children or grandchildren —they will love doing it. In fact, people often run out and buy a Donvier right after they have the Quick Fruit Sherbet. This is the recipe for those desperate last-minute occasions, such as when Cindy found herself turning the handle while stopped at red lights on the way to a potluck dinner!

Choose one of the six following
 Fruit Options:
1 pint fresh berries (strawberries,
 blueberries, etc.), mashed
 or 2 cups sliced fresh peaches,
 mashed
 or 1 cup finely chopped fresh
 peaches and 1 cup fresh
 blueberries, slightly mashed
 or 1 cup finely chopped fresh
 peaches and 1 cup very ripe
 coarsely mashed banana

or omit ¹/₂ cup sugar and use 1 cup
 very ripe coarsely mashed banana,
 ¹/₃ cup honey, ¹/₄ cup sugar or less,
 and 2 tablespoons freshly
 squeezed lemon juice (use
 1 tablespoon if bananas are less ripe)
 or 1 can (20 ounces) crushed
 pineapple, juice-packed and
 undrained
2¹/₂ cups buttermilk *or* nonfat
 plain yogurt
¹/₂ cup sugar

Choose a Fruit Option and combine mashed fruit, buttermilk, and sugar. Chill for several hours. Freeze in an ice cream freezer according to manufacturer's directions. Serve immediately for best texture.

— Per Cup —	
Calories:	122
Sodium:	108 mg
Fiber:	1 gm
Total fat:	1 gm
Saturated fat:	1 gm
Cholesterol:	4 mg
Cholesterol–saturated fat index:	1

Vanilla Frozen Yogurt

Everyone needs a good vanilla frozen yogurt to serve with apple crisp (and other crisps),
with fresh-from-the-vine berries (strawberries, raspberries, blackberries, including
marionberries, a large, sweet blackberry, etc.), or just to eat by itself. With a Donvier
Frozen Dessert Maker, you can have it ready in 30 minutes.

2$^{1}/_{2}$ cups nonfat plain yogurt
1 cup sugar

2 cups skim milk
2$^{1}/_{2}$ teaspoons vanilla

Combine yogurt, sugar, milk, and vanilla. Chill for several hours. Freeze in an ice cream freezer according to manufacturer's directions. Serve immediately for best texture.

·– Per Cup ·–	
Calories:	220
Sodium:	121 mg
Fiber:	0 gm
Total fat:	Trace gm
Saturated fat:	Trace gm
Cholesterol:	3 mg
Cholesterol–saturated fat index:	Trace

Baked Pears with Sherry Sauce

Firm pears, such as Anjou, work best in this recipe. Serve with Chocolate Sorbet *(page 314) for a special treat.*

3 medium firm pears (Anjou)
1/4 cup brown sugar
1/4 cup sherry
1 tablespoon freshly squeezed
    lemon juice

1/2 teaspoon cinnamon
1/4 cup water

Nonfat frozen yogurt (optional)

Preheat oven to 350°. Peel pears, cut in half lengthwise and remove core. Place halves, cut side down, in a baking dish that has been sprayed with nonstick cooking spray. Combine remaining ingredients and pour over pears. Cover and bake for 35 to 40 minutes or until tender. Spoon sauce over pears several times during baking. Serve with a scoop of frozen yogurt on the side, if desired.

·➛ Per Serving ·➛	
Calories:	100
Sodium:	5 mg
Fiber:	3 gm
Total fat:	Trace gm
Saturated fat:	Trace gm
Cholesterol:	0 mg
Cholesterol–saturated fat index:	Trace

Berry Rhubarb Crisp

1½ cups raspberries or strawberries
cut in half, fresh *or* frozen

3 cups fresh rhubarb, cut into
1-inch pieces

²/₃ cup sugar

3 tablespoons flour

Topping

¼ cup flour

½ cup brown sugar

¼ cup uncooked old-fashioned
oatmeal

2 tablespoons margarine, softened

Preheat oven to 350°. Spray a 9-inch square baking pan with nonstick cooking spray. Put berries and rhubarb in baking pan. Mix sugar and flour together and sprinkle over fruit.

For Topping: Combine flour, brown sugar, and oatmeal in a small bowl. Add soft margarine and mix with a fork until crumbly. Sprinkle topping over fruit and bake 35 to 40 minutes or until topping is brown and fruit is bubbly. Serve warm.

~ Per Serving ~	
Calories:	162
Sodium:	50 mg
Fiber:	1 gm
Total fat:	3 gm
Saturated fat:	Trace gm
Cholesterol:	0 mg
Cholesterol–saturated fat Index:	Trace

DESSERTS

325

Cranberry Orange Crisp

Crisps are the answer to the pie crust that is impossible to make low-fat. We were thrilled to find a crisp recipe that is perfect for the winter holidays. It was a great finale for our fancy holiday staff luncheon and it received raves when we served it to a group of hungry skiers.

6 large oranges, peeled and
   separated into segments
2 packages (6 ounces each) fresh *or*
   frozen cranberries
1 cup sugar

Finely grated peel of 1 lemon
$1/2$ cup flour
$2/3$ cup brown sugar
$1/2$ cup uncooked oatmeal
$1/4$ cup margarine

Preheat oven to 350°. Lightly spray a 9-by-13-inch baking dish with nonstick cooking spray. Mix orange segments, cranberries, sugar, and lemon peel and spread in prepared dish. Combine flour, brown sugar, and oatmeal in a separate bowl. Mix in margarine with a fork until it resembles coarse cornmeal. Sprinkle topping over fruit and bake for 30 minutes (45 minutes if cranberries are frozen). Top with nonfat vanilla yogurt or Frozen Maple Yogurt (page 316).

↝ Per Serving ↜	
Calories:	265
Sodium:	64 mg
Fiber:	3 gm
Total fat:	4 gm
Saturated fat:	1 gm
Cholesterol:	0 mg
Cholesterol–saturated fat index:	1

Fabulous Fruit Tart

As the name implies, this dessert is wonderful and definitely worth the effort. Make it when you have ripe, beautiful fruit to show off.

Graham Cracker Crust
1½ cups graham cracker crumbs
   (1 package of 11 crackers)
2 tablespoons honey
2 tablespoons vegetable oil

Filling
1 package (8 ounces) fat-free
   cream cheese
½ cup sugar
⅓ cup egg substitute
½ cup nonfat sour cream
1 tablespoon Grand Marnier *or* other
   orange-flavored liqueur
   or ¼ teaspoon grated orange peel
½ teaspoon vanilla

Orange Sauce
3 tablespoons sugar
4 teaspoons cornstarch
3 tablespoons Grand Marnier *or*
   other orange-flavored liqueur
   or orange juice
¾ cup orange juice

Topping
½ cup sliced kiwi
1 cup sliced strawberries
1 mango, peeled and cut into
   thin slices
1 whole strawberry

Fresh mint sprigs, for garnish

To prepare Graham Cracker Crust: Preheat oven to 350°. Prepare graham cracker crumbs by crushing with a rolling pin or using a blender or food processor. Combine graham cracker crumbs, honey, and oil and mix well. Press crumbs firmly onto bottom of a 9-inch springform pan. Bake 15 minutes. Remove from oven. Cool completely before adding filling.

To prepare Filling: Preheat oven to 325°. In a large mixing bowl, beat cream cheese and sugar until creamy. Add egg substitute and beat well. Add sour cream, liqueur or peel, and vanilla; beat until blended. Pour over crust and bake 30 minutes. Cool completely on a rack. If made ahead, cover and chill until the next day.

To prepare Orange Sauce: In a small saucepan, mix sugar and cornstarch. Add liqueur or 3 tablespoons orange juice and stir to dissolve cornstarch; add ¾ cup orange juice. Cook over high heat, stirring constantly, until sauce comes to a boil; cook 1 minute or until sauce is thick and clear. Remove from heat and cool to lukewarm.

To assemble Fruit Tart: Spoon ⅓ of the lukewarm Orange Sauce over cheesecake to within 1 inch of the edge. Place kiwi slices around outer edge of tart. Fill in center with sliced strawberries. Spoon a small amount of sauce over the strawberries. Arrange mango slices in a spiral over strawberries and kiwi. Put the whole strawberry in the center. Spoon remaining sauce over fruit to within ¼ inch of the edge. Cover; chill until sauce is set, at least 30 minutes or overnight.

To serve: Remove rim of springform pan and place on a serving platter. Garnish with fresh mint, if using. Cut tart in wedges with a sharp knife.

~ Per Serving ~	
Calories:	188
Sodium:	194 mg
Fiber:	1 gm
Total fat:	4 gm
Saturated fat:	Trace gm
Cholesterol:	Trace mg
Cholesterol–saturated fat index:	1

Fruit Trifle

1 package (3½ ounces) instant
    vanilla pudding
1¾ cups skim milk
12 ounces nonfat lemon yogurt
¼ teaspoon almond extract
1 prepared angel food cake
    (14 ounces)

4 cups sliced fresh strawberries
    (raspberries, blueberries, *or*
    peaches work well, too)
⅓ cup sliced almonds

Start this dessert early in the day or the day before serving. Place dry pudding mix in a bowl and beat in milk. When pudding has thickened, add yogurt and almond extract. Mix well. Cut angel food cake into 1-inch cubes and place ⅓ of them in the bottom of a deep glass bowl. Spread ⅓ of the pudding-yogurt mixture over the cake and top with ⅓ of the prepared fruit. Repeat layers of cake, pudding, and fruit two more times. Top with sliced almonds. Cover well and chill in refrigerator for at least 4 hours or overnight. Serve cold.

～ Per Serving ～	
Calories:	142
Sodium:	153 mg
Fiber:	1 gm
Total fat:	1 gm
Saturated fat:	Trace gm
Cholesterol:	1 mg
Cholesterol–saturated fat index:	Trace

Summer Fruit on Lemonade Squares

⤳ Makes 9 servings.

For the lemon lovers among us, this is a favorite.

Ginger Graham Cracker Crust
1¹/₂ cups graham cracker crumbs
   (1 package of 11 crackers)
2 tablespoons honey
¹/₂ teaspoon ground ginger
2 tablespoons vegetable oil

Lemonade Filling
¹/₃ cup frozen lemonade concentrate,
   thawed
1¹/₂ tablespoons (1¹/₂ envelopes)
   unflavored gelatin
¹/₃ cup sugar
¹/₄ teaspoon vanilla
2 cups nonfat lemon-flavored yogurt

2 cups colorful fresh fruit (e.g.,
   raspberries, strawberries,
   blueberries, *or* kiwi slices)

To prepare Ginger Graham Cracker Crust: Preheat oven to 350°. Mix graham cracker crumbs, honey, and ginger together in a small bowl. Add oil and mix well. Press into the bottom of a 9-inch square pan. Bake for 15 minutes. Cool before adding filling.

To prepare Lemonade Filling: Pour thawed lemonade concentrate into a small saucepan; sprinkle gelatin on top. Stir, then let sit for a few minutes to soften gelatin. Add sugar and heat mixture gently to dissolve gelatin and sugar. Stir in vanilla. Refrigerate until cold. When it begins to set, whip lemonade mixture until fluffy; stir in yogurt and whip again. Pour over crust and chill until firm. Decorate top of dessert with raspberries, strawberries, blueberries, or kiwi slices in an attractive arrangement (the colors are so pretty, they look good no matter what you do with them). Cut into squares and serve cold.

⤳ Per Serving ⤳	
Calories:	205
Sodium:	113 mg
Fiber:	2 gm
Total fat:	5 gm
Saturated fat:	1 gm
Cholesterol:	1 mg
Cholesterol–saturated fat index:	1

Summer Pudding

This cold summer pudding is traditionally made with stale bread, but fresh bread works well, too. This recipe is simple to prepare and has a delightful appearance and flavor. It is assembled and refrigerated 1 to 2 days before serving.

14 to 16 slices white bread,
  crusts trimmed
2 cups fresh *or* 1 bag (16 ounces)
  frozen blackberries, thawed
  and drained
$^1/_2$ to $^2/_3$ cup sugar

2 cups fresh *or* 1 bag (16 ounces)
  frozen raspberries, thawed
  and drained
$^1/_2$ cup nonfat vanilla yogurt
1 teaspoon lemon peel

Spray a 9-by-9-inch dish with nonstick cooking spray. Slightly overlap 12 slices of bread to cover the bottom and sides of prepared dish, pressing bread gently against sides so it will adhere.

Cook blackberries and half of the sugar in a saucepan over medium-high heat, stirring gently, until sugar dissolves and berries release their juices, about 2 minutes. Spoon berry mixture into the bread-lined dish. Add raspberries and remaining sugar to same saucepan. Cook over medium-high heat, stirring gently, until sugar dissolves and berries release their juices, about 2 minutes. Spoon raspberry mixture over the blackberry mixture. Cover with remaining bread slices. Cover the dish with waxed paper and set a plate on top of waxed paper; weight with heavy object. Refrigerate at least 24 and up to 48 hours. Meanwhile, combine yogurt and lemon peel in a small bowl and refrigerate.

When ready to serve, remove weight, plate, and waxed paper from pudding. Turn pudding out onto plate, spread lemon yogurt on top and serve immediately.

~ Per Serving ~	
Calories:	204
Sodium:	230 mg
Fiber:	4 gm
Total fat:	2 gm
Saturated fat:	Trace gm
Cholesterol:	1 mg
Cholesterol—saturated fat index:	Trace

Three Berry Cobbler

We were sorry when this recipe was finished, since that meant we would no longer have it at our tasting sessions. Served warm and topped with frozen vanilla yogurt, it is an all-time favorite of our staff members. Frozen berries are available all year long, so you do not have to wait for summer to have this great treat.

1 tablespoon margarine
1/2 cup whole wheat flour
1/2 cup white flour
1/2 cup sugar
1 1/2 teaspoons baking powder
3/4 cup skim milk

3 cups fresh berries (blueberries,
    blackberries, and red raspberries)
or 2 bags (12 ounces each) of
    frozen mixed berries, thawed
    about 1 1/2 hours

Preheat oven to 350°. Put margarine in an 8-inch square baking pan and heat in the oven to melt, about 2 minutes. Combine flours, sugar, baking powder, and milk. Pour batter over margarine but do not mix. Put berries on top of the batter (if using frozen berries, do not include the juice). Bake 35 minutes (frozen berries will take 45 to 50 minutes) or until a wooden pick inserted in the center comes out clean.

‧‿ Per Serving ‿	
Calories:	134
Sodium:	110 mg
Fiber:	3 gm
Total fat:	2 gm
Saturated fat:	Trace gm
Cholesterol:	Trace mg
Cholesterol—saturated fat index:	Trace

INDEX

halibut
    in garlic tomato sauce, 248
    lemon garlic, 250
    olé, 249
hazelnut coffee bars, frosted,
        284
herbed pita triangles, 39
herb tomato soup, 152
holiday corn bread dressing,
        221
homemade English muffins,
        65
honey dijon dressing, 130
honey dijon salmon, 238
honey ginger dressing, 126
hot and sour soup, 144
hummus, 38

ice milk
    chocolate chip mint, 313
    creamy chocolate, 315
Indian tea (chai), 55
Indonesian pasta salad, 118
ingredients, to have on hand,
        19–21
Italian biscotti, 308
Italian marinara sauce, 172

Jane's Asian pasta salad, 119
Japanese slaw, 108
Jenny's shrimp dip, 40
jollof rice, 211

kabobs, fish and vegetable,
        Asian style, 242
kate aloo, 191
Kung Pao chicken, 274
Kung Pao vegetarian style, 233

La Paz chicken and corn
        stir-fry, 275
lasagna, roasted vegetable,
        203
latkes, potato, 195
layered Mexican bean dip, 41
lazy daisy bars, 285
lemon
    blueberry muffins, 78
    cheese spread, 134
    chicken, 277

cookies, 312
dressing, 122
garlic halibut, 250
gelati, 320
sponge cake with glazed
        berry topping, 294
lemonade, strawberry, 59
lemonade squares, summer
        fruit on, 330
lentils
    peppers stuffed with, 224
    Syrian, with tomatoes,
        225
linguine, spicy sesame, with
        chicken, 279
lunches, menus, 22

mandarin orange and pineapple
        sherbet, 321
mandarin soup, 144
mango
    Megan's tossed green salad
        with red pepper,
        cucumber, and, 102
    salad dressing à la, 131
maple
    cranberry syrup, 91
    frozen yogurt, 316
Marie's seafood vegetable
        soup, 153
marinara sauce, 172
marinated asparagus or
        broccoli, 109
mayonnaise, garlic, 133
Mediterranean-style spaghetti
        squash, 173
Megan's tossed green salad
        with mango, red
        pepper, and cucumber,
        102
menus
    barbecues, 27
    breakfast, 22
    brunch, 22
    dinner, 23–26
    lunch, 22
    supper, 23
Mexican bean dip, layered,
        41
million dollar torte, 296

minestrone soup
    clam, 154
    special, 159
mint
    chocolate chip ice milk, 313
    citrus iced tea, 56
mocha squares, 286
Molly's balsamic vinegar
        dressing, 103
Molly's spinach salad, 103
Moroccan stew, 155
Mrs. Plancich's barbecued
        salmon, 251
muffins
    blackberry, 74
    chile cheese dinner, 75
    cinnamon applesauce bran,
        76
    English, 65
    fresh apple and pumpkin
        spice, 77
    lemon blueberry, 78
    pear almond, 79
    pie cherry, 80
    raisin bran, 81
    sweet potato, 82
    tiny pineapple, 83
mushrooms
    bok choy, and tomato
        stir-fry, 174
    risotto, 217
    roasted, 196
    and sausage spaghetti torta,
        276
mustard dressing, creamy, 107

Nancy's Puerto Rican rice and
        chicken stew, 156
noodles
    black beans with shrimp
        and, 237
    Pad Thai, 201
    spicy Si-Cuan, 205
    yakisoba stir-fry, 207
Northwestern salmon cakes,
        252
nutrients
    contents of recipes, 28
    standards, 27
nutrition, goals, 13–14

METRIC EQUIVALENCIES

LIQUID AND DRY MEASURE EQUIVALENCIES

Customary	Metric
$1/4$ teaspoon	1.25 milliliters
$1/2$ teaspoon	2.5 milliliters
1 teaspoon	5 milliliters
1 tablespoon	15 milliliters
1 fluid ounce	30 milliliters
$1/4$ cup	60 milliliters
$1/3$ cup	80 milliliters
$1/2$ cup	120 milliliters
1 cup	240 milliliters
1 pint (2 cups)	480 milliliters
1 quart (4 cups, 32 ounces)	960 milliliters (.96 liter)
1 gallon (4 quarts)	3.84 liters
1 ounce (by weight)	28 grams
$1/4$ pound (4 ounces)	114 grams
1 pound (16 ounces)	454 grams
2.2 pounds	1 kilogram (1000 grams)

OVEN TEMPERATURE EQUIVALENCIES

Description	°Fahrenheit	°Celsius
Cool	200	90
Very slow	250	120
Slow	300–325	150–160
Moderately slow	325–350	160–180
Moderate	350–375	180–190
Moderately hot	375–400	190–200
Hot	400–450	200–230
Very hot	450–500	230–260